INTERNATIONAL SCHOOLS AND THEIR ROLE IN THE FIELD OF INTERNATIONAL EDUCATION

INTERNATIONAL SCHOOLS AND THEIR ROLE IN THE FIELD OF INTERNATIONAL EDUCATION

BY

ROBERT J. LEACH

PERGAMON PRESS

OXFORD · LONDON · EDINBURGH · NEW YORK
TORONTO · SYDNEY · PARIS · BRAUNSCHWEIG

PERGAMON PRESS LTD.,
Headington Hill Hall, Oxford
4 & 5 Fitzroy Square, London W.1

PERGAMON PRESS (SCOTLAND) LTD.,
2 & 3 Teviot Place, Edinburgh 1

PERGAMON PRESS INC.,
Maxwell House. Fairview Park. Elmsford, New York 10523

PERGAMON OF CANADA LTD.,
207 Queen's Quay West, Toronto 1

PERGAMON PRESS (AUST.) PTY. LTD.,
19a Boundary Street, Rushcutters Bay, N.S.W. 2011, Australia

PERGAMON PRESS S.A.R.L.,
24 rue des Écoles, Paris 5e

VIEWEG & SOHN GMBH,
Burgplatz 1, Braunschweig

Printed in Hungary

CONTENTS

PREFACE

WHEN the Pergamon Press first suggested that they would welcome my writing a small volume on the general subject of international schools, I found myself involved in extensive travels to the States and Canada in the interests of the Development Program of the International School of Geneva. I agreed to undertake the assignment knowing in my inner heart that weeks would pass before I could begin seriously to think what this might involve. In the interim an opportunity was given me to re-read the personal journal which I have managed to write for nearly two score years. This glance back over my life, taken as it is in my fifty-first year, grants me perspective at least on my qualifications in presuming to speak with authority on international schools and, by implication, international education.

I was born in New England of a Yankee father and a Scots–Irish mother—in other words, the product of two not dissimilar cultures. The twentieth-century New Englander is subject in varying degrees to the dynamic reflected in George Santayana's *Last Puritan*. In my case, it drove me first to the middle west to "college"—and then to embracing quakerism, with its corollaries of meaningful community, equality of all peoples, simplicity or directness of approach and the peaceable resolution of conflict. I was indeed fortunate to be chosen for residence at Pendle Hill, the one Quaker Graduate Center for Social Study in America in 1939, to participate fully in a student body both international and inter-racial in composition. The Society of Friends in the twentieth century shows indisputable evidence of being one of the most vital religiously oriented thinking groups in the contemporary world. Its great virtue lies in putting its principles into dynamic action. There is scarcely an important social problem, political tension or international venture which escapes the vigilant Quaker eye and a concomitant expendible involvement of concerned Quaker activity therein. Usually Quakers are made welcome, even in the most unpromising places, in tribute to recognition of their basic motivation in working for universal good.

One consequence of believing and acting as though all divsons among men are of secondary importance is the notion that the national state is a temporary convenience or, in fact, an obsolescent institution. This point of view was made explicit in a Pendle Hill pamphlet *New Nations for Old* (1942) written by Kenneth Boulding, until recently Chairman of the Economics Department at the University of Michigan. I was then the employed Secretary of the Publications Committee which saw this essay into print. I must confess I have never since met a more stimulating point of view regarding the need for redeeming national patriotism. Subsequently, in line with Quaker peaceableness, I refused military service in the Second World War, and had, in consequence, the salutary experience of being estranged from my own nation in the sense that I did not share the war fever and in that the vast majority of my countrymen regarded people like myself as incomprehensible at best, traitors at worst.

With a return to a somewhat more normal peacetime atmosphere, there was ample opportunity offered the erstwhile conscientious objector to occupy a "respectable" position in society. For me, it meant teaching History in a small southern college—where very naturally I became interested in the international political potential as advocated by the United World Federalists at that time, as well as becoming very much aware of racial segregation.

A summer in Britain in 1948 brought home the absurdity of attempting to teach European History without having ever visited the continent. Two years later, I came to Europe— as it turned out, to live, to marry an English girl and to find a vocation in the International School of Geneva. Quite obviously, the communist–non-communist international tension postponed world federalism to an infinitely distant future, despite growing interdependence in such areas as in the Common Market. There was still the slower, surer field of building a sense of international community among young people of all nationalities. For me the problem of race was shelved for the moment.

When I entered the doors of the International School of Geneva, it was more than a quarter-century old; that is, it had existed long enough (and precariously enough during the dangerous Second World War years) to have developed its own character and techniques. Though I have served at the school now for more than 15 years, it was only after a relatively extensive apprenticeship that I was able to contribute to the basic ideas which are implicit in such an institution.

History fascinated me as a lad. I took my undergraduate and graduate degrees in the subject. My approach to any political, social or cultural configuration is therefore incomplete without depth perception. Naturally, this takes time to develop. In the case of dealing with the International School, it was complicated by the fact that when I arrived in Geneva I was essentially American—admittedly a half-Scots–Irish, Quaker, pacifist, historically oriented American. I had, for instance, served as president of my college "International Relations Club" and as adviser to its equivalent in the college where I taught. But I had still to learn how to move from being an internationally minded American to being an internationally minded internationalist.

Dag Hammarskjöld was one such! The arenas of his activities were, of course, those of governments feeling their way toward mutual accommodation. In a sense, his role was forced upon him. The imperative is not so great in an international school. It is easier and of less consequence to masquerade as an integral internationalist when, in fact, one is only a nationalist detached in some degree from the normal homeland or community to which eventually one expects to return.

I do not suppose one can ever escape what the French so strongly favor teaching, that is a *formation d'esprit*. I shall always find it instinctively easier to reason pragmatically and to feel at home with other pragmatic Americans. Yet I am spoiled for being only with Americans as their gamut of reactions is predictably limited. It is so much more fun, and of course miles more difficult, to move from one pattern of reasoning (and basic *a priori* values) to another. And, of course, to do so, that is to begin to become internationally international, is the basic starting point of the training which the genuine international school gives. This, in short, is the ideal of *formation d'esprit* of the rightly operating international school.

Once the formation of the integral international *formation d'esprit* is understood and practiced as central to teaching in an international school, its vocation is achievable. I must say in all honesty that I am not sure that the International School of Geneva hardly more than glimpsed this ideal until about 5 years ago, at least consciously. And in all honesty, I must claim that my own particular background (not the least being the fact that Americans are flexible as pragmatists) has played an important role in helping the International School of Geneva formulate its international internationalism. In this sense, this *apologia pro mea vita* is worth being set down as justifying my accepting the assignment from the Pergamon Press.

About 5 years ago the Geneva International School released me from a year's teaching to undertake the discovery of situations in other similar institutions in the Eastern Hemisphere. After 3 months of extensive travel, many generalizations could be made and were: the most impressive of these led me to become the original promoter of the International Baccalaureate, now so widely accepted and so promising for the future.

I have more recently been released from teaching (the ironic

reward of the successful teacher!) to undertake exploratory
work leading to a financial campaign to make the Geneva
International School so excellent in its vocation of integral
internationalism that its recapitulation a hundred times over
in the principal cities of the world will appear, self-evidently,
the course of wisdom. Thus I write from the position of one
who has engaged himself in favor of a definite type of internationalism. The advantage of such commitment in this case
is that in becoming *parti pris* I am so placed as to view objectively and systematically the multitude of other definitions
of internationalism which often only confuse the casual observer. And I have every intention of being (as in fact my
affirmation of integral internationalism would lead me to be)
as objective as possible in examining all institutions and movements of which I have knowledge and which apply themselves
in the field of international education.

Summer 1967

ROBERT J. LEACH

ACKNOWLEDGMENTS

DURING the 18 months in which I prepared this study, I had occasion to seek the advice of a number of people closely associated with the International Baccalaureate Office. To them I owe a debt of great gratitude; particularly to A. D. C. (Alec) Peterson, Director; Gerard Renaud, Assistant-Director, J. Desmond Cole-Baker, Nan Martin, Nansi Poirel, members of ISES Executive Committee; Ruth Bonner, Secretary, and Elizabeth Addossides, Secretary of ISA. Typing was undertaken by Marie Jordan (now McRoberts) and my wife Jean A. Leach, to whom I dedicate the work. The latter has borne the brunt of my involvement in International Education for most of our married life. Finally, a word of appreciation is in order to the long-suffering members of my own History Department at the International School of Geneva who have cheerfully given up innumerable hours to humor the never-ending inventiveness of their chief; especially to Eugene Wallach, Executive Secretary of ISES for 1965; Michael Knight, Acting Chairman of the Department when duty called me elsewhere; and Philip Thomas, who now acts as a most co-operative colleague in managing the newer Geography and Economics Department.

CHAPTER 1

WHAT IS AN INTERNATIONAL SCHOOL?

A. HISTORICAL BACKGROUND

When I was a fraternity "pledge" during "Hell Week" at my university, I was obliged to wear a dog-collar, which often encouraged others to inquire why. If asked (in the hearing of my fraternity brothers) I had to reply, "I belong to the *genus canis*, a carnivorous species identified by a marked aversion to that species known as felines—said felines reciprocating". One is almost tempted in replying to those who ask what is an international school to say, "It is a mongrel educational institution which upsets the basic prejudices of all pure nationally bred schools."

In fact, the first time I was ever asked the second question —and it was, significantly, in Paris by a clear-headed French educator—much as follows: "Alors, dites-moi ce que ça veut dire une école internationale!" I replied I had not the foggiest notion although I had taught in one for 10 years! It would be the French who would ask such a question! And it would be an Anglo–American who had not worked out the response. But, being stubborn, I did not let the matter rest there. Five years have elapsed since that time and I am prepared to have a go at the question now.

According to Toynbee, the first universal state, that is the one to swallow up nations which had already established traditions of government and regular means of transmitting such traditions to future generations, was the Persian Empire. In fact the Emperor or Shah-in-Shah was King of Kings and Lord of Lords. It would appear that each subject nationality was encouraged to keep its institutions intact (note the rebuilding of Jerusalem) which, of course, included the schools. In other words, the opportunity of creating international schools was not envisaged. The opposite seems to have been the case. Even today in the Middle East, built as it is largely on Islamic traditions—which, in turn, again according to Toynbee, represent the rebirth of the values of the universal Persian Empire—each culture maintains its schools more or less intact. In other words, the notion of consciously merging cultures is not a current Islamic ideal. The unwillingness of the Arab States to consider learning from Israel's experience in fighting the desert, to say nothing of joining common forces with the Jews against the mutual environmental enemy, is perhaps current evidence of what ancient Persia set in motion.

In sharp contradistinction to the Persian educational experience was the Hellenistic overlay, which was probably the chief result of Alexander's adventure. In many respects the "Persian" ideal was maintained but in others the universalism of the Greek interpenetrated. There is even evidence in inner China of Greek sculpture, in India of attempts to incorporate platonism into the Hindu notion of the Oversoul. The most startling Egypto–Greek sculpture is to be found in the catacombs of Alexandria, while the entire Coptic community in contemporary Egypt (United Arab Republic) is the result of a Greco–Christian–Egyptian amalgam. Above all, the revelations of the Dead Sea scrolls indicate that the Essenes were clearly the product of the interpenetration of Jewish and Greek ideas (perhaps earliest achieved in the Stoic School of Philosophy). By the transmutation of Jew for Barbarian and Greek for Gentile there grew the great Christian movement.

The Christian Church was, in effect, the end product of Jew, Greek and Roman tempered by the Germanic upheaval. In any case, the *Trivium* and *Quadrivium*, as they developed as disciplines, became the heart of a truly international, though very restricted, educational system. And when the Arabic horsemen swept out shouting "Allah Akbar", it was mostly the christianized Byzantine provinces in which they established themselves. Toynbee may be right that the Islamic way of life instinctively sought an accommodation of "live and let live" as known in ancient Persia, but particularly in Hispanic regions or in North Africa (Toledo and Kairwan) the "synthetic" ideal of the Christian world carried its influence into the Islamic community.

And when the superior technology and logic of the Arab teaching was transmuted within the Christian medieval cathedral school, it was the university which emerged. First at Salerno, then at Bologna and at Naples. Already, Paris had developed its own particular type. What is significant was that Arabic was the lingua franca of the world of the inland waterways, medieval Greek of Eastern Europe and medieval Latin of Western Europe. The national, tribal or clannish vernaculars were not the languages of instruction.

Only when the Caliphate broke apart, the Crusades ruined Byzantium and the Western Empire and Papacy strangled each other, did medieval internationalism lose its sway. The national state emerged, its monarch destroying the nobility, the guilds and the independent clergy in turn. The Italian city state like its classical Greek predecessor, attempted the stormy evolution through monarchy, oligarchy and tyranny towards democracy. In the resultant confusion, Italy was, however, crushed by rival national absolutisms. Curiously, the delayed action of the Italian Renaissance brought democracy to a most unlikely place—to the British Isles through the Stuart–Cromwellian and "Glorious" Revolutions. But England, far from becoming a universal commonwealth, was limited to a few islands and an amazingly widespread assortment of overseas colonies. Is it perhaps not to be wondered at that the Englishman casts himself in his own mind's eye as did the Classical Greek who enlightened a barbarian world. Perhaps this is the origin of the self-appointed superiority of the British–American from which, incidentally, the world has not yet ceased to suffer.

The only European rivals who seriously threatened British domination were Spain and France (Holland lost the game in the winning of the "Glorious Revolution" ironically enough). But Spain was too much devoted to the old Persian ideal, dressed as it was in monastic Catholic robes, to do more than overlay a Hispanic veneer in Latin America. And France delayed her democratic revolution until England had captured the dynamic of the industrial transformation.

The Germans then entered the lists, leading to two frightful world wars by which the leadership of mankind moved first to an unprepared United States, and has since been shared by America with the Russians, whose entrance into world power was by means of communist revolution. In modern times only the Middle East (Islamic–Ancient Persia), Indian (Hindu) and Chinese–Japanese civilizations somehow maintained some individual independence. And in the contemporary world their re-birth, along with that of Africa and perhaps the "Amerind" sub-structure of Latin America, constitutes the nature of the world as it is.

This rather breathtaking and I hope not too exhilarating super-survey of human history is undertaken largely to prove three points. First that medieval Europe constituted the only early fully developed "internationalization" in education. Second, that the emergence of nationalism supplanted the universalism of the Latin–Greek world: and third, that Anglo–American culture, having developed democracy first, imagined that its commonwealth values were more universal than the essentially national community in which they were nurtured. This applies to its educational values as well as to its concepts of "God, Mother and the Girl Scouts".

Naturally, I have oversimplified and, in fact, may well be in error at given points. It may also be pointed out that other national cultures, and not only those reinforced by new ideologies and rampant anticolonialism, uphold universal (philosophical) values for their own nationals within their own educational systems far beyond their inherent worth.

One outstanding such instance is that of the French who went so far by implication as to identify all culture with "Frenchness" and, at least in the colonial period, they seem to have regarded their civilizing mission as chiefly to spread French education and the philosophical values behind it.

B. PRIMACY OF NATIONALISM

However bitter is racial strife, however harsh economic conflict (both in colonial areas and between so-called capitalist and socialist blocs), however intolerant is religious and ideological opinion, it is nationalism which claims the primary loyalty of man today. In so doing, nationalism serves as the greatest divider of human kind. To some, this is surprising, unconsciously conditioned as they are by a Hobbesian-like logic, which allows them to fear that without the nation state, mankind would slide back into tribalism or something equivalently chaotic. How often arguments against regional or world federalism turn about the "folk wisdom" that the nation state is the best defence against tyranny. Even in federal unions such as Switzerland, or in the United States, the educational system does not often equip the citizen to think realistically how to apply the principles already functioning in his familiar governmental mechanisms to larger and more imaginative groupings of mankind.

It is deeply unsettling to come to regard secure governmental entities as obsolescent. In fact, each nation state tends to perpetuate the myth that it is permanent and somehow mystically essential to the identity of its citizenry. In short, in each country the schools teach national history as a kind of magnet around which to establish common national identity. Outsiders are technically "outlaws" as far as the national laws are concerned and often potential or actual enemies—in the view of certain national educational systems.

Since the First World War there have been, as we all know,

two not very efficacious international experiments in the forms of the League of Nations and the United Nations Organization. Both were established on mutual accommodation among sovereign states. Both have hesitated to get involved in other than comparisons of national educational systems. The Bureau of International Education, founded in Geneva in 1923, is devoted to developing an exchange of information between and among national Ministries of Education, and displaying a world-wide selection of textbooks. UNESCO, which developed in Paris in 1948, is mostly concerned with eradicating illiteracy, though the scope of its work is enormous, for the most part through national UNESCO commissions. Significantly, however, like the BIE, UNESCO has left concern for international schools as such to one side. Only in 1951 was a private non-governmental international body founded to promote international schools and this, the International Schools Association, received its first UNESCO contract only in 1963.

Not only would it appear that education is pretty universally recognized as a national prerogative for nations, but as well is so viewed by international organizations. There are, however, trends away from such thinking, as we will see later on. But the essential here is to realize that the international school is a sufficiently radical departure in the nationalist epoch in which we live as to be forced to build its own way without the normal governmental subsidies which are essential to make schools viable institutions.

C. TYPES OF INTERNATIONAL SCHOOLS

In 1964 the *Year Book of Education*, produced jointly by the London and Columbia Universities, applied itself to the general topic of education and international life. It is revealing that only one article of some 14 pages in a volume totalling nearly 500 dealt with international schools as such. Significantly it was the International School of Geneva which produced the 14 pages. Michael Knight drew a chart of equivalences between national examinations for university entrance, while Robert J. Leach wrote the text, in which a seven-way criterion was suggested by which international schools might be classified. There is still much validity in this criterion despite the passage of 3 years since it was formulated. But for the purpose of sharpening discussion, it is proposed here to reverse the order as presented in 1964 and perhaps to vary it at points.

It would appear to be common practice in a number of places to regard an international school as one serving or being composed of students from several nationalities. This definition leads into hopeless confusion, however, when, upon reflection, one realizes that practically every school in such a cosmopolitan centre as London or New York includes a number of nationalities in its student body. Such schools are mostly state-financed national institutions. There are, in fact a number of privately financed and some state-operated schools of an elite order in most developed countries, which pride themselves on being "internationally minded" and are, in truth, far more international in their orientation than the run-of-the-mill London or New York school. In most cases, however, the "internationally-minded" school (whether or not it belongs to the formal "Conference" of such institutions) is usually composed of students of one nationality, or mostly of one. It is significant that the internationally minded schools have been by far and away the chief promoters of exchange of students (not yet at university level). The Conference of Internationally Minded Schools, which was formed in 1949, has always worked very closely with the School Affiliation Service of the American Friends Service Committee (Quakers), which initiated the program of high-school student exchange soon after the Second World War. Yet the Conference has always maintained a sharp distinction between its member schools and international schools as such. This is probably because international schools have little need for recourse to student exchange.

In some countries the term "international school" indicates that it is "privately owned" usually by the headmaster himself, who is naturally a national of the country in which the school is located. This type of international school is juridically something quite different from the ordinary private (public) school in Britain or in the United States where a corporation with trustees operates a non-profit making, eleemosynary institution. Both types of institutions are independent of state control. Both offer a certain "snob appeal" as well. Some of these very private schools are so constituted that British, German, American or Italian university entrance examinations are offered—in part or all. But such practice is dictated by the clientele, not by intentional theory. No doubt a good bit of international understanding is achieved in such schools—but their primary purpose is to provide income for their owner–operators. They reflect in an intense manner the national psychology in dealing with a great influx of outsiders. They are, in fact, national international schools. Many such are to be found in Switzerland.

The next category of schools claiming to be international is the "overseas" grouping. These are, in fact, schools set up as personally owned, parent-owned or foreign-government owned in another nation and, in most cases, serve only the expatriate community. Each is international to some degree, at least if foreign residence is so considered. Closely associated with such schools are those institutions (often missionary in origin) incorporated and controlled in the nation of the founders but used by the nationals in the state in which they have been settled. A case could be made that the oldest post-medieval schools are such. Their evolution has, for the most part, allowed them to become binational schools reflecting both the founder's national educational orientation and that of the (often emergent) country in which they are located. The French *lycées* of Africa are one such grouping. Another are the Anglo–American Christian schools in the Indian sub-continent.

Among the more contemporary of these schools, as far as

origins are concerned, are to be found the so-called "American International", usually parent owned but subsidized by the US State Department provided they become demonstration centres of American education. Many of these schools are insulated, to use the description of Professor Redefer of New York University by "cellophane walls" from the national community in which they are located. For the most part, it is clear the overseas schools are devoted to preparing their students for rapid integration into the life of the nation of origin at whatever point their clientele goes home.

Practically none of these overseas schools, whether older missionary or more contemporary government promoted, are the product of bilateral national initiative. They are, in fact, national schools abroad, sometimes taking advantage of the international framework in which they could work. Usually they may be classified as French International, British International, American International, German International, etc.

A third grouping of international schools are those founded by joint action of two or more governments or national groupings. These are relatively few, though they include at least a few of the so-called binational schools of Latin America, those along the German–French border and, most recently, the John F. Kennedy School in Berlin. Even such an international school as that in Geneva resulted from the initiative of Swiss, French and American nationals working together. The most spectacularly successful of the multilateral grouping are the European (Common Market) schools, which grew out of a parent-owned institution in Luxembourg, when the six governments involved signed an agreement at Sèvres in 1956 allowing for a chain of schools leading to the European Baccalaureate and consequent admission in practice to most of the universities of the world. But like the internationally minded schools, the European schools draw a sharp distinction between themselves and international schools. This is partly due to their position as pioneers in achieving inter-state financial backing and partly that they do not pretend to be more than European.

The fourth grouping includes those who do belong to the International Schools Association (ISA), or could do so. But even here the lines are blurred, as the philosophy of ISA has been such as to accept for membership schools moving toward its criteria but not clearly already there. In addition, ISA has not laid down a sharp integral internationally international standard by which the genuine international school might be recognized. There are two reasons for this. First, the subject has never been thoroughly discussed by its board and, secondly, if a too rigid standard were adopted, it would find itself without member schools. However, implicit in the ISA criteria is the notion that no one government nor national grouping (especially the host nation and largest expatriate community) should control the international school nor hold half the seats in its board of governors, however selected. In addition, no special privilege may be given any social grouping, religious body or ideological point of view. It is, on the affirmative side, intended to educate young people to be at home in the world anywhere. The development, since 1965, of the International Baccalaureate, closely associated with ISA, offers an equivalent reality for university enrolment comparable with the European Baccalaureate. At least two of the ISA member schools, those in New York and in Geneva, are in receipt of annual gifts or pledges from the United Nations or its specialized bodies. Obviously, the success of a chain of internationally international schools will be dependent on a large governmental subsidy without consequent controls. At the present time, ISA is only beginning to explore this field of development—the International School of Geneva, as usual, taking the initiative.

Incidentally, there appear to be practically no international universities, which is an interesting commentary in itself on what has become of an authentic international institution founded in medieval times. The so-called College of Europe at Bruges, founded in 1950, comes perhaps nearest to it, though more than half its budget is given by the Belgian Government (with five other governments participating in its financing).

Only forty-six students are enrolled yearly for a post-university year, which is essentially European in approach. More than half its governing board are Belgian. One might almost be sure that this is a good example of Belgian internationalism.

The other university—International Christian, founded in Tokyo in 1952 and grown to a student body of 1250, is essentially binational in origin—Japanese and American. In this case, the tradition of Christian philanthropy in the United States joined with liberal Japanese of all faiths to confront bankrupt shintoism with the better Christian traditions. It has grown rapidly, reflecting as much as anything the impact of American influence in post-war Japan. Obviously, to become genuinely international this university should multilateralize, that is, assure that its board of managers and financial subsidy is not dominated by any nationality, especially not American nor Japanese.

D. TYPES OF INTERNATIONALISM

A rapid classification of schools calling themselves international forces one back to a more scientific analysis of the criteria involved. The field is fluid to an incredible degree. Each institution is different from the others (except perhaps among the six Common Market schools). In the light of such complexity, some observers try to find a non-juridical plumb-line. Sometimes it is suggested that bilingualism is the true touchstone, and a good case can be made that English and French as the commercial and diplomatic international languages should be equally used. This, however, takes little account of international schools located in Germany or India, or in Japan for example. A better case can be made for the school which consciously emphasizes the interpenetration of Occident and Orient at every turn—but how is this to be attempted in Physics or Chemistry? One is driven back to educational policy sooner or later along with the composition of boards of managers and financial subsidies which, in the end, determine such policy. I think it can be maintained that only when each national, financial and trusteeship interest is in the minority is it possible to achieve more than a national internationalism. There is, furthermore, no assurance that once every national interest is in the minority, more than an uneasy compromise between and among national internationalisms will be achieved.

To summarize, there is a phenomenon which dominates our age and has done for half a millennium—namely, nationalism. Each nation state cherishes its own way of life and develops its educational system to assure its continuance. Each nation maintains foreign relations intending that its own image be projected as creative, particularly as its internationalism. Thus each nation develops its own national-type internationalism. Those nations with extensive foreign commitments feel a sense of responsibility for their nationals abroad and often for the peoples in whose areas their national influence has spread. Frequently this takes the form of religious zeal. In any case, it is fairly easy to persuade governments to subsidize nationally dominated overseas "international" schools, particularly if they serve as "demonstration centres" for the country represented. Similarly, it has been easy to interest private and foundation charity in such enterprises. This type of internationalism is unilateral—it is concerned chiefly with its own personnel away from home.

After the First World War and particularly after the Second World War, the American Government, having emerged from isolationism—which is the domestic political concomitant of unilateral internationalism—undertook, chiefly through the agency of the Fulbright program, to launch itself into bilateral internationalism—that is exchange between and among students, chiefly at university level. The Institute of International Education in New York (itself an American incorporated institution with an American board and American finance) became perhaps the outstanding example of a unilateral international organization devoted to promoting bilateral internationalism. Nothing, incidentally, could be more respectable nor, incidentally, more conservative in this field. The celebrated Peace Corps is another similar activity. And it is significant that the small international Peace Corps group has never really grown.

What of course is needed is a practical application of the policy Jesus of Nazareth advocated to the man who wanted to know how to save his life. In other words, multilateral internationalism is necessary. In this case, investment of money must come from at least three national sources—no one of them dominant—and the trustees of such grants to educational institutions similarly distributed. This, I maintain, is the basic minimum allowing for international or multilateral internationalism to develop. More, of course, is required.

The truly multilateral international school must be devoted to the principle that the highest common denominator between and among the various contributing national elements is essential. Rather naturally, the whole world becomes the local parish for the multilateral international school. Each major tradition can be analyzed for its strengths and usefulness. Once this course has been decided upon and the essential unity of mankind therefore underscored, the possibility of achieving a result which will enrich each national heritage is made possible. Such a step seems, in retrospect, the only sensible course to have taken. This is the experience of a number of teachers in international schools which approach or have achieved multilateral internationalism.

The great virtue of educational multilateralism lies in its potential in demonstrating to at least a few leaders in the forthcoming generation that nation states may eventually follow similar policies politically without loss to their identity. It has been suggested in the adventurous *Discovering Art* publication that since the second World War all plastic art-forms have been interpenetrated by the influence of all others. If, as it has been postulated, the plastic arts are the most contemporary of man's activities in any given age, then by this token it would seem that the notion of multilateral international education has come into its own in our time. An educational programme interpenetrated by the major currents of value known in our world would be the equivalent of internationalism in the plastic arts. Where better to start this than in the multilateral international school?

CHAPTER 2

THE INTERNATIONAL SCHOOLS ASSOCIATION

THE academic community has not yet become very much aware of the phenomenon known as the international school, even though two doctoral dissertations have been undertaken on them and on the International Schools Association, the organization which binds them together. It is appropriate, therefore, to consider here in the first place the origins, development and achievements of ISA and later give some account of various international schools to illustrate further the problems they meet and to examine their possibilities.

The ISA is now 16 years old (although for the first 5 years of its existence it was known as the International Schools Liaison Committee). As an illustration of its growth it is interesting to note that attendance at its annual meetings from 1951 to 1955 averaged ten; from 1955 to 1960, thirteen; and from 1961 to date, forty. In point of fact, the history of ISA falls into three equal periods, the second break occurring at the time of the Social Studies Conference it held in Geneva in August–September 1962, which proved the most important turning point in the life of the Association. (This Conference was attended by sixty persons.)

The primary legitimate question to ask is why the Association gathered momentum so slowly.

In the first place only one international school survived the Second World War—that in Geneva. It was only in 1949 that similar institutions began to be established elsewhere: in New York, rather naturally, for the children of UN officials; in Paris for those of UNESCO and in Rome for those of FAO.

Since the Geneva School was unwilling at that time to create a kindergarten, a nursery school was established in Geneva along similar lines.

All these institutions, except for that in Rome, were represented on 20 November 1951 at Unesco House in Paris when the Liaison Committee was formed. Rather naturally, it was the Geneva School which took the initiative. The members of its governing board were also UN officials. It appears they hoped to develop close relations with UNESCO, but when this failed to happen, they managed to achieve consultative status with ECOSOC (in 1956)—this was secured through the personal interest of Dag Hammarskjöld himself, who asked Ralph Bunche when on mission to Geneva to look into the *bona fides* of ISA.

Up to the present the affairs of ISA have been handled for the most part by UN officials connected with the Geneva School. This largely for practical reasons: only the Geneva grouping was large enough at the outset to constitute an effective executive; most of the annual meetings could be arranged to coincide with visits of UN personnel in Paris and New York who could act on behalf of the schools in those places. Although serious attempts have been made in recent years to make the Association's executive more representative, the cost of bringing members to Geneva or of holding meetings elsewhere has tended to leave the Geneva contingent in day-to-day control. This situation is not unusual. Most international organizations are, in fact, structured essentially on location.

Paris might logically have become the center of ISA had the hoped-for international school there evolved. What happened was that the original school remained at nursery level. A few years later an *école active bilingue* was set up, originally on a private venture. Only last year (1966) was it recognized as the International School of Paris by UNESCO. It is now beginning to develop a secondary section. This School was rebuffed when it first sought membership with ISA in 1956, but after the Social Studies Conference in 1962 it became a member and has since become one of the most active participants in the affairs of the Association. A French committee to promote ISA was formed in 1964 and has worked closely with UNESCO to promote the interests of ISA, and at the same time has secured official recognition from the French Government.

New York might also have served as the logical center of ISA, since the international school there was the object of interest of even more influential members of the UN secretariat than those in Geneva, but the tremendous problem of financing a school in the Manhattan area has absorbed practically all the energies of its governing board. New York was content to allow Geneva the job of looking after the needs of International schools in general.

In 1956 the Association took the initiative of founding the International Schools Foundation (ISF) (later known as International Schools Services (ISS)) in New York and Washington to promote the work of international schools. Unfortunately, the Association had not yet arrived at a clear definition of what constitutes multilateral internationalism, nor did it exercise sufficient care to ensure that ISF should be juridically controlled by ISA. The ISF caught the interest of the State Department of Washington, which was looking for an agency to supervise the interests of national American schools overseas. Thus ISF came to be financed jointly by the Ford Foundation and USAID and found itself promoting schools which, by the very nature of things, competed with the internationally international schools. The board of the New York International School was involved in the initial stages of the work of ISF and found itself torn between promoting genuine internationalism in education throughout the world and co-operating with the American foundation world which looked with approval on Ford's grant to the ISF.*

*) Before the inevitable break occurred between ISA and ISF the two organizations had published jointly a brochure called *News Links*, which, ironically, served to get the Ford grant.

Rome never competed seriously as the headquarters of ISA. Only in 1953 did it send an observer to an ISA meeting and then joined in a half-hearted manner. No further representative attended from Rome until 1958, when it was reported that the School had become, in effect, an American school overseas to satisfy USAID requirements. Meanwhile, ISF was actively assisting it in staffing and educational materials. In 1961 Rome sent another representative to an ISA meeting, but resigned membership altogether in 1964. Obviously the notion of multilateral internationalism had not taken root in the Eternal City.

Money has been, of course, the root of the problem facing ISA. The original membership fees allowed for a total income of $40 yearly! Efforts to obtain a grant from a foundation (except as regards ISF) were uniformly negative. The Association represented too few schools, and foundations in general were unwilling to use ISA as a channel to finance schools whose liquidity was doubtful. Also, ISA found it difficult to formulate its objectives, which, in fact, it has grown to appreciate only gradually. Further, it failed to follow up a report made by the Paris American School in 1958, in which the technical "know-how" of American fund-raising was explained.

However, in 1958, a new system of subscriptions was put into operation: $15 annually for schools of up to 150 pupils, $75 for those of up to 400 and $100 for larger schools. Although this allowed for the appointment of a part-time paid secretary, most schools found it impossible for currency reasons to pay their dues, or imprudent to strain resources. A gift of $500 allowed for a new part-time secretary in 1961. A similar grant paid for the Social Studies Conference mentioned above. In fact, this was subsidized to the extent of $7500 by the loaning out of a full-time teacher from the Geneva International School to act as Consultant to ISA for the calendar year 1961–2. Another $2500 was raised by the Geneva School that year to underwrite the travelling expenses of the consultant, about $1000 of which was raised jointly by the Headmaster of the School and the consultant himself. The remainder of the travel costs was paid off by "ISA Day" fêtes held at the Geneva School—after being advanced by the School as a loan.

In 1962 the elaborate fee structure set up in 1958 was scrapped as unworkable, and the notion of an "ISA Day" was promoted. This, in turn, proved equally unworkable, and in 1963 it was agreed that each family with children in an ISA school would be asked to pay a (non-obligatory) annual fee of $3. This scheme has worked to some extent and in 1964 a full-time secretary was engaged; today the Association functions on a $9000 budget.

Since 1962 also four UNESCO contracts were undertaken, which provided $10,000, most of which, of course, had to be spent in accordance with the requirements laid down by UNESCO, particularly on the publication of the results of the work undertaken. The substantive aspects of these contracts will be dealt with later on in another chapter.

It should be pointed out that UNESCO recently—in September 1966—reclassified ISA as a category B consultative organization, as a result of its work for the International Examination programme. This upgrading should entitle ISA to a much fuller support from UNESCO in its future work.

It was only in 1955 that ISA made a serious attempt to think out what constitutes internationalism. An earlier rule of thumb had been the "self-evident" element of internationalism in staffing and student body, together with a close relationship to some UN agency. The 1955 formulation came as the result of bringing a cartesian logician, a French headmaster, into the daily working of ISA. Up to this point Anglo–Americans had played the dominant role.

A thorough rewrite of the standards of internationalism was undertaken by the consultant as the final task of his year's assignment. It was then that the notion of "multilateral internationalism" was made explicit. There still remains the question of which categories of overseas schools should remain the concern of ISA, even though they do not qualify for membership as multilateral schools. The question of membership itself might bear reviewing, provided the financial stability of the Association were maintained.

I think it may be postulated that the Liaison Committee was an essentially avocational activity of a few internationally minded public servants whose interests (largely of a protocol nature) determined the course of ISA. Then, till 1962, ISA was very much under the influence of a group of headmasters who used its meetings as forums in which to test out their own theoretical biases in the field of international education. Since 1962 ISA has been a proving ground of another group of international school headmasters, whose careers have included the classroom experience of international education. They have put into theory what in practice they have known to be true. I shall try to substantiate these judgments in the following pages.

Until 1962 no headmaster of an international school served as an officer of ISA. Even the Education Subcommittee was chaired by international officials till 1956 (except for one period which did not prove productive). The Liaison Committee was concerned with such considerations as acquiring the right to report directly to the Secretary-General of the United Nations, helping push forward educational allowances for UN employees and the promotion of General George Marshall's opinions on the importance of education for peace. The achievement of consultative status with ECOSOC (1956) was a continuation of this trend, as was the proposal of an ECOSOC-sponsored world meeting of international educationalists for which ISA circulated a draft agenda. This conference was never held, but "face" was saved by representation at the 1959 Human Rights Conference, at which a paper dealing with the problems involved in eradication of prejudice and discrimination in textbooks was presented by ISA. To prepare this paper ISA sponsored a series of meetings held at the European Center of the Carnegie Endowment in Geneva. It is interesting to observe that no teacher in any international school sat with the group of international public servants chosen by ISA to act on its behalf. An attempt to get UNESCO to finance this singularly unrelated activity failed.

After 1955 the Annual meetings of ISA were divided into general sessions and those known as official business meetings. This division encouraged the headmasters attending to consider their common problems. The meetings tended to be dominated by the Headmasters from Geneva, Brussels (member since 1957), The Hague (1956) and New York. Curiously, a good many subjects spoken on by the headmasters concerned dealt with fields in which the individual headmaster felt personally unhappy: for instance one whose business management was considered inadequate spoke in 1957 on "Financial Control and Education" The panacea proposed was that international schools be subsidized by local governments. Parenthetically, it never occurred to ISA to think of obtaining the services of an international auditing company, or to call on an international firm of lawyers to work out its statutes. They saw no anomaly in turning to Swiss auditors and Swiss legal counsel.

Another headmaster suggested, in 1957, that a postgraduate course be offered to recruit teachers for international schools —a course involving Comparative Education, Philosophy of Education, Social and Applied Psychology and Social Anthropology. Still a third headmaster, in 1957, discussed the model plant for an international school based on a "social wing" complete with plural gymnasia, swimming pools, television, projection rooms, etc.—amenities which, until the new New York School is built, have been totally absent in all international schools. In 1961 still a fourth headmaster led the discussion on "Physical Education"—his school was innocent of all facilities in that area of activity. The same headmaster had discussed teachers' contracts in 1957, displaying a marked

3*

aversion to collective contracts and teachers' associations in general. The headmaster who had proposed the postgraduate courses, on another occasion led a discussion on student government and democracy in the student body—both of which he only partially approved. By 1961 these men had talked themselves out—no funds had materialized. (Finally Brussels resigned in 1964, having been "Americanized".)

The crisis was met by the new Headmaster in Geneva who proposed the loaning out of a consultant, as before mentioned. The consultant's travels to schools of international interest in Europe, Africa and Asia not only brought together the first ISA conference planned for one subject, but underscored the absolute necessity of creating international examinations for a recognized international graduation certificate. Without this no school could afford to go all the way with its internationalism. Concurrent with such an examination programme was the necessity of the reconstruction of curricula. The ISA then had before it a practical target of tremendous proportions.

It is interesting to read that in 1953 the Education Sub-committee of ISA had reported that co-ordination of curricula at the Secondary Level was "difficult if not impossible". Even so, by 1956 the general meeting discussed the possibilities of "establishing equivalents for university entrance examinations". In 1957 a damper was put on the interest in developing international curricula by the declaration that since parents were not fundamentally international, neither could their children be. It was also stated that classes in the mother tongue ought to be limited to eighteen students, but those not in the mother tongue to eight. A year later it was declared categorically that "it was impossible to teach in a second language". Such negative approaches put off visitors from the Tangiers and Athens American Schools, as well as discouraging the Association from looking into university entrance equivalents.

In 1962, with encouragement from the French UNESCO Commission, the Institute of Education of London University and the American Federation of Learned Societies, ISA crystallized its thinking regarding the need and practicability of developing multilaterally international syllabuses and examinations set bilingually. The International School of Geneva was prepared to encourage its History Department to develop the first pilot project in Contemporary History 1913–63.

At the same time ISA established its first Headmasters' Committee, which continued to meet at fairly frequent intervals in the next few years. Its first task was to negotiate the first UNESCO contract, which led to a special seminar in Paris in the spring of 1963 to formulate how best ISA could contribute to the "Mutual Appreciation of Cultural Values of East and West". This credit allowed for the publication of syllabuses and examination papers being prepared in "Contemporary History 1913–63" as well as formulating a program of exchanging certain educational and cultural materials between and among international schools.

A year later the second contract was granted to deal with "The Co-ordination of Academic Standards and Criteria among International Schools". This grant led to the publication of a report which was formulated by one teacher from the Geneva School who had not only participated in the formulation of the Contemporary History program but had also been given leave to visit key ISA schools.

Meanwhile, another participant in the History program undertook a visit to Great Britain to sound out education authorities in general and discover their reaction to what was in process of formulation as an International Baccalaureate. So affirmative was the reaction that it was decided that Ministries of Education throughout the world should be circulated with the Contemporary History program.

In 1963 the regular meetings of ISA were held conjointly with a seminar on the teaching of Modern Languages with British, French, German, Italian and American specialists brought in. The meeting looked forward to the creation of pilot international examinations in Modern Languages. But at this point discussions as to the form the entire baccalaureate should take interposed, so that actual preparation of the language examination was postponed to the autumn of 1964 when a colloquium sponsored by ISA was held at Atlantic College. By that time the French educational authorities and those in the United States had become sufficiently interested for ISA to envisage creating a separate legal entity to administer the International Baccalaureate program. Thus, on 1 January 1965 the International Schools Examination Syndicate (ISES) came into being. Its story is reserved for the next chapter of this study.

ISA decided against holding a subject conference coincident with its business meeting in 1964: rather, it approved a policy of constructing international curricula from the nursery school upwards. In line with this decision the 1965 meeting was devoted to teaching the new Mathematics in the primary school, while that of 1966 was given over to a general conference on the whole of the primary curriculum in international schools. This last was attended by some fifty teachers and in many respects proved as important as the Social Studies Conference 4 years previously.

But in this instance the ground was carefully prepared by the Headmasters' Committee—which in the meantime had become known as the Education Committee.

It might seem peculiar, on the surface of it, that ISA should appear to be so much more interested in primary rather than secondary education. In fact, the member schools composing ISA determined this situation. It will be recalled that of the four schools which originated the Association, two of them were nursery schools. The New York School only developed its secondary section some years after its foundation, while Rome, though a fully-fledged school was early Americanized. The secondary section of the Brussels School became totally Americanized as it grew up, owing to the competition from the local "Common Market" European School. The International School of The Hague was similarly American in its main secondary section. A German primary and secondary school which was loosely affiliated with it broke away, though its headmaster once attended an ISA meeting. The Hague American secondary headmaster worked on the Headmasters' Committee—but unhappily he was drowned when on holiday in Israel in the spring of 1965. Since then, the Hague School has been relatively inactive in ISA. The International School of Paris is only now beginning to develop a secondary section.

It might be useful at this point to note the changes in membership of schools associated with ISA—most of which joined through personal contacts. Several international schools have been created, as it were, *in vacuo*, and only later on have discovered that there are others.

First a word on nursery schools. These were very much overlooked during the period of the Liaison Committee and almost equally so during the "theoretical" period up to 1962. More vocal school authorities took the floor at the annual meetings. Then the Hellerup (Denmark) Nursery School joined as a result of contacts developed by the consultant. This school is rapidly expanding and is now known as Bjorns' International School, with both kindergarten and primary classes. It is being consciously developed on a multilingual basis. In 1966 the kindergartens shared in managing one section of the Primary Curriculum Conference where they were joined by the new nursery-school section being set up by the International School of Geneva.

The Djakarta International School joined ISA in 1956 at the same time as the International Schools in Rome and The Hague. But then they were all swept into the American overseas schools orbit and, in 1962, were dropped from the membership. The International School of Yokohama (which, though founded in 1924, closed in 1940, and only re-opened in 1955) learned of ISA through the consultant and hastened to become a member in 1963. Its headmaster was able to participate in the 1966 Conference, where he took a leading part.

A strongminded refusal to be influenced by the Americanization normal in the Far East was a major motive in determining
Yokohama's adherence to ISA.

In 1957, at the same time as the Brussels International
School, the Karachi Grammar School in Pakistan asked to be
admitted. The question of its membership was left open for
5 years as the grammar school appeared to be a Christian-
oriented institution in a Moslem country. By the time (1962) a
decision was taken in favour of admission, the school had
become nationalized, and when the consultant visited in that
year, its status as an international school had vanished. In the
same year, 1957, the Vienna International School presented
and then withdrew its candidacy. The School was suffering
grave dissensions resulting from its breaking up into a British–
Indian section and an American–Canadian section. The latter
was drawn into the Social Studies and Paris/UNESCO Conferences, in spite of its very American orientation. In 1963, the
American International School of Vienna, as it came to be
called, applied for membership of ISA, but when, shortly
afterwards, the headmastership changed hands, the application lapsed. The Karachi and both the Viennese Schools have
secondary sections.

An even more complex situation was presented by the request of the Kabul International School to join ISA in 1959.
This struggling primary school existed in competition with
several overseas schools, none of which was constitutionally
recognized by the Afghan Government. The ISA consultant
engaged in a series of careful negotiations to bring about a
merger of a number of these institutions, so that one strong,
multilaterally international school might arise, with the indirect encouragement of the Afghan educational authorities. Not
long afterwards, however, the ISA school went bankrupt.
A number of parents and diplomatic officials in the American
expatriate community took the opportunity to create a financially viable school in modern buildings—admittedly American
in orientation and character—with the help of USAID funds.

The merger came about in 1964 but at cost to ISA and possibly with the loss of an international school which might have secured collaboration between the USSR and the USA, as Kabul is genuinely a cultural "no-man's land".

A contrast is offered by the Community School of Tehran, which joined ISA in 1962 after a visit by the consultant. It played a role in the Paris/UNESCO Conference of 1963 and the subsequent 1964 Cultural Exchange program. It has declared itself genuinely interested in the International Baccalaureate, but so far has been content to experiment on its own. Its pro-international orientation comes in large part from the fact that Tehran offers also the facilities of a large American grammar and high school.

Some remarks are called for here about the Indian subcontinent, which was also visited by the consultant. In Delhi he was given the opportunity of explaining the operation of British GCE examinations to the American board of the American International School there. They expressed themselves as interested, and even more so if the projected International Baccalaureate were created. It will be interesting to observe how receptive such overseas schools prove to be when that far-off day occurs.

In Bombay the newly created international school might well have associated itself with ISA—it has advertised through ISA for a headmaster—but as it is essentially a bilateral Indian–American venture it has remained unassociated. This was not the case of the Overseas School of Colombo, which promptly joined ISA after the consultant's visit—though it never developed a secondary section as has its next-door neighbor, the American School.

Quite recently, ISA has been drawn into consultation on the setting up of an international school in Katmandu in Nepal. At the same time the opportunity was taken for an ISA headmaster who acted as consultant to travel to Bangkok and Manila (at the latter place to attend a Conference of American Overseas Schools). It is overwhelmingly clear that in neither place did he meet with genuine understanding of or respect for the idea of internationalism without American control, approach and finances.

Three schools have recently attracted the interest of ISA. The first of these, Brummana High School, in the hills above Beirut, like St. Hilda's School, Octacamund, which learned of ISA in 1965 and applied for membership, was the product of nineteenth century missionary endeavour, but has, in effect, found a wider orientation in helping to educate "emergent" groups. The consultant visited Brummana in 1962 but it was only in 1966 that it finally joined ISA. As a high school oriented towards the British GCE, it will be interesting to see what role it will give the International Baccalaureate.

The same comment applies to the English School of Nicosia, which became a member in 1964. Admittedly the Cyprus crisis rather interfered with the Nicosia School doing more than holding its own. In consequence it has not played any significant part in ISA affairs to date. The third school to join ISA from the Middle East area is the United Nations School in Gaza, which became a member in 1966, but was closed down in consequence to the "dune" war of 1967 in the Middle East.

Finally, note should be taken of the American School of Alexandria, which sent a delegate to the 1962 Conference but whose candidacy for membership was turned down— partly because of its frankly American orientation, but also because it is a Presbyterian school catering for the children of missionaries. This school likewise fell a victim to the Middle East war.

Very little interest has been expressed by ISA in international schools located in the Communist sectors of the world. It would appear that only the most tenuous connection has been established with the English-Speaking School in Prague, the Anglo–American School in Moscow, and the American School in Warsaw. On the other hand, the International

School of Belgrade was granted associate status in 1959. In this case, the School can only exist under the wing of an embassy—in Belgrade, as it happens, that of the USA. Consequently, the "internationalism" of the Belgrade School has depended upon the "internationalism" of the American community at any given time. The Yugoslavs connected with the school try at all times to promote the ISA connection, but their voice is muted. This is a primary school.

The relatively new International School of Trieste has, on various occasions, made approaches to ISA but to date still remains outside. In contrast, the International School of Milan has been an ardent supporter of ISA. Recently, troubles inside the school have prevented a more active collaboration. Another of the members, joining in 1962, is the Zurich Inter-community School, which has become, with the École Active Bilingue of Paris, one of the most active supporters of ISA. Its headmaster has made extensive trips for ISA through Africa, Northern Europe and Asia in recent times. Unlike the Trieste and Milan Schools it is a primary school only. Recently, the Headmaster of the Zurich School has been engaged in negotiations for the establishment of an international school in Düsseldorf.

It is unfortunate that the English-speaking school in Bern has shown very little interest in the ISA. The St. Jean International School in Fribourg (Switzerland) did show an interest in 1965, but was not encouraged as it is a Catholic boarding school, and recently became a member of the Council of Overseas Schools founded in New York under the auspices of the International Schools Services (successor to the ISF). This is an unusual step for Fribourg to take as it is supported by an international religious order and only recently decided to start an English section. This is a school which should welcome the International Baccalaureate.

There is no member school of ISA located in Germany. The International School of Frankfurt is wholly American in orientation: the International School of Hamburg is largely

British: the International Gymnasium in Bonn is purely German. The John F. Kennedy School in Berlin is bilaterally German–American. In Copenhagen, the Bernadotteskolen has shown a limited interest in ISA, as has the International Folk High School in Elsinore. But the second Scandinavian member is the Viggbyholmsskolen of Stockholm, which only joined in 1966. This school is very much interested in the International Baccalaureate.

Another ISA member admitted in 1966 is the Eerde en Rhederoord International School of Holland, which professes great interest in the International Baccalaureate. This school sent delegates to the 1962 Conference.

At this point reference should be made to the two NATO international schools of St. Germain-en-Laye and Fontainebleau, which did not join ISA owing to the fact they are official French schools, but which have, on occasion, maintained friendly contacts. The 1962 Conference brought as well an observer from the Brussels European (Common Market) School.

One of the strange facts that appear in studying the configuration of ISA membership is to find that only one school in Great Britain is a member. This is Atlantic College, a "sixth-form" institution intended as a prototype for others about the rim of the Atlantic Ocean. Its membership dates from 1964, when it joined in bearing a major responsibility in planning the International Baccalaureate and was the second school to present candidates for pilot examinations in 1967. It has not, however, played a significant role in the work of ISA itself.

Equally strange is the absence of member schools in the New World. New York was somewhat inactive in ISA affairs after 1962, though it is taking an active part in the work for the International Baccalaureate, and sent a large contingent to the 1967 Conference. The "Committee for Establishing an International School in Washington" has worked closely with ISA, but has so far only led to the establishment of a very small primary school, set up by one of the members of the Committee. It recently applied for membership in ISA. In 1965 the French School in Toronto did join ISA. This School is also a primary school. In 1962 the Waldorf School in Mexico City expressed an interest which proved abortive. In fact the only pan-American school to make a serious bid for ISA contact is the Santiago College of Chile. A school in Montevideo and another in Port-au-Prince, Haïti, have also recently shown their interest. Two private schools in Spain have also applied for membership.

This leaves us Africa as the last major region in which to make inquiry. There, the Headmaster of the Geneva school undertook yeoman service after the consultant had made his initial trip. Two other ISA visitors have also left their impact on the continent. The first school to join ISA was the Ghana International School in 1958. It has served as a nexus of ISA interest in West Africa, and has generally been co-operative. In 1963 the Dar-es-Salaam International School was formed under the care and advice of ISA.

In 1964 the LAMCO International School of Liberia became a member—this School has now withdrawn from ISA, however, believing, as an industry-sponsored institution oriented towards Sweden, that it can get along best by itself.

Neither the International School of Freetown, Sierra Leone, nor that of Ibadan, Nigeria, have joined: nor, in fact, those in Libreville nor in Leopoldville. The Corona Trust School of Kano, Nigeria, joined in 1966, as has the Ridge Church School of Accra and the Tema Parents' Association School. Except for the Ghana International School, none of the ISA schools in Africa is at secondary level as yet, though there are active plans for a secondary international school at Moshi in Tanzania, which is envisaged as being wholly integrated into the International Baccalaureate.

It might be useful to summarize the membership of ISA as follows:

1951 Four
1956 Six
1961 Eleven
1966 Twenty-six

In any case, more specific references to individual schools will be made later on in this chapter, when it should prove more possible to evaluate the future prospects of the Association.

In the autumn of 1958, ISA started to publish its *Newsletter Bulletin*. Five issues appeared during that academic year, followed by one in 1959–60. The impression given was of a struggling news-sheet trying to establish itself and hardly succeeding. Only one issue appeared in 1960–1 and a further one on the third anniversary of the original issue. Only in the late winter of 1961–2 did the publication revive. It now appeared monthly giving first accounts of the consultant's travels and then full reporting during the "third" period of ISA activity of conferences, contracts, applications for membership and developments in curricula, and specifically the International Baccalaureate. The consultant continued to edit the revived *Newsletter* until the mid-spring of 1964, when the ISA Secretary took over the responsibility. Since the beginning of 1965 it has appeared every two months but with a greatly increased format. During the 1962–4 period the *Newsletter* was, in effect, a testimony to faith, which has subsequently appeared to have been justified.

The ISA has existed in a rather curious isolation from other school associations, at least till the 1962 Social Studies Conference. The most curious of these situations concerns its relations with the Council of Internationally Minded Schools (CIS), a body which was founded in Paris in 1949. The CIS early secured consultative status with UNESCO and undertook extensive work-camp, "outward-bound" and cultural festivities, with its support. The researcher in the field of International Education will be astounded to discover that the Geneva International School was a founder member of the CIS, but after 1953 played no role whatsoever in its activities, nor did the practical experiences of the CIS appear to have been known to ISA before 1962. At that time the Geneva School again became active in the CIS, acting as host to one of its conferences—on International Organizations—in 1963. The CIS conference in 1965, which was held in Colorado, was attended by a very large group of teachers from ISA schools, thus making possible a confrontation between international schools and schools which though juridically national, were eager for as wide an international experience as possible.

This latter category may well find a growing common interest in the International Baccalaureate, though the CIS as a body is more concerned with student exchange than examinations.

In 1959 the National Association of Independent Schools in the U.S.A. extended ISA free membership of that body, an offer which was not taken up (probably because it still hoped to secure a workable *modus vivendi* with ISF (ISS)). Now, 8 years later the Hon. Secretary of ISA was asked to address the annual meeting of the NAIS in Boston. Admittedly there are anomalies in having an international association join a national organization—but without any such connections it is difficult to secure publicity for the work of ISA. To affiliate to a number of different national assocations could only be useful both to them and to ISA. Parenthetically, it should be observed that in 1966 much better relations were established with the International Schools Services (ISS) as the notion of multilateral internationalism has gained adherents within the US State Department, and the orientation of ISS has changed in such a way as to appreciate rather than denigrate what ISA has set as an ideal.

After 1962 the regular meetings of the Headmasters' Committee which was formed at that time (later known as the Education Committee) has supplied much of the insight and drive in the current period. As has been indicated, curriculum and examination preparation has been markedly successful—also negotiation of UNESCO contracts, the third of which paired several international schools in the Orient and Occident in the exchange of teaching materials.

In the area of staffing, ISA has had a more limited success. A certain amount of interviewing has been carried out by ISA officials—but the cost of doing this effectively throughout the world is prohibitive. In tackling in-service training, which poses particularly difficult problems, ISA has been able to interest colleges of education in the USA and Britain. So far, only a few teachers in training at the Oxford University Department of Education take their practice teaching at the International School of Geneva. Since the establishment of a regular office (1964) in Geneva, a steady flow of visitors interested in the work of ISA stop by at headquarters to obtain information about its activities.

An attempt to establish sports competitions between ISA Schools has not gone well—one reason being the scarcity of secondary sections capable of producing adequate teams. The sponsorship of a study of prejudice in textbooks met with very little success. Most potential participants were just too busy to get on with the additional burden of reading and judging. A good critic needs to develop sensitive antennae not only to glaring injustice but also to more subtle unfairnesses arrived at by selecting materials in such a way as to convey unstated judgments. Obviously a trained and highly-paid staff is needed for effective work in this field. If ISA eventually becomes involved in sponsoring the writing of manuals and the preparation of programmed materials for integral international teaching, the more negative work of judging extant national texts will become somewhat less academic.*

The second subject conference held by ISA involved Modern Languages (1963). Obviously, international schools are

*) It was along this line that the extensive textbook exhibition assembled by one headmaster at the Social Studies Conference tended to go. In

particularly placed to develop languages, yet it would appear that "language laboratories" have tended to develop outside ISA schools. There is much to be learned. It would seem that the Language of Instruction and Foreign Language panels of the International Baccalaureate have gone far to remedy in theory what will need to be put into practice at this point.

The third subject conference (1965) was devoted to teaching the "New Mathematics in the Primary School". Here it would appear that some international schools are as advanced as any in working with the new concepts and methods. Perhaps the very environment of the international school proves conductive to the universal logic of the new system.

The fourth (1966) subject conference of ISA, devoted to the whole spectrum of primary education, found its participants open to the notion of interdisciplinary environmental studies which both the French speaker and the speaker from the Nuffield Foundation saw as appropriate to international schools.

Obviously, the implementation of International Baccalaureate standards at secondary and ISA standards at primary level (as suggested in 1966) will require a tremendous amount of in-service training. The natural inertia of the human being and the security of sticking to known ways of doing things stand in the way of innovation. Add to this the need to respect national standards (practically every teacher has been trained within a single national system) and any movement is brought to a standstill. What ISA and ISES have proved is that for those who venture into genuinely comparative educational

---

this case a huge labour of love was expended in collecting some thousands of texts (in English—too many actually American). They were carefully analyzed and grouped, with result of proving them nearly all too ethnocentric, too Occidental and too Judeo–Christian in value judgments to be universally useful. The American texts were, in addition, often too juvenile for the highest common denominator required by the genuine international school.

approaches, the whole matter becomes tremendously exciting. Objectivity is assured, and sometimes highest common denominators are found and adopted. Altogether, perhaps eighty schools have been drawn into this work sponsored by ISA— perhaps this is more significant than growth in membership.

In the spring of 1964 a particularly important Symposium on International Education was held at the Pedagogical Centre at Sèvres under the auspices of the French section of the Association of European Teachers. The Common Market, NATO and ISA schools met to discuss common interests. Two British institutions were represented: Atlantic College and the Oxford University Department of Education. The former had been offering bilateral agreements with Ministries of Education and universities in general. The second had a multilingual staff-member serving as expert for the Commission on Education of the Council of Europe. For both, the pilot program developed by ISA towards an International Baccalaureate was a step ahead of anything else they had met with. As will be seen in the next chapter, both these institutions have become closely involved in promoting the ISES program. The interest of the French Government in the baccalaureate is not unrelated to the Sèvres Colloquium of 1964.

Still another initiative of ISA to help prepare the teaching of Science in the primary school was the extensive trip across the United States and Canada of another teacher detached from teaching at the Geneva School in 1966. In this case, the materials collected and the "know-how" were shared with international schools in Africa before being discussed at the Primary Curricula Conference. In reporting to UNESCO on this Conference, ISA has emphasized that in reality its curriculum work is only just beginning: that it should undertake an imaginative program involving in-service training and the creation of cross-disciplinary programming at all levels.

With category B status granted ISA by UNESCO, there is every hope that a real partnership between the two will be worked out. This achieved, it may be possible to estabish organic links with all the member schools. In another decade membership of ISA should run between 50 and 100 schools. It should be stressed that the extensive and attractive report on the 1966 ISA Conference on Primary Curricula was financed by a fourth UNESCO contract.

In addition, it is interesting to examine at least some of the member schools of ISA to discover to what extent they merit being called international. First, there is the International School of Geneva, which was technically organized as a non-profit-making association under the Swiss Civil Code. It was founded in 1924. Its statutes were revised in 1948 and 1960. Negotiations have been undertaken to transform the association into a foundation under Swiss law, to be finalized in 1968. This will ensure Swiss oversight of the institution financially speaking and place its control in a self-perpetuating board of trustees rather than in the existent democratic assembly of theoretical stockholders—open to anyone interested in the School. At least current regulations require that only three of the nine board members elected by the assembly can be of the same nationality. Three are nominated each year for a 3-year term (total two terms) by a committee representative of three agencies: the board of the school, the parent-teachers association, and teaching staff.

Unfortunately, since 1955 the School has been organically divided into two linguistic sections with co-equal directors— one French and one English. The evolution of these two sections, each preparing for two national university entrance examinations (Swiss–French and British–American) has been very different. The French-speaking section, being about one-quarter of the whole School, is beset with an understandable feeling of inferiority aggravated by its having kept more nearly to the traditions of the original School than has the English section. (The total student population (1500 in all) is nearly half from the USA.) The teaching staff on the French "side" is overwhelmingly local Swiss. The teaching staff on the English "side" is overwhelmingly British. The property occupied by the School belongs to the Canton of Geneva, which maintains the buildings and thus subsidizes the School. Of course, if the local school authorities had to absorb the total student population of the School, the cost would probably be ten times what it costs the canton now. Against this can be balanced the value of the property which is lost to the canton as the International School uses it. If, however, the School were not there, the various international organizations in Geneva might be tempted to go elsewhere as educational considerations often determine whether or not a given post is taken on by the official involved.

Nevertheless, it can be demonstrated that there is too much Swiss influence, too many British staff, too many American students.

A major campaign to acquire capital would also seem to be called for, not only to acquire the title to the property which the School uses, but to construct more appropriate buildings. There is a relatively small boarding department which could be considerably increased to bring in capable students from developing countries. Such a development would tend to balance the linguistic imbalance (many developing nations use French) and offer a confrontation of developing with developed society, necessary if an international school is to escape the charge of serving only the rich.

In recent years the tension between the English and the French sections of the School has been so great as to a parody internationalism. In 1966 a serious attempt to unify the School under the English-side headmaster aroused the fears of the French that their identity would be lost—swallowed up in a British–American combine. It happens that the School was over-staffed, largely because of irrational student-loads imposed by the dual nature of the School, and its financial security was thus seriously undermined. Unless some rationalization was achieved, the oldest and most important of international schools may well go bankrupt. The 1966 effort ended in a draw: the French staff were able to stir up sufficient reaction in the community—among parents, alumni and Swiss who wanted a continuation of the original School as it was, to prevent the board from implementing the assembly's majority vote to go ahead with amalgamation. A mediation commission under the chairmanship of a distinguished retired diplomat has issued a report which calls essentially for what was attempted in 1966—except that it should be carried out under a headmaster chosen from outside the School. In consequence a bilingual Director-General has been appointed.

The controversy could ostensibly be solved by the adoption of the International Baccalaureate in the place of the four current national examinations. Such a change would pose few problems for the French and American streams.

The development of the International Baccalaureate has been supported by the English-side headmaster, the American staff, French staff and a good many of the British staff from the beginning. It is they who have been mainly responsible for the subject about which this book is being written. To them it is unthinkable that the International School of Geneva should be paralyzed in pursuing its vocation by a small minority. A separation into two entirely separate international schools is regarded as equally unthinkable by the board.

The United Nations Nursery School of Geneva dates from 1949. The year before it became one of the four founders of ISA. It has never provided for more than fifty children. It is technically governed by an assembly who elect a board of managers. Its regulations are less complex than those of the International School. Recently, the Nursery School has been considering plans for growing into a fully fledged primary and secondary school, and there is certainly a need for this.

About 6 years ago a privately owned *Collège du Léman* opened its doors to the Geneva international population and now prepares students for three examinations: Swiss *Maturité*, GCE and US College Board. More recently a co-operative venture known as the Lycée des Nations was also created to teach in English at Primary and Secondary Level.

The CERN (Centre Européen de Recherches Nucléaires), also located in Geneva, has been exploring the possibilities of developing a large international school near the Research Center. The situation in Geneva illustrates the problems facing the development of international education.

Paris is a much larger city than Geneva and therefore has tended to have more national "overseas" schools available for the children of expatriate groups. Among these is to be found the excellent American School, incorporated in Wilmington, Delaware. With the establishment of UNESCO a movement developed to establish a fully fledged international school: but as education tended to be regarded as a "political" matter, initiatives had to be taken by the governments. Only the Staff Association of UNESCO went on record as supporting the Paris International School, with the result that it remained a nursery school with a governing board which is essentially an adjunct to the UNESCO Staff Association.

In 1951 the NATO (SHAPE) International School was born to meet a definite need, but one which, by its very nature, could not easily include eastern Europeans. To secure a financial subsidy the NATO School, situated at St. Germain-en-Laye, became technically an annex to the local *lycée*. This rather tied the hands of the director, who found he was caught between the NATO supervisory authority and the French Ministry of Education. An international certificate was developed for foreign students not taking the French baccalaureate (which was regarded as the normal procedure). The language of instruction was French. In 1956 a similar NATO international school was developed at Fontainebleau. With the withdrawal of France from NATO the future of these schools remains problematical. It should be pointed out that the great majority of American children whose parents were stationed in France attended American dependent schools controlled by the US Armed Forces.

The second attempt to set up an international school in

Paris began in 1954 with the École Active Bilingue, as the venture of a private citizen. In 1956 the School was accepted by the French Ministry of Education as an accredited private primary school, received a subsidy and was recognized by UNESCO as the International School of Paris. By 1960 the School had grown so much that its incipient secondary section was transferred to Sèvres, where it became an international section of the local *lycée* (itself part of the Centre Pédagogique. This group numbers about 200, while the École Active Bilingue itself has double that number in its original premises, and has opened up another primary section in another part of Paris for another 500 children. A number of elaborate schemes have been put forward for setting up a fully fledged international school. It should be mentioned that in 1964 a branch of the École Active Bilingue was opened in Cannes, but it was forced to close down after a couple of years.

The New York United Nations International School, the final founding member of ISA was created in 1949 by parents connected with the United Nations. Geneva sent its (at that time) headmistress to lay down the guidelines. It is incorporated as a private school in New York State run by a self-perpetuating board of governors, who usually manage to co-opt about as many again of permanent delegates to the United Nations. Its status as an international school was unique as its budget was supplemented by the General Assembly of the United Nations.

Despite its favorable diplomatic position, the New York School had hard going till 1965 when it became the recipient of a munificent gift from the Ford Foundation of $7·5 million (to which another $2·5 million are to be added). This will enable the School, to date housed in a condemned public school, to acquire its own property. The New York School suffers from being sited in Manhattan. Few UN officials live in the city. The French send their children to the French *lycée* so that it has only been possible to maintain a French-speaking section for the primary school. The majority of the students are American, though the staff is not. Preparation is, however, given for the GCE, though so far only to O-level. The School is very much interested in the International Baccalaureate program. It has undertaken a really original initiative in seeking to have staff seconded from Eastern European countries. It has about 700 students.

Although Atlantic College was only established in 1962, it deserves special mention as being the most active after Geneva in promoting the International Baccalaureate and the only member of ISA in Britain. Unlike most international schools it is an elite institution, with students from both sides of the Atlantic and even from Eastern Europe. So far, the School has only prepared its students for GCE A-level but from 1970 onwards will offer the International Baccalaureate to all leavers. The governing board of the school is almost entirely British and the staff mostly so. The School may, therefore, be described as a liberal form of unilateral internationalism, but once a series of Atlantic Colleges is established, the superior council will have to embrace multilateral internationalism. The present institution, a boarding school located in South Wales, is a " sport " as compared to other international schools.

The Dutch are regarded as perhaps the most international of peoples. For this reason the International School of The Hague should have developed as a model of internationalism, but the story reads otherwise. Started in 1953 by the French and British diplomatic communities, it soon elicited interest from German and American groups. Almost from the start the German and French sections became essentially independent schools financed by their respective Ministries of Education. The British early resented any trend towards Americanization and set up their own school, an example followed by the Americans. All that was left to be governed by the Council elected by an assembly was a small Anglo–American section which somehow survived. When a secondary section developed it was entirely American in curriculum and staffing.

What finally developed was a very loose confederation of schools presided over by a Dutch headmaster (or rector, as he is called). Each section has its own campus and buildings scattered over the city. Another section developed at Dordrecht which proved essentially American, and another in Amsterdam which is Anglo–American.

In contrast, the Milan School tends to use more Italian, especially as it grew out of an institute teaching English to Italians. It suffers from private ownership, which tends to judge results by the values of an Italian private school.

The International School in Accra dates from 1954. It has remained British or British Commonwealth in orientation despite being a local entity, governed by five appointees of the host (Ghana) Government and by six ambassadorial representatives. The pattern is suggestive for other emergent nations. Currency restrictions pose restrictions on the development of the School. The language of instruction is English. The School takes some 800 children.

The School in Dar-es-Salaam was set up as a limited company in which the Tanzanian Government, the expatriate groups and the local industrial firms participate. This formula was worked out by ISA itself and has offered a serviceable framework for the development of other international schools. The most obvious shortcoming is the "anglophone" nature of the school. Swahili is not a language in which the expatriate community seeks instruction, and French, though the vehicular language of half Africa, is regarded as a foreign language.

The problems of international schools lie in the dichotomy between expatriate and local populations, in the decision as to which language is to be used as the language of instruction, in the gap between privilege and under-privilege and in the tension between attachment to known national systems of examination for university entrance and the desire to experiment with genuine multilaterally international certificates. This last problem gives rise to the subject treated in the next chapter.

BIBLIOGRAPHY

ISA *Newletters* and *Bulletins* Nos. 1–45 inclusive (1958–67).
Minutes of Official Business Meetings of ISA (1951–67).
Profiles of twenty-four schools of International character (see Appendix).
Theses of Richard Purkiss and Sally Ronsheim.

APPENDIX

During his year (1961–2) as Consultant to ISA the author prepared a questionnaire of eighteen pertinent questions regarding how international schools operate. He took the headmaster through the questions personally and then submitted his draft of the responses elicited. These were then reproduced and given to all who "took" the questionnaire. These were offered for publication by UNESCO but considered to be too topical—too quickly out of date. They have served as authority for much of what has been written in this text. The complete list (most with official statutes enclosed) include:

*Accra, Ghana
 Alexandria, Egypt
 Athens, Greece
*Belgrade, Yugoslavia
*Brussels, Belgium
*Colombo, Ceylon
 Fontainebleau, France
 Frankfurt, Germany
*Geneva (Ecolint) Switzerland
*Geneva (UN) Switzerland
*The Hague, Netherlands
 Hamburg, Germany
 Hellerup, Denmark
*Kabul, Afghanistan
 Luxembourg, Luxembourg
*Milan, Italy
*Ommen, Netherlands
*Paris (Bilingue), France
*Paris (US), France
 St. Germain, France
 Tangier, Morocco
 Thessalonika, Greece
 Vienna, Austria
*Zurich, Switzerland

Twenty-four schools (total) in sixteen countries (three continents).

* Members of ISA (thirteen).

CHAPTER 3

INTERNATIONAL SCHOOLS EXAMINATION SYNDICATE

PERHAPS the most important consideration in encouraging the spread and development of multilateral international schools is the prospect that graduates of such institutions may be assured of university placement. It was this consideration which led the Consultant to the International Schools Association to place the subject of an eventual International Baccalaureate on the agenda of the Social Studies Conference of 1962. There the reception was affirmative.

"Following [discussion of] the topic 'The Social Studies programme in international schools appropriate to preparation for an International Baccalaureate', the conference asks ISA: That the development of a joint Social Studies final examination be explored by ISA as a first step toward the establishment of basic standards".

That autumn the ISA *Newsletter* announced that the Social Studies Department of the English Language section of the Geneva International School was already busy preparing an experimental examination for use in June of 1963 along the lines laid down by the Social Studies Conference. By February two examination papers in Contemporary History plus a list of thesis (research paper) topics had been dispatched to the printer, the cost of which was met by the UNESCO–ISA contract on the interpenetration of Occident and Orient. Though originally written in English these and all subsequent papers published for the baccalaureate programme have appeared as well in French. Bilingualism became a cardinal principle from almost the onset of the program even though its first implementation was undertaken by staff members who used the English language for preparing the program.

All during the academic year of 1962–3 the above-mentioned Social Studies Department held a series of extraordinary discussion meetings to formulate what seemed, in the light of their experience, to be the most desirable considerations for training up young people to understand the nature of the contemporary world in which they live. Since this pilot program provided the launching platform for the financing of the International Baccalaureate, it is perhaps interesting to note in some detail the principles employed in the creation of the "Contemporary History 1913–63" examination. Most History courses in most schools stop at the Second World War. Most offer no Economics and relatively little Human Geography. Few educate in Contemporary Fine Arts. Those preparing Political Science often limit themselves to ethnocentric institutions. Such omissions the Social Studies Department set out to rectify.

It was decided that a 2-year course involving seven periods weekly (36 weeks) was sufficient time to prepare for two 3-hour written papers, and allow for the writing of a research paper of from 5000 to 7500 words (which was to be examined orally) at the end of the 2-year preparation. The research papers were to be selected from ten topics of a general type involving background material as well as evolution during the last half-century. The written papers, roughly speaking, dealt with Occident and Orient in turn.

The first paper was planned to cover equally Northern America, Latin America, Western Europe, Eastern Europe and Siberia. The second paper similarly involved Africa beyond the Maghreb, the Arabian–Indian region, South-east Asia and Australasia, as well as the functioning of international institutions. Both papers contained twenty-four questions divided equally among the four sections involved. In addition each group of six questions was divided into two political, two economic and two social types. Thus a maximum variety was guaranteed. But since the writing of coherent essays was considered of primordial importance, only four of each twenty-four were indicated to be answered. But this choice was governed by a complex system of elimination which restricted the choice in such a way as to prevent the candidate from dealing with a limited area or type of question. He had first to choose a quotation question (one such was to be found in each of the three types). Next, he was to assure that a question in each of three areas was to be answered. Finally, he was to be sure that in choosing these the other two types that he covered in the quotation question were also dealt with.

The complications this involves for the candidate were the object of a number of negative criticisms from examination experts who scrutinized the questions. Curiously enough, however, no single candidate among the fifty or so who have taken this examination found the restrictions onerous or confusing. Admittedly, 15 minutes was allowed for the candidate to make his choice. Subsequently, it was decided to double the questions in the area in which the school is located at which the candidate is studying. In point of fact such additions have only been made for Western Europe, where especially it does seem an unnatural limitation to be allowed only two political questions in a gross total of forty-eight offered in a given year. Once the pattern of the entire baccalaureate was emerging and as no other subject had envisaged its examinations as covering a similar geographic and technical spectrum, some radical change in the Contemporary History program were well in order. How to preserve its basic intention in a less complicated form was naturally of importance to the future of the program.

At a meeting of History teachers and examiners held in late autumn of 1966 it was agreed that instead of writing a thesis the candidate should present a few essays on a chosen topic and submit to a more rigorous oral than was originally envisaged. Instead of two 3-hour papers, one of 3 and another of 1 hour were proposed. The larger paper would deal with one of four areas: North and South America combined, Western and Eastern Europe combined, Africa and Arab world combined, India and South-East Asia–Australasia combined. It would consist of answering three of twelve rather than four of twenty-four questions, while distinction as to quotation or tripartite type of question was dropped.

The second paper would require answering one of three questions chosen by the school from a list of twelve to fifteen proposed by ISES: half of these would be of world-wide importance (replacing the eighth area in the original project) and eight from other regions than that chosen by the school for its first examination paper. In addition, a small oral to cover the three second-paper questions would be included. Obviously the change indicates a move away from encyclopedism. It necessitates, however, the candidate dealing with some topics outside the area in which his school is located. (Probably schools will choose to emphasize their "own" local region.)

Four candidates passed the examination in Contemporary History in June 1963, that is, each gained at least a C^+ average. The Social Studies Department, acting as a team, certified the results, one of whom used his certificate as partial qualification for entrance into his sophomore year at Harvard University. One member of the Department then visited rather extensively among British educators and examination syndicate officials, which bore important results in bringing a number of influential British educational figures to the spring 1965 Curriculum Conference in Geneva. This was the Conference which first studied the overall possible configuration of the International Baccalaureate. What was of even more interest at the time was the general reaction that the then constituted ISA Contemporary History paper would be regarded by British University authorities as equal to an A-level GCE History paper.

Meanwhile, negotiations with UNESCO led to the granting of a second contract to ISA—this time to study the possibility of an interchangeable curriculum between and among international schools. This study had the effect of pushing co-ordinate primary-school studies which, in turn given the composition of ISA, has become its major interest. Partly because of this fact, and also because of the hesitancy of the board of ISA to launch itself into a huge examination program whose acceptance was not assured, it seemed best to set up a separate legal entity to handle the formation and operation of the University Entrance Examination program.

Consequently, the Geneva International School agreed to patronize the examination program until such time as a substantial foundation grant would make another arrangement necessary. In preparation for this eventuality, an ISA Examination Advisory Committee was formed in the autumn of 1963 by which members of the staff of the Graduate Institute of International Affairs of the University of Geneva were brought into the practical work of planning for the 1964 papers, and to collaborate in examining candidates. This Advisory Committee underwent a metamorphosis in the spring of 1964 to become the Executive Committee of the new International Schools Examination Syndicate. Meanwhile, the Geneva School employed a geographer–economist to help insure that adequate preparation of the Contemporary History program was achieved. In fact in another year the popularity of Geography in this school was to lead to a division of the Social Studies Department with the new appointee heading up the new Geography department. The portion left renamed itself the History Department. These two have subsequently worked in closest harmony with each other. The consequence of this bifurcation to the International Baccalaureate has been such as to establish Geography as a full-fledged subject for its long-range program. Discussion of Economics as a baccalaureate subject has now taken place.

During the summer of 1963, the ISA Language Conference in Milan explored the possibility of baccalaureate examinations in the English and French languages, though nothing concrete was put into effect, as was hoped for, by the June of 1964. However, this Conference did have the effect of mobilizing the interest of some members of the French linguistic section of the Geneva International School, which proved particularly important as the baccalaureate program could be presented convincingly at the Pedagogical Institute of Sèvres in the spring of 1964 as a genuinely bilingual operation.

This presentation occurred at a conference patronized by the French section of the European Teachers' Association at which the European schools, NATO schools, Atlantic College, the Oxford University Department of Education and French Ministry of Education people were first confronted with ISA and ISES. The consequences of this Conference proved more far-reaching than the mission to England of the preceding year. It was no doubt interesting to the Sèvres Conference to learn that UNESCO was at that time arranging its third contract with ISA involving the exchange of Occident–Orient materials between matching international schools in different parts of the world.

Language teaching proved to be the area in which Atlantic College found itself drawn into the work of ISES (and, incidentally, into ISA, of which Association it became a member). In the autumn of 1964 an invitation was given ISES, still technically a subcommittee of the governing board of the Geneva School, to visit St. Donat's Castle in Wales to share in the discussion of linguistic problems. This confrontation brought Atlantic College into the Executive Committee of ISES as full participating partner with the Geneva School.

Meanwhile, soon after the Sèvres Conference, an effective mission to the United States was organized by ISES to present a carefully prepared "offset" memorandum to highly placed government, education and foundation officials. The reception in the office of the US Commissioner on Education was most favorable, while that of the State Department was certainly, by constrast, critical, if not hostile. It should be pointed out that this reaction has subsequently practically disappeared in favor of sympathetic interest. Education and World Affairs, which co-ordinates bilateral educational exchanges, was affirmatively cordial. CEEB wished to keep in touch. The foundation world was cautiously interested, though the Twentieth-Century Fund proved in the end to be sufficiently adventurous as to grant $75,000 to ISES for "action research" and to contract a book on the program with Martin Mayer, a free-lance educational expert. This contract was negotiated in the summer of 1964 and came into effect in January 1965. Martin Mayer's book appeared in the summer of 1968.

Anticipating successful issue of the American negotiations, the Advisory Committee not only set up the Examination Board but before becoming an executive committee helped form a group of sponsors composed of distinguished educators and international public servants in the neighborhood of Geneva. They, in turn, selected a directorate which was clothed with final authority in large decisions and directives. Actually, when the formal statutes of ISES were written the directorate and sponsors were coalesced into a council. At this time a number of additional members from different countries were co-opted. The first formal meeting of the sponsors group was held on 6 June 1964, which date is now chosen as the legal point of departure for ISES although it was only 6 months later that the statutes were actually filed with the *Registre de Commerce* in Geneva. Thus ISES (IBO) is technically a non-profit-making association governed by Article 60 *et seq.* of the Swiss Civil Code.

The International School itself took cognizance of what was taking place by arranging for International Schools' Day in May in which all departments in the School, of both linguistic sections, examined what an International Baccalaureate might mean for their particular subject. From this gathering came the first overall schema of many which have followed. The executive was actively working on draft proposals to be put before the Twentieth-Century Fund. At first these were oriented to the relevancy of the International Baccalaureate to

STR 5

developing nations, but gradually broadened their scope. At the same time a 5-year plan of action research was drafted. It was hoped that visitors from the Ford Foundation would appear in Geneva, an anticipation which had to wait for 2 years.

In June an effort was made to interest the local cantonal authorities in the International Baccalaureate but without marked success. This initiative did, however, lead to a serious attempt both in 1964 and in 1965 to contact national educational delegations who were in Geneva in July for the Joint Annual UNESCO–International Bureau of Education Conferences. Already copies of the pilot History program had gone to Ministries of Education the world over—evoking an unusually wide generous response. All four of these initiatives, while unproductive in themselves, did encourage further work, that is to say the response of junior officials in Ministries of Education was cautiously favorable.

In the autumn of 1964 August Hecksher, then Executive Director of the Twentieth-Century Fund, spoke at the Annual Rencontres Internationales sponsored each year by the city of Geneva. This gave him opportunity to talk with members of the Executive Committee and sponsors, particularly with Desmond Cole-Baker, Treasurer of ISES and Headmaster of the Geneva International School. This discussion led the groundwork of the grant which became a reality 5 months later. The International School kindly seconded one of the teachers who had been active both in the pilot History program and on the Executive Committee to act as Executive Secretary for one year. With him went one of the staff of ISA as office manager. Additional office space was made available at the International School (which had accommodated ISA since early 1963).

The prospect of sure financial subsidy on a substantial scale not only pushed forward the formulation of legal statutes for ISES but encouraged fuller work on the part of the Examination Board. In June of 1964 a number of History candidates had been examined jointly by the Board and Ecolint staff. This included some who sat only the Occident half of the program and others who prepared a "pre-baccalaureate" examination covering the world from 1713 to 1913. This examination was divided into three areas—two of which were Occidental—but the Orient had to be treated. Quotation questions followed the contemporary pattern but two rather than three types of questions were involved. No thesis was involved for the half program nor for the pre-baccalaureate examination. During 1964–5 not only were thesis questions formulated jointly by the Examination Board and the Ecolint staff but a second battery of examinations was produced, complete with syllabus. This second set (which came to be known as modern beta as compared to the alpha contemporary) took its framework more from the pre-baccalaureate examination of 1713–1913 than from its parallel set-up of 1913–63.

The reason for a second stream was twofold. First, many "orthodox" historians regard the post-1913 period as "Current Events" rather than History. Secondly, Ecolint had been markedly successful in preparing the O-Level (GCE) British examination in Medieval History in a world-wide syllabus and wanted to put that program within the ISES program. The beta program was discussed by the History section of the March 1965 Curriculum Conference and noticeably modified. For example, instead of using quotation questions, certain precedence was given asterisked questions. The pre-baccalaureate paper on Medieval History was approved as having three-quarters of its questions on the area of the inland waterways system from Gibraltar to Aden, one-quarter outside. The two baccalaureate papers (beta) were to cover the time span from 1500 to 1950, to be broken in 1793. Also it was agreed that the first of these would contain two equally balanced areas of the world, thus to bridge from the pattern in the medieval area to that in the 1713–1913 paper (the latter of which was used explicitly in the 1793–1950 beta examination). In 1965 the papers of the alpha candidates were jointly corrected

5*

as in 1964 while those in the beta stream were handled by the school itself.

Earlier in the spring a series of seminars sponsored by the Examination Board were held to discuss possible answer outlines submitted by the participants. Martin Mayer, then in residence in Geneva, participated in these sessions. Obviously an imaginative initiative was undertaken as regards evaluating the History program. On the other hand it was running the risk of moving so far ahead of other parts of the program as to get out of touch with the overall requirements of the International Baccalaureate program. Probably no harm was done inasmuch as the History proponents moved to logical conclusions within the framework of their own subject—while keeping an open mind as to adjustment which was proved valid in the autumn of 1966. One outstanding virtue of that adjustment was the drawing together of alpha and beta streams, at least as far as patterns were involved. Six months earlier, it was agreed that as no other subject had developed them, the pre-baccalaureate examinations would have to drop. This enabled the autumn 1966 reform to extend to the beta dates, which now read 1750–1913 or later instead of 1500–1950. That no candidates sat the beta papers in 1966 helped promote the changes. No radical revision of the History program took place until the Ford grant was actually made. It was then quite clear that the primary stage of ISES was concluded.

I have dealt with the History program in detail as it was not only proposed but put into practice. No other subject examination in the ISES battery was sat before June 1967. The 1965 examinations constituted the high-water mark of the pilot History program. Those candidates who accepted the beta program also undertook the equivalent of A-level GCE with interesting comparative results. In 1966 only half the contemporary alpha program was sat. The pre-baccalaureate alpha was regarded as a strictly Ecolint examination though prepared, as were all the 1966 examination questions, half by Atlantic College, half by Geneva. At least those that were officially graded were certified by the Examination Board alone—as was to be the case henceforward.

The notion of some International Baccalaureate subjects being taken at Higher Level, others at Subsidiary Level was first seriously put forward in October 1964, when Atlantic College invited Ecolint to discuss their provisional pattern at a colloquium held at St. Donat's Castle in Wales. There the possibility of three higher and four subsidiary subjects met with most general approval. This has since been reduced to three and three. At the Syllabus Conference of March 1965 the History panel produced two subsidiary papers, the alpha drawing on one question of each of the eight sections in the higher-level paper. This reduced examination of 2 hours duration was acceptable to French and German examination candidates and was sat in 1965 by the French section at Ecolint. The beta subsidiary paper was drawn in such a way as to be acceptable to students preparing the Swiss *Maturité*, that is it took two questions from each higher-level beta paper, two from the pre-baccalaureate medieval and two questions formulated on Classical History. This paper was never used.

When radical reform was in order in the autumn of 1966, each subsidiary paper was brought in line with its higher-level prototype, to be drafted so that of twelve questions each, four would apply to the chosen main region, four to others and four to the world-wide scene. It was agreed that treatment of an original document would be required as part of the final section. In reality the subsidiary papers in History have become more complex, but more universal. It would be fair to state that the original higher-level beta papers were prepared with an eye to providing acceptance in streams leading to the British GCE just as much as the original subsidiary History examinations were geared to national European streams. Obviously, overall policy regarding the International Baccalaureate would take precedence over that undertaken by one subject, however well developed and flexible.

The notion of a so-called "package deal" was first raised at the Atlantic College Symposium in October 1964 and has since been justified as the only viable approach to the International Baccalaureate. Otherwise the use of subjects as individual pawns in the university entrance game would eventually undermine any basic multilaterally international approach. This overall consideration has gradually shaped the work of ISES progressively in the past 3 years. Soon after the Atlantic College Symposium, and partly because the Geneva School was celebrating its fortieth anniversary, an exploratory conference on fund-raising for Ecolint, ISA and ISES was held. Obviously the time was not yet ripe, though the notion of an International Education Foundation was talked about. This has now become an ideal toward which ISES is working.

Two important contacts were made in November which have since borne fruit. First, the Council of Europe was agreeable to the proposition that ISES would be officially represented at an educational conference sponsored by the Belgian Government in the autumn of 1966. For this development ISES was indebted to the Swiss representatives who had followed the program closely from 1962 onwards. Secondly, the idea of the International Baccalaureate was presented officially to the Programme Committee of UNESCO by joint resolution of the Swiss and Belgian Governments. This was undertaken with the support of Robert Dottrens, Rector of the University of Geneva, then a member of the ISES Sponsors Committee. Although the Swiss–Belgian resolution was technically too late to be considered by the Programme Committee, its reception at the time was very cordial. Members of UNESCO staff spoke warmly regarding the seriousness of the project. Subsequently it was possible to present the substance of this reception to the committee dealing with the International Co-operation Year (1965) program so that its inclusion in the findings of this committee was assured. In other words, the General Assembly of the United Nations, in accepting the ICY report, recommended to UNESCO that a favorable eye be

kept fixed upon the development of an International Baccalaureate. The granting of category B status to ISA largely
because of the International Baccalaureate program (1966),
no doubt relates to the UNESCO Programme Committee
discussion in the autumn of 1964.

Perhaps of equal importance were negotiations in the autumn of 1964 with officials of the French Ministry of Education which followed up the spring contacts made at Sèvres.
In any case, there were six *inspecteurs générals* present at the
three formal syllabus meetings which followed (and as well
at the ISA Primary School Conference of summer 1965).
The interest of the French was so pronounced as to lead them
to offer Sèvres as the gathering place of the crucially important
"Policy Conference" of 1967. Mme l'Inspectrice Générale
Hatinguais allowed her name to go forward as a member of
the Council of ISES. As the *doyenne* of the French Inspectorate
her support is of great value. The co-operation of the French
reflects their sensitivity to significant program in education,
and mirrors their appreciation of a bilingual English–French
venture, by which an international clientele is offered relatively
secure access to French universities, and further appreciation
of the culture they represent.

The first meeting of the General Assembly constituting
ISES as independent of the International School of Geneva
met on 25 January 1965 at which time the statutes were approved, the Council elected, the Executive Committee confirmed
and M. le Recteur Capelle of Nancy selected as the next
French member of the Council.

Already, late in 1964, the sponsors had agreed to become
the Council and to assume full responsibility for the financial
side of things. This was fairly easily done as the Chairman of
ISES was John Goormaghtigh Director of the European
Office of the Carnegie Endowment for International Peace
and as well Chairman of the Board of the Geneva School.
With him was Dr. Sarwate, Secretary-General of the International Telecommunications Union then Chairman of the

Finance Committee of the School Board (since deceased in 1967) and Mr. Cole-Baker, then Director of the English-language section and Treasurer of ISES. It was agreed that the Executive Secretary would serve *ex officio* on the Council and the confirmed Executive Committee.

Planning for the March Colloquium to deal with History, Geography, Modern Languages, Biology and Mathematics took up the time of the Executive Committee in the early weeks of 1965. The English language section of the Geneva School likewise mobilized itself for the coming event. This Conference consisted of sixty attenders—in fact equalled the 1962 ISA Social Studies affair in size and importance. Among the attenders were some distinguished educators who were constituted into a "sixth" commission to examine the International Baccalaureate as a whole.

It was at this commission that the representative of the French Ministry of Education proposed the formula which satisfied the Executive of the GCE Board who was present. In other words, a French initiative met with a British assent—a procedure which appears to have much merit in contemporary political agreements. It might almost be said the most important political hurdle had been cleared. Otherwise certain areas were explored including formulae regarding range of subjects, types and length of examinations, examiners and particularly the ratio of Higher and Subsidiary Level.

The five subject commissions each got on to some extent. History has already been reported. Geography recommended more materials be collected. Modern Languages indicated they wished both written and oral examinations. Biology went further than the other "new" subjects in agreeing to draft syllabuses, and Mathematics was united in the necessity of a "mathematical literacy" test for students not electing the subject at Higher or Subsidiary Level. In other words a good start was made in four disciplines and a fundamental overall agreement achieved. It should be perhaps mentioned that an interdisciplinary study of key cities was tentatively proposed

—an initiative which came from the Ecolint History Department, and which has borne fruit at a joint History–Geography panel held in June 1967.

Perhaps the most important indirect result of the March Colloquium was the appointment of staff at Atlantic College on the Executive Committee. In other words the range of participation in day-to-day planning was materially widened. At the first Executive Committee held after the Conference, Martin Mayer urged the absolute necessity of getting on with actual syllabuses and sample examination papers. There was, however, a curious lag in this development. Such is "probably traceable to the unfortunate academic habit of being purely "academic" about new ideas, however good. Other departments at the Geneva School (i.e. other than History) wanted assurance that work for the International Baccalaureate would not be futile. Once other groups were involved, the very physical problems of getting on with collective work tends to delay matters. However it may be analyzed, only in the spring of 1967 have there appeared the papers for which Mr. Mayer asked.

Another reaction to the March Colloquium came from a member of the French section of Ecolint who urged that a pedagogical committee be formed to oversee this vitally important syllabus work. Obviously the energies of the executive secretary and the Executive were torn between the necessary promotional work falling upon a new venture and shepherding educational development. This advice was followed a year later though in point of fact the staff of ISES found itself undertaking the work which would have been the prerogative of the Technical Committee simply because of pressure of time—brought on by the prospect of the Policy Conference of 1967.

Two subsequent projects which arose from the discussions of the March Colloquium were written up, but not acted upon. One had to do with financing the "cities" project referred to above. The other called for systematic analysis of the development of ISES as it went forward. In fact the essential contact which should have been made with various European foundations was postponed for a variety of reasons. At least some tentative connections with the Polish Ministry of Education were made, an effort which underscored the necessity of reaching out into the so-called Socialist world.

A number of contact trips were undertaken in the late spring of 1965 chiefly by the executive secretary and Martin Mayer, Then the summer took most people interested in ISES on personal holidays. Notwithstanding, a number of interesting developments took place. First, ISES moved from Ecolint to a villa nearby, which it shared with ISA. Secondly, twenty-five Ecolint teachers travelled in the United States and Canada to inform educators generally regarding international schools and their interests.

Mr. Cole-Baker himself was asked to go to New York by CEEB authorities to discuss the International Baccalaureate program with representatives of the Twentieth-Century Fund, the Ford Foundation, the State Department, etc. Obviously the impact of the March Conference was being felt. Negotiations with the Ford Foundation were entered upon seriously in the autumn in consequence. The appointment of A.D.C. Peterson, Head of the Oxford University Department of Education and member of Council of Atlantic College, constituted another important development. Mr. Peterson was to accept the post of director-general *ad interim* for the next 12 months and go to Geneva to devote his best endeavours personally, as he expressed it, to help forward a program of the "utmost importance to the world".

The initial Executive Committee was concerned that it might be replaced by a steering committee of the Council. This seemed the more likely as an *ad hoc* "education subcommittee" had become operative to push the development of curricula. Obviously a "highly unsatisfactory" administrative situation was developing. In consequence a weekly "information session" was created, at which it was suggested that another *ad hoc* education subcommittee be set up at Atlantic College. Incidentally, Atlantic College members of the Executive had been instrumental in getting the NATO Parliamentary Conference in New York in October 1965 to affirm "total support" of the International Baccalaureate program.

Two more curricula conferences were then held—each double headers as it turned out. One at Atlantic College with thirty attenders divided into Language of Instruction (English and French) and Foreign Languages sections. No less than three *inspecteurs générals* were present at the request of the French Ministry of Education. It was suggested that a compulsory section of the Language of Instruction include World Literature in Translation. As far as foreign languages were concerned the notion of vehicular versus foreign languages studied for reading ability essentially, was made. And for the first time a sufficiently large contingent of German-speaking participants allowed for the report of this colloquium to appear in three languages.

Simultaneously, in Geneva, a Mathematics–Physics Conference was held composed of forty attenders including two French *inspecteurs générals*. The outlines of Mathematics and Physics papers at both levels were agreed, but the pattern of "mathematical literacy" was far from formulated. In fact the Geneva gathering got on more slowly than that at Atlantic College. These two were the last full-fledged curriculum conferences to be sponsored by ISES before the Policy Conference, which was already in the air by early autumn of 1965. The main reason for abstaining from full-fledged conferences was their cost. By November 1965 ISES was virtually without funds. It was time for a serious rethinking of the whole administrative set-up.

This was undertaken at an "administrative conference" held at the Carnegie Endowment European Centre in Geneva at which confidence was renewed between the Council and Executive, and certain principles regarding remuneration put forward. This Executive was enlarged to include Dr. Hans

H. Fischer-Wollpert of Frankfurt who also joined the Council. Dr. Fischer-Wollpert has been able to establish the reputation of the International Baccalaureate in influential German circles and in recent months chaired Executive sessions planning for the Policy Conference.

Soon afterwards representatives of the Executive Committee and the Examination Board put their points of view to the Council in official session. The Council did not accept these in full, notably to establish full independence for the Examination Board. Fees were set for work undertaken for the Syndicate and extracts of the minutes were sent to the Executive Committee and Examination Board. Perhaps the most important decision that was taken was that to replace the executive secretary by an administrative secretary in the figure of a retired public international servant.

The enlarged Executive Committee met late in 1965 to set the pattern for the next year. It was agreed that meetings should be held five times a year, that the Policy Conference (now actively requested by the Ford Foundation be held in November—actually February 1967) be arranged, that seven subject panels be formed (each with a CEEB representative—which did not materialize) and that "mathematical literacy" be introduced. The pass–fail standard was discussed but without ready decision. A new business-like tone was brought to the discussion very largely introduced by members outside Geneva.

Despite the creation of the enlarged Executive, those members who lived in Geneva had to be responsible for the day-to-day decisions. In consequence, a private monthly news-sheet was sent to other members by which they were kept in close touch. This proved a useful exercise till the appointment of an acting director-general in June. Such a vehicle was the more important as the original chairman of the Executive Committee was on leave in the United States for most of this 6-month period.

In the meanwhile, the Pergamon Press had reprinted an

article by Desmond Cole-Baker in *Comparative Education* which introduced the International Baccalaureate. Another statement issued by the Syndicate Council indicated that a "well-trained" rather than a "well-filled" brain was the end desired, and that the International Baccalaureate would establish aptitudes primarily.

Representatives of ISES now made trips on its behalf to the Council of Europe, to the European schools, etc. The enlarged Executive then met in March to summarize activities and formulae for the International Baccalaureate to date. The augurs were good as it was announced that the Ford Foundation had granted ISES $300,000 over a 4-year period with a similar grant envisaged if the results were satisfactory in 1969. (In point of fact the question of tax exemption and other similar matters held up payment of the first $150,000 for 6 months.)

The dates not of seven but of eight subject panels were fixed—that for Modern Languages was still floating. A brochure to introduce the whole program was tentatively postponed. Suggestions for enlarging the Executive and working closely with ISA were raised and an exhaustive discussion of hours to be devoted to higher and subsidiary subjects engaged upon. Actually no less than thirty directives issued from this meeting. One of these had to do with approving revised statutes to meet the needs of a dynamic, growing institution. These, however, were not acted upon by the second Assembly, which met in June 1966. Thus the legal structure of ISES still needs reworking. That much of the good work of this executive session remained a dead letter is due to the natural new orientation flowing from the appointment of a director-general in June.

The first of the panel meetings was that for History for which ample documentation was provided. Its chief work was to evaluate a huge bibliography in the English language (those for the German and French languages are still to be produced). The panel suggested a grant be given the New York International School which participated (as it had at the second

Atlantic College and Geneva conferences) in developing some version of the cities project. Also it suggested a grant to Ecolint to similarly establish a philosophical syllabus, and one to Atlantic College to set up a variant philosophical approach. All three of these have lain fallow. The recommendation to set up a history library has only recently been implemented.

The Mathematics panel next met with nine participants as compared with the twelve for History. Its results, however, were meagre as compared with the pilot program. Each subject had had the benefit of two conferences as well as the panel meeting but, in the latter case, only one improvement was arrived at—that is to call mathematical literacy "mathematical comprehension". And that was only finalized at an autumn panel meeting in November 1966. History held its final revision meeting then as well.

In connection with the New York's interest in the Baccalaureate, their Headmaster, Desmond Cole, was named to the ISES Council. This appointment followed the line which the Ford Foundation suggested, as they were desirous that UNIS work out its curriculum revision within the framework of ISES. It will be recalled that UNIS was the recipient of a munificent grant from the Ford Foundation. However, New York's participation was complicated by the fact that, being situated in the United States, they have not yet established a thirteenth grade as is the case with European schools. Most of their graduates go to colleges in the USA. Thus, if the International Baccalaureate is useful there it must be offered in the eleventh and twelfth grades. Furthermore, a high-level pass–fail could only interest a small proportion of their students. In consequence, one of their staff produced a well-documented proposal that ISES use a scheme not dissimilar to the 200–800 range of the CEEB ratings. This document was the object of lively discussion at the opening Executive in 1967 when a compromise proposed by Mr. Peterson was favorably received, namely, that the international certificate should become a Baccalaureate at a certain level and an International Baccalaureate *cum laude* at an equivalently higher level. It was hoped this would meet the needs of UNIS and in fact a number of schools, but after discussion at Sèvres, this received still further definition and arrangement, as will be pointed out later.

The third panel to meet was Physics (seven participants). This panel got things pretty well tidied up, though some of its members took a traditional Laboratory Science attack on the Study of Man as a required field of study. The fourth panel was for one of those under attack, namely Geography, which insists it is, at least as Physical Geography, a Science alternative. Still another incident in the Science *vs.* Humanities dichotomy was the insistance that Social Biology (a plan for which appeared in the summer of 1966) was in fact a Study of Man to be made equivalent to History or Geography.

At the end of May the Executive met again, this time coincidentally with the Council and the Assembly. Once again the tempo of activities changed as it had 6 months before. This was the occasion to form a new Executive (the majority of which were Council members) and to reconstitute the old Executive as a Technical Committee, in effect reconstituting the Education Subcommittee which had evaporated 6 months before. The Assembly met with Professor George Panchaud in the chair. Panchaud had become an active Council member—a year before having taken an active part in the two History panel meetings. As Director of the School of Education of the University of Lausanne he had played an active role in Council affairs. He announced the appointment of Alec Peterson as director *ad interim* to be assisted by two consultants, Gerard Renaud of the Geneva School staff and Dr. William Halls of the Oxford Department of Education staff. Both had been active members of the old Executive Committee, in fact Renaud had served as its most recent chairman. At this point, the treasury was taken over by the administrative secretary, while Mr. Cole-Baker was to accept the post of Director of ISA. The Policy Conference was pushed back 3 months, and it was announced that the accounting firm of Price-Waterhouse would audit the accounts.

This threefold gathering was followed by two jointly assembled panels—one for Chemistry, the other for Classics—each with eight attenders. Both did yeoman service considering that nothing formal had been done in either field. The History examiners then became active and left this time written comments regarding their impressions of the program and the year's candidates. Then the office slid into the summer routine. It seems that no one attended the annual UNESCO–BIE conference in 1966 (nor. in 1967). Everyone waited for policy to be put forward by the new administration.

In retrospect, perhaps the most important single event to take place in early June was the active participation of Dr. Harlan Hanson, Director of the Advanced Placement program of the CEEB, who had become an ISES Council member. In addition Sir William Hayter, Warden of New College, Oxford University, and Dr. Andre, rector of the University of Stockholm were asked to join the Council at that time. Thus the Council consisted of twelve distinguished international personalities of whom three were British, two French and seven from other national backgrounds; half are normally English speaking and one-third French speaking. Thus as near a sound multilateral balance as could be expected had been achieved.

The Executive then produced a progress report for the first 4 months of 1966. Mr. Peterson followed with one for the second 4 months—naturally, considering the holiday, this was geared to what had to be achieved in the next months. He had already undertaken to talk with heads of departments at Atlantic College, to line up some possible fifty-five candidates (forty-five at Subsidiary Level) for June 1967. A discussion held at Ecolint among department heads revealed a similar need for negotiation there, which Mr. Peterson undertook 3 months after that done at Atlantic College. At that time it was uncertain whether other than partial program History candidates would be presented at Geneva in 1967, though the Governing Board at Ecolint had encouraged as full co-operation as heads of department felt was feasible.

Important as he considered the development of experimental courses, Mr. Peterson did not see his way clear to recommending the allocation of funds from the Ford grant to such activity. Rather he was able to get the Twentieth-Century Fund to agree that its final payment be so used. The prospect of systematic research and promotion of experimental course work is far from being overlooked. In fact planning for it is well advanced, even to the extent of inquiring into probable subsidy.

In addition, planning was well in hand for the Policy Conference, which was envisaged as dividing for part of its time into Commission A intended to deal with formulae for the baccalaureate and its standards, under the care of Mr. Renaud; and Commission B to develop plans for the Examination Board, procedures for testing, etc., under the care of Dr. Halls.

The initial meeting of the Technical Committee in September 1966 applied itself to these reports. Its chief activity was to select key members of each of the subject panels to bring each curriculum report in line with the economy of hours possible for teaching, homework and actual examinations. This, of course, was undertaken with an eye fixed on the all-important Policy Conference. The following day the new Executive Committee held its initial meeting to set *per diem* expense arrangements, to approve the budget and to plan for panels which had not yet gathered. One important decision taken was to approve the "package deal" outlook regarding the International Baccalaureate, though strictly speaking this fell within the province of the competence of the Technical Committee. Use of the ISA *Bulletin* as a journal for ISES was left in obeyance. It appeared that no panel meeting was considered necessary for either Language of Instruction or

Foreign Languages, largely because the key people involved were members of the Technical Committee and thus managed to produce papers meeting the requirements of the two subjects. Similarly the biologists found it possible to do the necessary work without a panel meeting. Mathematics and History had to meet as before mentioned while Physics, Geography and Classics could be brought into line as a result of their spring meetings. It was decided that Fine Arts would be left till after the Policy Conference but late in September seven participants met at Sèvres to produce a Philosophy paper. Some progress was made, particularly in producing a "Theory of Knowledge" course, which came to be considered as even more essential for all International Baccalaureate candidates than "mathematical comprehension". The Philosophy panel also produced general titles for groupings of subjects for the International Baccalaureate, namely "Languages", "Study of Man", "Laboratory Sciences" and "Mathematics".

The second Technical Committee met in early November when it was decided that the first full Baccalaureate would be offered in June 1969—one year only behind the schedule originally put out in the late spring of 1964. As the Technical Committee was invited to the subsequent Executive Committee meeting, it dealt with both categories of decisions at this meeting. In principle it was agreed that Technical members would be on hand at Sèvres to see that documentation, reporting, *précis* writing and similar activities be adequately handled. The ideal put forward in Commission B papers that ISES would become only an Examination Syndicate met with sharp criticism, though that was envisaged at the earliest as taking place in June 1975. Attendance at the Policy Conference, which was envisaged as including Great Britain, France, United States, West Germany, Sweden and Switzerland, was enlarged to include, Poland, Bulgaria, Cameroons and Tanzania. Report was made of the initial payment of the Ford grant and a visit of Dr. Ralph Tyler, Director of the Center for the Advanced Study of the Behavioural Sciences, which reinforced the interest of American educational authorities in the ISES.

Early in December just before coming to live in Geneva, A. D. C. Peterson met the two consultants in Oxford to streamline the work for the next $2\frac{1}{2}$ months. This coincided with the final History panel meeting. Then, early in January 1967, the Technical and Executive Committees met jointly to finalize work for the Policy Conference, though the Executive also met separately to deal with budgetary and Council matters. Papers dealing with the two commissions were completed as well as a marking scheme approved. It was also decided that a brochure containing both the *raison d'être* of the baccalaureate, and lists of participants in its meetings to date would be issued. All syllabuses were reported prepared and in process of being published. (These, with the ISA Report on Primary-School Teaching, form a basis of the next chapter in this study.) In other words the appearance of Mr. Peterson in Geneva had galvanized the organs and secretariat of ISES to achieve remarkable success.

Early in the new year it was decided that the original Examination Board, which had, of course, applied itself only to History, should come under direct control of the director-general, at least until the program is permanently established (1975). In recognition of the vision and generous help on the part of its chairman, Dr. John Siotis was made a member of the ISES Council. Dr. Siotis, a Greek national, is Professor at the Graduate Institute of International Affairs at the University of Geneva.

The ISES Policy Conference at Sèvres rose higher than its proponents dared to expect. Not only was the pattern of the International Baccalaureate accepted in principle by a distinguished gathering of educators, but they also undertook (unofficially, of course) to seek to procure acceptance of the IB program in the universities which are located in the ten countries involved—for 500 candidates from ten or so carefully selected schools in the 6-year period from 1970–6. This was the extent of the request which Mr. Peterson made of the Conference. Attendance was limited to fifty participants, which made it, in fact, a smaller conference than those of 1962 and 1965. In addition to the ten invited nations the following bodies were represented: UNESCO, the Ford Foundation, Twentieth-Century Fund, British Education Development Overseas, CERN, CEEB, the Organization for Economic Co-operation and Development, the Oxford and Cambridge Schools Examination Board, the Council of Europe, the British Schools Council and the European (Common Market) Schools. For the first time in history the Director of College Board Examinations, the Director of the French Baccalaureate, the Director of the Oxford–Cambridge Board and the ex-Director of the Swiss Federal *Maturité* sat down to discuss educational matters together. A number of universities were represented: Stockholm, Nancy, Goteborg, Geneva, Oxford, Sofia and Lausanne. In other words a highly responsible cross-section of educators was in attendance.

The Conference opened at UNESCO House with note being taken by the hosts of the important work being undertaken. The major deliberations followed at the Pedagogical Institute of Sèvres in Commission A devoted to "Structure, Standards and Syllabuses of the Courses", while Commission B introduced the "Organization and Procedure of the Examination". The attention of Commission A was drawn to a comparison between the higher-level courses and GCE A-levels (not such a wide range of information but comparable intellectual ability) and as regards major branches of the French Baccalaureate (slightly higher level). It was pointed out that guides will be issued to teachers instructing IB courses, and that liason between chief examiners and heads of schools will be assured. The notion of co-ordinators for each subject received sympathetic hearing at the January 1967 planning sessions, but since then the preferability of regional co-ordinators has been suggested. At least ISES inspectors are envisaged. The basic syllabuses which were presented are to be disclosed, as before indicated, in the next chapter.

As far as the Examining Board is concerned it is envisaged as a creation of the ISES Council, composed of chairman, secretary and chief examiner in each subject, director-general and secretary-general *ex officio*, and two representatives of participating schools. Other examiners are to be named by the Council on nomination by chief examiners. Delegation to local examiners and nomination by national educational authorities of additional examiners subject to council consent are likewise envisaged. The original configuration of examinations will be the province of the Examining Board—but later, subject panels will take an active role in revision of syllabuses and examinations.

No regulations were proposed for pre-baccalaureate years, though marking and compensation schemes were proposed (see next chapter). Times of holding examinations, and its "security" regulations were likewise proposed and some questions were raised concerning types of questions, the oral, etc. In addition, a series of papers including proposed questions with some suggested answers were made available: at Higher Level in Language of Instruction (English–French), First Foreign Language (English–French), Philosophy, History, (alpha–beta) Geography (in English only), Physics (same) and Biology (same). At Subsidiary Level they were offered in: Language of Instruction (English–French), Latin, Geography (in English only), Physics (same) and Biology (same). Those were read with interest by the participants. In addition a complete dossier of the experimental History program at all levels was available for scrutiny. Seldom has a conference been as well prepared and documented. This fact, plus the efficient work of the chairman, staff and *rapporteurs* probably played a large role in the success of the Policy Conference.

There was some "floating" between the two commissions but a good nucleus stayed put. Commission A under the chairmanship of Dr. Fischer-Wollpert and spoken to by Mr. Renaud as consultant wound its way through most of the documented material. At given points the more conservative continental approach clashed with more experimental outlooks (Scandinavian, British, American, socialist Eastern Europe) but on the whole the papers were given an *imprimateur*. Commission B, guided by Robert Blackburn, Vice-Principal of Atlantic College, used the capacities of Dr. Halls as consultant to prove itself slightly larger and more controversial.

There, in connection with the Examining Board, it was proposed that university as well as increased school participation would be useful. Also it was strongly emphasized that experts in professional testing be included, and that special arrangements be made for syllabus revision. It was suggested that chief examiners be appointed for a 5-year term to assure continuity. Even more interesting was the vivid disagreement regarding the role, reliability and usefulness of objective type testing as opposed to the more traditional essay method. As one participant noted, the subject raises emotions. But the confrontation was perhaps the most valuable of the whole conference, particularly as the more radical group acted with genuine honesty, straightforwardness and humility.

A joint session to iron out differences preceded the concluding plenary. Here it was considered essential that profiles of students entering IB courses be assembled beforehand to determine the eligibility of the candidate to enroll for the course. Obviously some form of orientation must be given such a student as he enters the program. It was also agreed that a profile of performance would be prepared for each candidate in each of his six subjects, so that if the baccalaureate level is not achieved, his work may stand him in some stead. In fact the very absence of conflict in the joint session seemed to encourage some contradictory remarks in the plenary.

There, Dr. Goormaghtigh presided, with Mr. Peterson acting as consultant (as the latter had handled the joint sessions). There, the Germanic–British–American tradition of using internal validation within schools was put forward—but of course this concept ran on to the rocks of the extreme dissimilarity of international schools, particularly as to standards. This left the Conference to deal with the IB program, which the Council of Europe representative seemed to recommend be referred to national educational authorities, a perfectly normal procedure for them, but for the ISES an almost certain dispersal of the project. In response a number of voices rallied, in range from those most intimately involved to others who felt disinterestedly the importance of the project to international personnel. It was interesting that both the Polish and Bulgarian representatives were forthright in promoting the IB. In fact, Bulgaria had gone so far as to accept the project on the basis of documentation received. It was further reported that a number of universities in several countries would most certainly agree to participate in the project. Oxford University had already set the pace. Countries with centralized educational systems would have to proceed through certain channels, but no representative from France or Germany saw any clear obstacle in the way of achieving this. Perhaps the most convincing argument was given by Mr. Hampton of CERN a member of the ISES Council, who stated that only the problems presented in the field of International Education stand in the way of the success of such an agency as theirs, and CERN was willing to recommend their thirty member nations that they stand in favor of the International Baccalaureate. The UNESCO observer indicated that the first question an international public servant asks upon considering an appointment is "What schooling is available?", secondly, "What housing is available?" and thirdly, "How near is the school to the house?". On this pertinent note the Conference concluded.

Thus, in concluding this chapter, in retrospect it is clear that the Geneva International School first drew members of the University of Geneva into the International Baccalaureate program, then turned it over to an independent association. This body first attracted Atlantic College personnel, then personalities associated with Oxford University, finally those attached to the New York International School and at least one German educator.

With Sèvres successfully negotiated ISES appeared to have come of age. The Technical Committee was then abolished; its functions being taken over by the Executive Committee which met in the spring and autumn of 1967. Mr. Peterson remained in residence in Geneva into June, and has made periodic visits subsequently. In the summer, Gerard Renaud became a full-time assistant director replacing the administrative secretary. The office of ISES was then moved to a very attractive *maison de campagne* in Cologny near Geneva. There, in the autumn, the third General Assembly of ISES met to approve the year's work and to change the name from ISES to the International Baccalaureate Office (IBO). Recently, Mr. J. Sellars, formerly testing expert affiliated with the Greater London Council schools, has joined the staff of IBO on a part-time basis, also as assistant director. Originally it was hoped that the College Board program would be in a position to second someone in this capacity.

In December 1967 the first of a series of printed reports issued by A. D. C. Peterson appeared. This four-page document calls attention first to the printed report of the Sèvres Policy Conference which was published in May. It then points out that the Council has been enlarged to include eminent educators in the following countries: Cameroons, Lebanon, Morocco, Poland and Uganda. The Cameroons and Polish appointees were present at the Sèvres Conference.

As far as recognition is involved—that is for a limited number of candidates in the 1970–6 period—the Governments of France and West Germany have accorded recognition (except for their own nationals studying in participating schools in their own countries). The British Government has undertaken to grant annually a token financial contribution, while fifteen universities in Britain have accepted the IB (including Oxford, Cambridge and London). In the United States the College

Board has circulated a memorandum to universities recommending acceptance. In Canada McGill University has already done so. In Switzerland the Universities of Geneva, Zurich and St. Gallen have also accepted the IB as equivalent to the Swiss *Maturités*. In Sweden negotiations are in progress. Thus the thorny problem of *recognition* seems to be resolved.

Secondly, attention must be drawn to acquiring widespread financial support. The Gulbenkian Foundation and the Dulverton Trust Fund in Britain have both replied affirmatively, while the Twentieth-Century Fund has undertaken to equal its pioneer donation. Plans are actively afoot to achieve subsidy from both private and public sectors.

The following schools have provisionally agreed to submit candidates during the 1970–6 period:

International School of Geneva, Switzerland.
Atlantic College, South Wales, UK.
United Nations International School, New York, USA.
International High School ⎱ Copenhagen, Denmark.
Soborg Gymnasium ⎰
Goethe Gymnasium, Frankfurt-am-Main, West Germany
International College, Beirut ⎱ Lebanon.
Brummana High School, Brummana ⎰
Santiago College, Santiago, Chile.
John F. Kennedy School, Berlin, Germany.
Lycée de Sèvres (Int. Sect.), Sèvres. ⎱
Lycée d'Hennemont (Int. Sect.), St. Germain-en-Laye ⎰ France.
Phillips Academy, Andover, Mass., USA.
Iranzamin, International School of Tehran, Iran.

The Examination Board has been established under the presidency of Dr. William Halls, consisting of ten chief examiners representing six nationalities. Three co-ordinators to handle Languages, Human Sciences (Study of man) and Experimental Sciences–Mathematics have also been named.

Attention is drawn to the fact that in 1967, 148 trial candidates presented themselves in nine different subjects, mostly at Subsidiary Level. Also a full battery of trial examinations is expected to be offered at the Geneva International School, at Atlantic College (the participants in 1966 and 1967) and at the International School of Copenhagen. Correlations between these examinations and similar GCE and CEEB achievements will be studied by independent examination experts.

At least eleven subject panels were held in 1967 after the Sèvres Conference. The first of these was Physical Sciences, held in April, producing a subsidiary paper—partly Physics, partly Chemistry. The second dealt with Philosophy, which, of all subjects offered at Sèvres, needed working through. The third handled Economics. (Only the higher-level syllabus was here worked out.) Both Philosophy and Economics panels met in May. In June the Study of Cities was envisaged by a joint History–Geography panel. When Fine Arts gathered only the Plastic Arts received treatment. Then, in October, Mathematics was considered particularly to plan for a teachers' guide. During the same month Physics met for a similar purpose. In November Language A was considered, where solid work needed doing. Finally, in December, three panels met. One developed the Physical Sciences first tackled in the spring. Another looked critically at Biology (a subject, like Language A, requiring attention) and finally a third examined the possibilities in an Anthropology syllabus.

Early in 1968 three more panels are already planned, one each for Psychology, Sociology and Fine Arts—Music. Obviously this account stops in the midst of intense pedagogical and administrative activity. The IBO appears to have attracted to itself the best national and international educational techniques which are available.

CHAPTER 4

INTERNATIONAL SYLLABUSES DEVELOPED BY ISA AND ISES

UP TO this point this book has been concerned with basic theory and the experience of the two integral international institutions dealing with multilateral international education. It is now time to discuss the substance which ISA and ISES have developed. In other words, it is interesting to examine critically their recommendations regarding what should be taught in international schools and in schools concerned to be internationally minded. One can start with such recommendations most easily in the nursery school or at the terminal university entrance year (though, of course, a division between primary and secondary education offers a third possible starting point). As ISES was developed for the second of these starting points, ISA has concentrated on the first. The consequence of this has been to leave a vast "no-man's land" from the onset of the seventh year through at least the tenth, in which very little has been formulated. It is perhaps interesting to observe that these "neglected" years are specifically those which are now being most carefully programmed by the History Department of the International School of Geneva. It will be recalled that this Department was largely responsible for developing the pilot project in Contemporary History which served as the occasion for the creation of the International Baccalaureate program. If History is any sure guide for future development, the next few years will no doubt witness the formulation of international standards in the junior secondary school.

Even now it is possible to predict that there will be a clash between the basic philosophy inherent in international primary education and that which undergirds the International Baccalaureate. In a recent issue of *Punch*, Elspeth Huxley notes that the psychology of the nursery school has invaded the primary division (at least in Britain). Since the ISA is dominated in the final analysis by British educators, who are sensitive to *école active* procedures in France, and sympathetic to the American progressive school, there is every reason to expect to find that "child-centered" project-oriented education is upheld as ideal internationally. On the other hand the rigorous selectivity of continental universities in their admissions policy dictates an "elite" syllabus and examination structure at the conclusion of secondary international education. Furthermore it would be ludicrous to imagine that the 2 terminal years' preparation for the International Baccalaureate can be undergirded by purely permissive student interest studies. At least two or three IB syllabuses specifically mention a 3–5-year pre-baccalaureate training. Hence the obviously predicted clash in educational philosophy forecast for the international junior secondary school.

Before analyzing the ISA report on the Conference on Primary Curricula in International Schools, which has been prepared as a partial fulfilment of a fourth UNESCO contract (1966), it is interesting to note what, in fact, is the basic philosophy of integral international education. Here no specific formula has as yet been worked out. But I would venture to put into words what my colleagues in this field are feeling after. First it would seem reasonable to postulate an education free of "culture shock"—that is, to put it in a more affirmative stance, to incorporate not only the highest common denominator between and among known national and ethnic education techniques, but to exclude nothing that is common to man. Second, it would seem reasonable to stress those elements which affirm the solidarity of mankind as an entity in such a way that the one-time international school students will find themselves "at home" in all cultures and human situations. But more important, they should feel their lives incomplete in less than universal situations. How this identification is to be assured is more problematical.

In the first case, the majority of students in international schools are and will probably be there "by accident". Not more than a quarter of these will grasp the essence of the multilateral internationalism and be converted to it. But how many in any "captive" situation anywhere rise to such a percentage of commitment? In other words, soundness cannot be measured by immediate results. If, however, the great mass of students in international schools were to be transformed by their experience, then more weight could be given to primary (free) as compared to secondary (controlled) patterns. If, however, it is clear that the mass of international school leavers are to seek admission to national universities, high standards must be exacted. Controllable high standards cannot be other than teacher directed.

It may well be that the true end of the International Baccalaureate program may be to abolish university entrance examinations for those who eminently and evidently qualify. When that day arrives the self-directed project program may well replace examination dictated syllabuses. Short of that eventuality, it would appear that the secondary junior school will be drawn along with its senior department.

The underlying assumption of the 1966 ISA Primary Curricula Report is that essentially of Jean-Jacques Rousseau, a name not unknown in Geneva. Basically, what the pupil "will need to know about the world" involves getting away from "what to learn" toward "how to learn". The Report indicates that a revolution in education is in the wind, as the International Baccalaureate program seems to prove. Actually this assumption betrays some unclear thinking, as the ISES approach is in fact almost diametrically opposite to that proposed by ISA.

From the French and most continental vantage points the ISA Primary School program is revolutionary. At the same time it is contemporary to British approaches, and *vieux jeu* to many Americans, who have observed on many occasions that academic standards have dropped seriously in schools which went over to "progressive" education as early as 40 years ago. In fact the International School of Geneva was created partly as an interaction of Winnetka (Chicago) experimentation in progressive education with *avant-garde* thinking at the Institut Jean-Jacques Rousseau of the University of Geneva. Surely a revolution 40 years old is not the one to which the ISA Primary School Report makes reference. There is no question but that the post Second World War academic standards at Ecolint are much higher than those during the first quarter century experience of the school when, in fact, the "progressive" pattern obtained.

But perhaps I am being unfair, as a bit later on in the ISA Report it is suggested that "knowledge", *savoir faire* and a responsible attitude towards life are the basic aims of international primary education, as well as a respect for different points of view. It is also noted that the speed-up of contemporary technology calls for the universal reading of technical texts, maps, graphs, tables, etc. These aims are to be achieved by individual project work and group activities, with the teacher acting as guide and counsellor. In other words, there would appear to be a paradox presented here. Let us see how it can be explained. The second chapter of the Report deals with "the role and responsibility of the teacher", which should give some clue.

First it is suggested that the primary-school teacher should understand his own prejudices, be prepared to promote international understanding, react flexibly and responsively to children, be ready to promote self-government in his class and principally help develop an "aptitude for change" among his pupils. Incidentally, he should be bilingual to some degree. Except for the final qualification, the standards would seem normal for most primary-school teachers. What seems to be specifically lacking, at least in line with the earlier technological reference, is specific ability to impart the specialized skills involved in graphs, tables, etc. Equally important would seem to be specific knowledge of varying ethnic patterns in order to be able to use them intelligently as opportunity presents.

The Report goes on to deal with the development of a common language of instruction, a problem to be met with in all great metropolitan centers as in international schools. At this point, the ISA study does show a more genuinely revolutionary character—post-Montessori one might say. Here, reference to Gattegno's *Words in Colour*, to Freinet's printing press, to comprehending language as "a form of behavior", all indicate that the more contemporary revolutionary programs are known and appreciated and lead to wide use of flannel graphs, puppetry, debating and dramatics, and culminate in the proposal to construct individual dictionaries.

It is pointed out that grammar, style and fluency are indirect by-products and that creative writing is more rewarding than language exercises (chosen by students?). Certain books are recommended as their logic is essentially child-like, others, equally good, reflect the adult outlook. In fact, there seems to be a balance upheld between student and instructor which would remove both a sense of resistance on the part of pupils at being pushed about constantly—a criticism levied at teachers in traditional classrooms—and the inverted resentment of the child who exclaims "Must I do what I want to today?".

Even more convincing is the ISA proposal that in Mathematics the teacher should become a research worker standing alongside the child as he adventures into the new Mathematics—into a "sensorial" experience suggested by Cuisenaire, Dienes or Stern, for example. Despite individual approach, "rapid mental calculation" and the development of logic are widely appreciated. Obviously, these developments are tied to the "computor epoch", and a brief outline of accomplishments to be achieved is listed for the 6 years in question.

Not only this but a key bibliography covering forty specific topics is appended. Quite obviously ISA intends mathematical progress and offers very satisfactory clues to any school adventuring into that subject, a subject which was formerly notorious for alienating many of its participants.

Nowhere near as satisfactory treatment, however, is given "environmental studies", which are envisaged as a combination of Experimental and Social Sciences. Obviously the notion of combining disciplines has great appeal. Often, as in the case of the union of History and Geography into Social Studies as happens in the United States, Geography lost out "hands down". So in this union, Social Science is to all intents and purposes pushed into a very subordinate place. Given the fact that the basic ideological divisions of mankind are of human origin, and that the primary school-age child is least fixed in irrational prejudices, this preoccupation with weather, life, water, energy, food and power as the key concepts in each of the six grades can hardly be considered other than reactionary. This must be said in the face of an otherwise suggestively interesting Science program.

At least ISA postulates the world as the parish of the child, which, if one proceeds from the known to the unknown, might well mean from the macrocosm to the microcosm. Such, however, appears to be an afterthought lip-service paid as it were to the international school as being different from the typical British school, whose example in developing environmental studies was intentionally promulgated at the conference as useful in international schools.

Curiously, the discussion of teaching foreign languages was divorced from consideration of the common language. Particularly at this point attention was drawn to the relatively brief average period of attendance of students in international schools. This fact is intimately related, of course, to the short term of service of most diplomatic personnel. Adaptation classes are noted as primordial—though this is even more important for learning the "common language".

At one point the Report confesses to essential ignorance as to how students in international schools do learn foreign languages. It does point to the usefulness of "hardware", especially language laboratories, and stresses that listening, speaking, reading and writing are four separate skills each to be mastered in turn. Is this judgement a contravention of the permissive student-led orientation in the common language? Perhaps foreign languages can only be taught by teacher-directed activities. In that case it were well removed from consideration of a child-organized common language study.

The two final areas of study for primary schools have to do with "creative Activities" and "Physical Education". The first is taken to mean Music and Art with special attention to singing and appreciation of art forms. The second has to do with physical training, particularly with "apparatus". Both are obviously incomplete in treatment, as Creative Activities should cover a host of artistic and occupational interests which could be central to a child-directed educational program. Nor is account taken of games—sports, which are again particularly well adapted to student interests. In fact, physical training, as proposed, could only be performed in a gymnasium extensively equipped. No international school has such. Furthermore, it is postulated that the second half of each lesson is entirely teacher directed. In the case of the Fine Arts, basic psychological values are cultivated. In Physical Education, selection, modification, clarification and repetition make up the teacher-directed stages for achieving expressive and objective movement. It would appear that Physical Education in international schools is the least revolutionary subject taught.

In conclusion, the ISA Report rather surprisingly declares that "in every educational situation the decisive factor is the teacher". This is probably true as he should possess the essential authority which makes for a proper learning situation. It is he who permits the student-directed activity to take place within limits. Given my quarter-century experience teaching I should say that it is also his province to take initiative to organize data which otherwise remains in childlike or childish chaos.

In my experience there is no violence done the class by a sensitive and ingenious teacher in communication with his pupils at a number of levels, some unconscious, or nearly so, who utilizes his authority and experience to make vivid a lesson which otherwise would make a much poorer impression on his class. This does not mean that he does not encourage his class to create a laboratory experience of their own choosing. It simply means he is responsible for timing both activities.

The ISA Report concludes with a good many pages of useful source material (the Environmental Science section had already done this; as had Mathematics). Also included is a reprint of an article which I wrote on the nature and variety of international schools, which is not too relevant to the Report but perhaps indicates after all that, since international applicability is conspicuously absent from the treatment of most subjects, this Report applies to international schools. A more serious criticism may be put forward, in concluding this analysis, by pointing out that what is recommended is pretty "academic"—that is any resemblance of a given international school to the syllabuses recommended is purely coincidental—and remarkable if discovered.

The teaching profession is probably one of the worst offenders in putting forward theoretical arrangements which never get tried. Admittedly no progress is made if no one holds a plumbline and advocates change. This criticism is not put forward to denigrate the work of individual gifted teachers and administrators who are constantly experimenting in their own domain with self-authenticating methods. What is said here is that no one single international school resembles this Report in its general configuration, nor has any single school undertaken to remodel itself on the lines of this Report since its appearance. Finally, it is my judgement that the Report is insufficiently international in its general outline (and specifically deficient in the areas of History, Geography, Fine Arts and Sports), it serves as only a first exploratory step in creating the ideal primary international school. As to the role of the teacher in multilateral international education, a much more serious inquiry needs to be made.

To compare the ISA Primary School program with the ISES baccalaureate syllabuses is unfair to the former. But it should be recalled that for 2 years previous to the 1966 ISA Conference, both annual meetings and a series of ISA Education Committee meetings were devoted principally to primary education. Over the same period, but admittedly with a much larger budget available, ISES prepared its syllabuses for the Sèvres Conference of February 1967. The sheer volume of ISES work is naturally much greater, particularly when one considers the 2 earliest years devoted to the pilot program in Contemporary History. Notwithstanding, certain comparisons may be in order.

The common languages of ISA emerge as Language A (Language of Instruction), in this instance English and French. Both are treated as the first subject requiring attention and examination in the International Baccalaureate program (with World Literature in Translation annexed). Mathematics appears in both syllabuses (though treated as the last of eleven subjects elaborated for the IB and compulsory only as "mathematical comprehension" if not taken as a regular subject). In both instances the new Mathematics makes impressive inroads. In addition, an undeveloped syllabus in Applied Mathematics appears among the options listed under the sixth grouping of IB subjects.

Environmental Studies undergoes the greatest transformation of all the subjects proposed by ISA. In fact from six to ten disciplines emerge depending on the counting. Three Experimental Sciences (listed as eight, nine and ten of the IB subjects) are Physics, Chemistry and Biology — one of which must be sat at Higher or Subsidiary Level. In addition a composite Science subject has been developed at Subsidiary Level. Thus

7*

four legitimate heirs of environmental studies may be discerned. In addition two less legitimate descendants make up the IB subjects: five, six and seven. The first of these is Philosophy, the second History, the third Geography, the fourth Economics, and the fifth Anthropology. One of these must be sat at Higher or Subsidiary Level and, in addition, a Theory of Knowledge studied by all IB candidates as a key to interdisciplinary arrangements in the syllabus. A fourth subject for this grouping as yet undeveloped, is Physical Geography which is envisaged as one of the general grouping of electives—though not yet prepared. Finally a combination of History and Geography similar to the composite Experimental Science paper may well be prepared. Thus the total of eight subjects dealing with the Study of Man may be compiled. And as the History syllabus divides into Modern and Contemporary sections, it can be clearly stated that the neglected area in the ISA environmental studies has produced more than double the IB syllabuses of the more favored Science section. In any case no other ISA subject is ancestor of two compulsory IB examinations.

The ISA foreign-language teaching section has evolved into two examinations, one (Language B) which must be offered unless the candidate can take a "linguistic competency" test (similar to "mathematical comprehension") or produce work in another course in the language required—the other (Language C) which may be offered among the electives listed with Physical Geography. In point of fact these two examinations are being presented in three languages initially: English, French and German. Like Language A which is a "descendant" of common language, one required IB examination appears to follow from the foreign language as seen by ISA. There still remains the study of Classics (Latin) which must be grouped with the three modern-language examinations. And as well, a similar program is envisaged for Greek and perhaps for other classical languages. These are listed, however, as purely optional examinations. In any case a total of four examinations spring from this area, similar to the Experimental Sciences in number.

Creative activities still claims a place (similar in importance to classical languages) inasmuch as optional examinations in the Plastic Arts and in Music are envisaged for preparation. Finally, Physical Training disappears altogether as an examination subject, though it is not inconceivable that a creative international sports syllabus could be prepared. It would seem in retrospect that except in the area of environmental studies, the ISA Conference envisaged a reasonably good overall scheme to meet the needs of an eventual baccalaureate— though such planning was only in their minds to the extent of being aware of its existence.

In turning to the ISES program itself, certain preparatory discrepancies in preparation of syllabuses are immediately evident. Previous to the Sèvres Policy Conference (February, 1967), Languages came off best with three panel meetings — leading to three examination programs, two essentially obligatory. Mathematics came next also with three panels, but at their own insistence refused to offer an obligatory examination (except as "comprehension"). History officially came third (despite 4 years of practical experience) with two official preparatory meetings which lead to a double-headed subject examination. This subject will probably prove to be the most popular in the "Study of Man" series—one of which is obligatory.

Physics came fourth with two meetings (like History) leading to an examination as important as History, especially if one considers that Physics is also offered among the optional subjects. Geography likewise met twice, and in addition to sharing equally with History in the pattern of the Study of Man subjects, projected a Physical Geography alternative which cannot be taken concurrently with the main Geography course. Biology, Chemistry, Classics and Philosophy each had to be satisfied with one panel meeting, while Economics and Fine Arts were put off altogether. Biology and Chemistry occupied positions in the ISES syllabuses identical to Physics, while Classics was given, at least in theory, two optional places. Philosophy, although the most recent subject elaborated, not only shared a place with History and Geography, but had secured a universal study of its epistomological "Theory of Knowledge" course, similar to "World Literature in Translation".

Having given this much general introduction to the IB pattern, it is appropriate that each subject be discussed in turn in detail. In doing this I have chosen to follow the arrangement of courses which was suggested at Sèvres, rather than to elaborate the ISA primary school arrangement or that pattern which is related to panel gatherings discussed just above. It should be pointed out here that post-Sèvres arrangements are discussed at the end of this chapter.

There is only one subject which is listed as obligatory among the six which the candidate takes for the International Baccalaureate. This subject is the Language of Instruction (Language A) which includes World Literature in Translation. The combination of these two subjects would seem to constitute a normal procedure, as appreciation of both the vehicular language and world-wide contributions in literary form meet the needs of the educated internationally minded person. That pointed out, it must be added that this examination may be taken at either Higher Level or Subsidiary Level and in both cases in English or French—which means a total of four different examinations which are offered—only one of which is actually obligatory.

It is postulated by ISES that an average of five lessons weekly in a school year of 180 days would meet the requirements of higher-level syllabuses and three periods similarly weekly for subsidiary. It is further postulated that the higher-level examination should average 4 hours' written work, while the subsidiary involves 3 hours'. On the basis of periods given to each level for instruction a case could well be made for a $2\frac{1}{2}$-hour examination average for the subsidiary. Certainly most subsidiaries tend to take on an importance somewhat greater than space originally allowed them in the program. The Sèvres Policy Conference recommended a ceiling of 18 hours for written examinations, which is exceeded by 3 hours if an average of 4 for Higher Level and 3 for Subsidiary Level is adhered to. Even allowing subsidiary examinations $2\frac{1}{2}$ hours the ceiling is topped by half an hour.

In the case of Language A (Language of Instruction) certain introductory explanations should be examined before turning to their internal regulations. The first of these is indicated as clarifying the relationship of the language of instruction (English or French) to mother tongues. For those candidates where identity of the two tongues is established there is no problem. However, a case is made for those of French mother-tongue treating the English Language A examination as a Language B (First Foreign Language) and vice versa. In both cases the candidates would be allowed to reverse the roles of Languages A and B. Still another category contains those whose mother tongue is neither French nor English. These could be allowed to take a "qualifying examination" in their own language, which would exempt them from taking Language B and thus allow them full concentration on Language A. It is also envisaged that where possible a student might prepare other than a language examination in his own mother tongue, and thus qualify for exemption from Language B. Obviously such sensitive regulations reveal sharp awareness of the linguistic problems faced by international schools and unquestionable competence in facing up to them. The purpose of Language A (and for Language B when it stands in place of Language A) is threefold—to develop powers of expression, to appreciate its literature and to deepen understanding of human experience. World Literature in Translation is cited at this point as being particularly useful. A balance is intended in Language A between a study of literary periodization and set texts: while the values of literary composition form a third dimension involved in the overall approach.

In turning to the syllabus of the higher-level examination for Language A, an even more specific outline is presented. Here again the tripartite approach is kept. Study of three set texts from one or more authors; consideration of characteristic works of four selected authors; appreciation of the literary period of one set text or specified author: these are the substance presupposed for the examination. Attention is then drawn to the proposed basis of World Literature in Translation— where, incidentally, a third tripartite characterization is engaged upon. Here biblical, oriental and classical texts stand first; followed by European medieval texts; and concluded by modern European texts. To explain its Occidental preoccupation this outline is described as a "guide for schools of Western culture".

Here at last is a glaring weakness. Did ISES expect to create a guide for schools of Eastern culture? Why should the syllabus of a basic compulsory subject offer options, particularly at this point? There are in print today a good many competent collections of texts offering extracts from the medieval Orient and the Orient in modern times. It is "notoriously" Occidental to deal with the inception of Oriental philosophy in ancient times and then to pretend that what has followed is too obscure or too difficult to be taken into account at least till the contemporary era. By that time classical, medieval and modern Oriental writings may be conveniently forgotten. The consequence is a distortion of the Oriental mind, so that today it is a general practice not only for Westerners to know practically nothing of flourishing contemporary Eastern cultures but also for the Christian church in India to have lived in the heart of hinduism without knowing or even wishing to know the greatest Hindu thinkers.

Because international schools are dominated (of necessity) by Occidentals, they can easily fall into mentality of the "colonizers' enclave" if they do not intentionally reject "guides for shools of Western culture". At this point the whole purpose of Language A is seriously compromised. The English and French languages—useful and magnificent tools that they are—were also the two principal languages of nineteenth-century imperialism and are today of contemporary cultural imperialism. At least the Sèvres Conference called for a wide geographical spread at this point.

Unfortunately, this unconscious Occidental slant is not the only criticism which may be levied against Language A at Higher Level. Upon turning to the pattern of the examination itself, it would appear that the principal written paper (of 3 hours' duration), which was proposed to deal with language rather than literature, offered two options. One option (B) consisted of an essay upon one of three set subjects plus an exposition and commentary on one set item of verse, or one set item of prose. To observe that this type of examination exists practically only in English-speaking countries is to cavil, except inasmuch as the other option (A) asks for a 3-hour essay only on a single one of three subjects offered. This only reinforces the impression that the Language A examination was, in fact, only an unsatisfactory compromise between the two linguistic cultures in which the examination was offered. This impression is changed to certainty when one reads the footnote inserted by ISES that students intending admission to British and North American universities will normally take option B.

The second written paper for Language A (dealing with literature) of 1 hour's duration, fortunately offered no options (which, incidentally, ISES condemns in principle). In this case, an essay was required dealing with prescribed texts or selected literary periods. I am not sufficiently conversant with the relative values of a language as a mode of expression in contrast with the appreciation of its literature to judge whether or not a 3-hour language and 1-hour literature paper offer the right balance—particularly as the larger paper offered options, both of which affect the real proportions proposed. I am not, however, clear in my mind that this balance had been worked out on principle. Neither am I convinced that the American ideal as worked out in Advanced Placement examinations (roughly equivalent to IB Higher Level) have been fully considered in arriving at the pattern offered.

In addition to the normal 4 hours of written papers, Language A offered two orals which together might total another hour. The oral was envisaged in "dialogue" form (though what else an oral is puzzles me) on the general subject of World Literature in Translation (at least common in ground for both English- and French-speaking students). What proportion of marks the two orals might take was not suggested. It is clear that they raised the total examination time to about 5 hours. This grand total was equalled only by History and Physics among the other ten subjects offered but was surpassed by Mathematics by a half hour. The excuse given by the linguists for 5 hours was that, after all, the language takes precedence. The historians point to the fact that History is the one completely international subject and that they have reduced their requirement already by $1\frac{1}{2}$ hours to meet the pattern imposed by a "six-subject package" arrangement. It would appear that Physics should be drawn in line with the other Experimental Sciences, and that Mathematics should at least adhere to the vehicular Language–History ceiling.

The subsidiary examination in Language A (intended for those who specialize in Mathematics and Sciences for the most part) offered a normal written load of 3 hours, and two orals bringing the total to $3\frac{1}{2}$. This grand total was equalled by Latin, History, Chemistry and Biology, and was exceeded by Mathematics by the space of its usual half hour. (This last should be reduced as for the Higher Level.) Curiously, Physics might well be encouraged to raise its subsidiary requirements by a half hour to bring it in line again with the other Experimental Sciences. Similar arguments could be used for Languages B and C and for Philosophy.

The subject farthest out of line at this point was Geography which ran an hour behind the subsidiary examination offered by Language A. It could be argued that Geography has more nearly grasped the correct ratio which should obtain between higher and subsidiary subjects. This opens a whole new area of principle which needed full airing. Short of this it would seem that the geographers should raise their subsidiary grand total by 1 hour. I think it quite tenable to ask that all subsidiary subjects occupy the same grand total of time allocated to Higher Level. Curiously, the 5-hour–$3\frac{1}{2}$-hour grand-total ratio between higher-level Language A and subsidiary-level Language A more nearly met the need of a proper balance between those levels than did the ratio between their written examinations, which ran as earlier mentioned—4 hours Higher; 3, Subsidiary.

The subsidiary A examination merited criticism first inasmuch as it omitted only the 1-hour written paper on literature, though the lesser oral at that level and the smaller "dialogue" over World Literature probably saved another half hour. (Unfortunately no clear indication is given as to what this, in practice, might mean.) It may well be maintained that the subsidiary candidate should know less literature, for the "anglophone" language examination proposed the substitution of its higher-level exposition and commentary on a set piece of prose or verse by an hour's exercise in comprehension on a hitherto unseen passage. The ideals set forward earlier concerning set books and authors lose still further their place as justifying the examination.

An even greater dichotomy is to be discovered when it is realized that in the francophone option the original higher-level dissertation appeared transposed without any change. Thus, in point of fact, at Subsidiary Level there is even less attempt to achieve synthesis between British and French viewpoints. All that can be said is that the anglophone version approaches the American point of view to the extent that it moves away from its "higher-level" orientation. If this is an intentional development, no clue is given to that fact. To sum up, the proponents of Language A show competence in linguistic expression, undue hesitation in overcoming national prejudices and alarming unawareness of how Occidental they are in fact.

The fourth subject listed on the general schema of the International Baccalaureate is Language B (First Foreign Language). It is interchangeable with Language A for that category of student whose mother tongue is inverse to those two examinations, and is omitted by those whose differing mother tongue may be tested as observed earlier. The principle, however, remains that students in international schools must acquire, at Higher or Subsidiary Level, another language than that which serves as vehicular for them in normal instruction.

It is, it seems to me, a sound principle to require a second language, though it complicates the choice of other subjects enormously. Interestingly, a 5-year period of preparation is presupposed for Higher Level and three for Subsidiary. In other words, preparation reaches back into the second or third year of junior secondary schooling. The basic purposes are stated to be: achieving linguistic competence; understanding of the culture lying behind the language; and development of appreciation of its literary contribution. The range is understandably somewhat less universal than for Language A.

In turning specifically to the higher-level examination we find that its syllabus prescribes fluency and comprehension at a standard equal to "natives"; four prescribed works; and six specified topics dealing with the life and civilization of the people speaking the language.

The set authors and emphasis given literary periods in Language A tend, it would seem, to disappear here. As far as duration given to examinations is concerned, an equivalence between Languages A and B appear identical, at least as to written exercises, but half an hour less on orals is suggested at both Higher and Subsidiary Levels. Notwithstanding these superficial resemblances, the examinations for Language B are conceived after an entirely different and, from my point of view, more satisfactory angle.

For example, instead of deleting a written paper on literature, as took place in the transition of Language A from Higher to Subsidiary Level, here the subsidiary attempts portions of both higher-level papers—which, on the face of it, seems to be a much more rational arrangement. More important, there are no anglophone–francophone options. In other words, a genuine synthesis of cartesian and utilitarian attitudes has been achieved.

Why was this not done then for Language A? The only rational answer would seem to be the attitude of almost "holy reverence" with which both British and French tend to regard their respective languages, an attitude which extends to the methods which each has developed for examining them. Another innovation with Language B is to reverse the importance of literature and language examinations. Surely this is what is needed in international schools. Linguistic fetishism is a strong nationalistic ingredient needing to be displaced.

In any case the 3-hour written literature examination includes both commentary on one of two set passages and one essay chosen from a series set on the life and civilization associated with the language in question. In addition, note may be taken of independent work which may have been prepared during the 2 years preceding the examination. For the first time in the IB program the notion of taking into consideration that which normally makes up the credit structure for admission to American universities appears. It is put forward tentatively in a continental atmosphere where uncontrolled independent work is immediately suspect of being essentially plagiarized.

The language paper of 1 hour's duration is likewise revolutionary in suggesting that it consist of many short objective questions—and then be reinforced by an oral of half an hour's duration, before which the candidate is given 15 minutes to absorb the literary data upon which he is to be questioned. At this point the more reliable but less versatile examination patterns, developed for the most part in the United States, make their first appearance. In addition, the use of the "open book" oral is adopted. A word might usefully be put here to indicate that for the British (except in foreign languages) the use of the oral is practically unknown. Thus, in retrospect, Language A demonstrates that much innovation (though many taking Language A are, in fact, taking a foreign language).

The Subsidiary Level of Language B also offers creative innovation. First, there is a 2½-hour written paper comprising essays on two of a number of set literary subjects and a less searching short-answer objective question section on language. This is followed by a 30-minute comprehension oral; then 10 minutes of this is given over to reading literature aloud, and 20 minutes in which the candidate discusses in depth one page of thirty selected pages of text which he has submitted. It is also envisaged that the full subsidiary examination could be taken in the penultimate year as the linguistic comprehension test excusing the candidate from sitting Language B. Here the regulation would appear open to question, as ISES allows IB candidates the right to take two subsidiary subjects in the penultimate year. Does this in effect mean that three subjects may be taken on the assumption that one of them is only a "linguistic comprehension" test? It would seem the course of wisdom to develop a third type paper not dissimilar to that which the mathematicians regard as the basic minimum for all candidates.

With the exception of interchangeability of the subsidiary and linguistic comprehension texts, the entire profile of Language B stands out as unquestionably superior to the Language A pattern. How, then, can these totally dissimilar grouping of examinations be used interchangeably by anglophone and francophone students studying inversely in the two languages? This eventuality is still obviously a purely academic exercise.

The second foreign language (Language C) is listed as the first option under point six of the subjects listed by ISES. Like Language B it appears in English, French and German at both

Higher and Subsidiary Levels. The configuration of the two groupings of languages is absolutely identical except that during the first 10 minutes of the oral, at Subsidiary Level, the reading of a piece of literature is combined with conversation. This nearly complete identity can only be justified, of course, by the level of the questions used in Languages B and C.

Until a full battery of examinations is developed and offered, it will naturally be difficult to assess the wisdom of parallel exigencies for differing standards of performance. Nothing is said regarding interchangeability between Languages B and C, which only sharpens the divergence from Language A (in which interchangeability with B is envisaged). Certainly, if Language C is performed at a level 2 years below Language B, its subsidiary would be more useful as a linguistic comprehension test than would the subsidiary in Language B. As the B and C syllabuses are grouped together in the paper presenting them at Sèvres, their difference in standard is not specifically clear.

The last of the language syllabuses deals with Latin as the first of two or more classical languages, all of which are to be offered alongside Language C as an option under section six. The purpose in introducing "extinct" languages is that they undergird and give a common basis to a number of subjects offered in the International Baccalaureate (how this applies to ancient Persian, Sanskrit and classical Chinese is not quite clear, though hellenistic Greek may meet the qualification). Also, Classics are apparently to be encouraged as they give clue to ancient cultures.

As far as the specific syllabus is concerned it is suggested that grammar in the abstract should be avoided, and that translation from prose into vehicular languages should be encouraged rather than to use poetry (which is more "tricky") or to translate into the classical language itself. Dictionaries are encouraged to be used in examination. Nothing is said explicitly concerning the possible uses which classical languages offer to multilingual students, though this is probably implied. Not as great parallelism with living languages is to be expected either in theory or in practice but in looking over the examination structure suggested for Latin, the subject appears to run more parallel to Languages B and C than to A, which indicates that at least the anglophone–francophone approaches to Latin have been harmonized.

Instead of one 3-hour written paper followed by a second 2-hour paper (or vice versa), two 2-hour written papers appear both involved equally in language and literature (not as in the living languages). The first of these higher-level papers offers translation of prose (and simple poetry) into English or French. The second paper apparently offers some translation into Latin if desired, and seeks out information regarding Roman civilization and daily life. These two are followed by a 20-minute oral (with 20-minute preparation) on prepared and/or unseen texts. There seems to be some uncertainty between the syllabus and the examination proper regarding the use of poetry and translation into Latin. This uncertainty probably stems from the regulations still intact for certain faculties in British universities. The resolution of the problem should lie in the "package" acceptance by these universities. Most of these also exact their own individual admission examinations even from candidates whose GCE results are unquestionably good. It will be recalled that Classics has benefited from only one panel.

Subsidiary Latin is envisaged as offering one 3-hour written paper (which exceeds the amount required by Languages B and C by a half hour). Its accompanying oral is identical to that at Higher Level, except that the questions are "easier". The written paper is therefore interesting to examine. It calls for a $2\frac{1}{4}$-hour written translation into English or French from easy Latin authors. The remaining $\frac{3}{4}$ hour is devoted to answering three to four questions from a total of six to eight which are set. Those deal with Roman life and civilization and could terminate with a few sentences to be translated into Latin. Though somewhat different from Languages

B and C, the Latin configuration is obviously superior to that of Language A. It would seem wise to bring all the linguists together to compare the merits of the three systems proposed. Not least in such a discussion would be the extension of the Classics examinations to Greek.

The second grouping of IB subjects go under the title "Study of Man": offering in theory four subjects to match the four languages. In fact, however, they are not spread over the spectrum of the six branches of the IB program as are the languages, but rather are grouped as comprising subject two—one branch of which is obligatory for the candidate. Although History is the central subject which has proliferated into the Study of Man, it is given second place after Philosophy. The reason for this is clear inasmuch as the obligatory "Theory of Knowledge" grew out of Philosophy, and is attached to the Study of Man much as World Literature in Translation is attached to Language A. However, the Study of Knowledge does not form a part of any examination but seeks its *raison d'être* in offering itself as an epistomological guide to the whole configuration of the baccalaureate and the basic philosophical approaches which unite to create a sophisticated internationalism.

Philosophy, like Latin, suffered from obviously inadequate preparation, and in the latter case, it is clearly a francophone contribution. Attention is drawn to the fact that Philosophy plays a leading part in the European Baccalaureate (but not to the reason that it was incorporated there specifically as a result of the pressure of the French authorities). The basic IB syllabus is composed of consideration of psychological phenomena, while at Higher Level this includes some existential problems. Three philosophers are noted as demanding special study: Plato, Descartes and Kant. (The first two of these significantly have more to do with the francophone approach than any others who could be brought to mind.)

Without doubt both the Theory of Knowledge and the course in Philosophy can constitute one of the most original aspects of the IB program provided their substance is built upon the highest common denominator of leading Occidental and leading Oriental cultures. So conceived, this would fulfil the inspired promise which the French most appropriately put forward in insisting on philosophical soundness. Should the final result prove to be |French-dominated, this would constitute its ultimate betrayal. A parallel is to be found in an ancient Israel which would want to keept the insights of the second Isaiah regarding a universal Jehovah for its own tribal embellishment.

As might be expected the proposed higher-level Philosophy examination consists of one 4-hour francophone-like disser-tation with possible comment on a philosophical text. A half-hour oral is envisaged on the same theme. Not only is such an essay too limiting (as in the case of option A of Language A) but there was no opportunity to deal with schools of philosophy as such. This syllabus came under specific heavy criticism at Sèvres, as neglecting behavioral psychology alto-gether. One gets the uneasy feeling as it is presently consti-tuted that it promotes the deductive *formation d'esprit* which the French cherish above all else in their educational system. Obviously, French clarity is a useful ingredient in the inter-national mind-set—but only in competition to other, perhaps less self-authenticating systems. As for the Subsidiary Level in Philosophy, it was envisaged as offering a 3-hour (rather than 4-hour) examination on psychological phenomena, no doubt as understood by certain philosophers. There was no oral nor any discussion offered of existential epistomology.

History, in contrast to this most unsatisfactory syllabus, was several times declared at Sèvres to be the most thoroughly thought out and internationally satisfactory. This description was natural considering its circumstances of being hammered out in the hard school of experience—4 years of it (which no other subject had to its advantage). Attention has already been drawn to this experience in the chapters on ISA and ISES, and so the account here will only sketch in the pattern as presented at Sèvres. History, unlike any other subject (except Languages B and C), is composed of two streams—alpha (contemporary) and beta (modern). The reason for this bifurcation (and some would like a combined paper drawn from the two) is the fact that the contemporary world is the world of incipient integral internationalism. The great mass of conservative orthodox historians prefer the opening of state archives (normally after half a century) before wishing to commit themselves to definitive historical judgements. At least in maintaining two streams, the motives are extra-national; and absolutely parallel arrangements occur for the examination procedures in both. (It is pointed out that alpha questions on paper one are divided into political and non-political groupings. In point of fact the same arrangement is followed in paper one, beta stream. The only reason for this is to assure that non-political subjects get a fair hearing.) At the Higher Level both streams offer two written papers and two orals following the outline pattern of Language A. The first paper is of 3 hours' duration, during which time three of twelve questions must be answered. These are set upon one of the four geographical areas of the globe. Normally the area examined will be that in which the given international school is situated. The second written examination is of 1 hour's duration and seeks out information on one of fifteen subjects set (seven on world-wide movements, eight on historical events taking place within the three areas of the world not examined by the first paper). Two others of these are examined by an oral running 20 minutes. In addition, each candidate is questioned orally on a topic in depth which he has selected from a list of twelve to fifteen, and upon which he may write a series of essays which are handed into the examiner a month before the oral.

These essays do not grant marks to an eventual total but help guide the examiner in noting the work of which the candidate is capable. A total of 30 per cent of grade is envisaged for each of the two later exercises in examination, while 40 per cent attaches to the first paper. It is interesting that the historians have always been specific in the internal weighting of their examinations, as contrasted to most other subjects. No doubt practical experience explains this difference. The motivation behind the tripartite History program is clear. In the first place, the student should know his selected area (contemporary or modern) well. He should be able to deal with the three outside areas and with world-wide events at a more superficial level during the time of his specialization. And he should be able to organize basic historical material in such a way that by composition and oral discussion he proves mastery of a limited specific historical topic. This seemed to the historians as much as a candidate could do given the limitation of the six-subject package to which the IB is pledged.

At Subsidiary Level a 3-hour paper is offered, one-third of the questions applicable to the "home" area, one-third to the other three areas and the last third to world-wide problems in the time span covered (contemporary and modern). To this is added one half-hour oral in which one page of an original document is examined. As in Languages B and C, the student will have studied thirty pages from which the one to be examined will be chosen. This exercise should be useful in teaching students how to handle primary documentation. It would appear that this overall pattern contains much which might recommend itself to the field of Philosophy. The Sèvres Conference recommended that a second subject listed under "Study of Man" be included in the general sixth grouping of IB subjects. As Physical Geography meets this objective, probably the appearance of History in that grouping was envisaged, but this is not clear.

The Geography syllabus describes that subject as a Human Science serving as a bridge between the Arts and the Experimental Sciences, and as offering useful contrast between the Orient and the Occident. Further, it offers discrimination and correlation in dealing with one's immediate environment.

Like Language B, Geography envisaged 5 years' training to the point at which the Higher Level is taken. Geography thus resembles History in its international spread and interest in interdisciplinary approaches. This having been said, the syllabus at present seems curiously unprepared, not as in the case of Philosophy, but because it seems academic and unstructured. Although the higher-level syllabus calls for four areas of work, viz Physical Geography (land, climate, soils); Human Geography (population, settlement, economics); Regional Geography (in a world setting); and for local field work, the 3-hour essay and 2-hour short answer examinations are not related to the four fields. The oral (time unspecified) has to do with local field work.

Similar lack of clarity characterizes the subsidiary examination (of only 2 hours duration) except that the following subjects are noted in relation to its substance: Population, Technological Improvement, Culture Pattern, Spacial Interaction and Major Problems Facing Man. The case study at this level is listed as being worth one-third the total subsidiary grade, but the only method of examining the candidate on this work is an oral of unspecified length. If this means that independent project work is to be counted toward the examination grade, an innovation is proposed here which was specifically discouraged at Sèvres. What proportion project work bears in relationship to Higher Level is not in any way indicated, though one might hazard a fifth, if the written examination at Higher Level is worth twice that at Subsidiary. The overall pattern is not unlike the approach to History but it badly needs finalizing.

The geographers alone among the Study of Man participants also carry an option in the sixth section of the IB set-up. This subject (for which nothing has been prepared to date) is described as Physical Geography, and would, I presume, be an enlarged development of the first quarter of the present higher-level Geography syllabus. Just why this should exist as a separate subject is not made clear. Still another unsettled geographical question is a constantly recurring proposal to offer a joint History–Geography paper, the contents of which were not all clear, though an anthropological approach has been discussed along this line. The pressure for such a paper comes from the francophone elements, who are used to such a composite paper in France. Its effect would be such as to denigrate History as a discipline, as is the case in France. At Sèvres, the only subject to receive strong support for its being pushed forward on a par with Language A was History. It is difficult to envisage a joint History–Geography paper having any other effect than to run sharply counter to the approach recorded at Sèvres. Unless a uniquely valuable international quality can be attached to such a joint paper it were better forgotten. There is obvious need of clarification in the geographical field.

Finally in connection with the Study of Man there is a proposal for an Economics examination at Higher and Subsidiary Level. Obviously this is greatly needed at the Secondary Level and, if imaginatively enough prepared, will serve as an important element in the IB program. It is a curious generalization to be able to make that despite the pioneering work in History, the overall language program is more solidly thought out and developed than the "Study of Man". What is needed in both areas are ringing statements of multilateral international principle around which subject regulations may be rationally drawn, so that although international linguistics and international humanism use different approaches and techniques, they do, in the final analysis, apply themselves fundamentally to the basic ideal.

The third area of syllabuses is that of the Experimental Sciences, in which Physics has had the greatest opportunity among the three to get its thinking integrally international. The claims of the physicists are not particularly modest, indicating that their subject puts forward the scientific method, develops technological knowledge and offers the key to civilization itself. (Parenthetically, one group of ISES physicists went on record in favor of moving History, then the only "Study of Man" offered, to the sixth group of options, leaving the second required subject as well as the third required subject to the Experimental Sciences.) Probably this impression of the importance of Physics as a discipline accounts for its asking for 5 hours of written examination which was matched only by Mathematics (and exceeds Language A by a full hour).

Physics also puts forward a minimum claim of seven periods' training weekly, two of which are to be given over to laboratory work. The conditioning behind this approach is British. The GCE Experimental Sciences are accustomed to nine periods weekly and the Physics panels seemed to be particularly concerned not to approve an ISES paper which would be "softer" than the British A-level. At this point the overall six-subject packet arrangement should be brought to bear to reduce the Physics requirements at least to the more realistic Chemistry and Biology recommendations.

Physics naturally emphasizes the importance of practical work, in this case envisaged as developing both logic and skill. For the physicists demonstration and free inquiry are both of vital importance, and justify the emphasis on extensive laboratory activity. The Physics work paper then produces an impressive list of 134 obligatory items required of higher-level students under the headings: Body Behavior, Molecular Activity, Atomic Behavior and Wave Activity. This is followed by an additional 73 optional topics under such headings as: Fluids, Materials, Electronics, Thermodynamics, Atmosphere and Universe—though only two of these must be dealt with. For the Subsidiary Level only 25 of the required higher-level 134 are needed, while another 57 topics listed under such subjects as Atmosphere, Astronomy, Communications, Machines, Music and Photography are also given. As with the optional topics at Higher Level, only two of these need attention.

The effect of reading this encyclopedic listing of literally hundreds of topics is overpowering to the uninitiated. On reflection, however, they still seem over-comprehensive. The sample listing of texts to be used in English and French for Language B preparation take on a simplist appearance by contrast. No doubt scientists need to "program" their courses in such a way that their colleagues appreciate the competence of their endeavors.

Notwithstanding this, the IB Physics program appeared to advertise its wares as the "best possible of all worlds" to the extent that it is simply impossible to achieve. This was the case with the experimental alpha History program (which endeavoured to cover the politics, economics and social life of eight geographical areas of the contemporary world). To pull one's course into line with reality is not a confession to incompetence but rather an acknowledgement that the ideal arrangement is elusive. A second impression gained from Physics is the fact that the subsidiary examination was at least three times more possible than at the Higher Level. In no other subject does there exist a 2-hour differential between the two examinations. As in the case of Geography, the proportion of time may prove to be more in line with reality, than is the case with other subjects. Notwithstanding, "the cards" appear to be "stacked" against the higher-level candidate.

At Higher Level two written $2\frac{1}{2}$-hour examinations are envisaged (usual in British A-level). The first of these requires that six topics listed among the compulsory 134 be discussed— four to be categorically designated. In addition two of six topics listed from the optional 73 must receive treatment. The second paper likewise is envisaged as containing two parts. After attempting a large number (unspecified) of short-answer questions applying to the 134 obligatory subjects, the candidate must answer two of three essay questions set upon practical work, also involving the famous 134 items. As well, there is some question as to whether or not an oral should be set upon the practical notebook kept by the student.

At Subsidiary Level a single 3-hour written examination is envisaged containing 20 short-answer questions, 11 of which are chosen in such a way that 6 come from each major section of the optional topics (57 altogether)—but of these only 2 should be answered, while the other 5 come from each major section of the compulsory topics (25 altogether). It would appear that a total of 16 questions would be answered in 3 hours or 15 minutes given per question. There is no doubt that an ingenious mind could be set to work to develop this examination and it may well be a very practical exercise. The complication of regulations for the uninitiated are, however, not inconsiderable. As in the case of Higher Level the question of an oral is suggested to deal with a Physics notebook. It would appear that at least 1 hour of laboratory each week in addition to three lessons would constitute a minimum for the preparation of the Physics subsidiary course.

The chemists, similar to the physicists, have listed their obligatory and optional topics at Higher Level. Here, however, a total of 61 as contrasted with 134 and 11 as compared with 73 make up the list. Unfortunately, no other list was prepared for the Subsidiary Level so that it is less possible to make a meaningful contrast there. Notwithstanding, if the overall Chemistry figures apply at both levels, then the contrast with Physics goes as follows—compulsory 61 and 25, optional 11 and 57. In other words the dichotomy between Higher and Subsidiary Level is nowhere near as great in Chemistry as in Physics. By the same token the higher-level Chemistry examination is a less intimidating vehicle. The Chemistry work paper stresses the fact that the discipline encourages accurate observation and develops a critical sense. In addition the student is introduced to technological processes. In conclusion a "cosmos" type box for practical Chemistry work is recommended.

In comparison with the claims made for Physics, Chemistry is indeed modest. Yet its compulsory areas include: Atomic Structure, Bonding, Quantitive Relationships, Periodicy, Kinetic Theory, Precise Equilibria, Energetics and Organic

Chemistry: while its optional subjects cover: Biochemistry, Nuclear Structure, History of Science, Philosophy of Science, Chemistry of the Universe, Macromolecules, Chemical Industry, Petrochemicals, Chemical Analysis and UN Projects in Chemistry.

The higher-level examination in Chemistry is composed firstly of two 2-hour written examinations (in other words two equal papers like Physics). The first of these consists of 25–40 multiple-choice questions and six short-answer questions from among ten. In conclusion two or three quantitive problems must be resolved. How much of this comes from the compulsory areas and how much from optional is not stated. The second examination is the more traditional type, consisting of two or three essays chosen from four set. One of these is compulsory. Again no indication is given as to the origin of the four questions to be set. No oral is indicated except at Subsidiary Level (and then for 20 minutes). Strangely enough, this is the only Science oral to be securely established.

The rest of the subsidiary-level Chemistry examination consists of a 2-hour written paper covering 25 multiple-choice questions and six short-answer questions from a group of ten (as for Higher Level) and two stoichiometric calculations —and a 2-hour written paper in which two of three set essays must be answered. As with Higher Level, no indication is given as to the origin of the material to be tested. Obviously there is need of working over the Chemistry material more carefully. Even more important would be a colloquium composed of the three Experimental Sciences to draft a joint statement of the role of their subjects in international education and also to discover if more common procedures could be established. It has been suggested that an interdisciplinary General Science program might be developed, as is currently the case in France. The pros and cons of such an innovation could well come before such a colloquium.

Finally, in the area of Experimental Sciences there appears Biology, which, like Chemistry, had not been favored with more than one panel meeting. Yet that syllabus has got on with, if anything, more felicitous results than have been registered by its peers. The purposes of Biology as stated in the ISES syllabus encompass the nature of living things and the human predicament. It also claims the virtue of instilling sound experimental habits and opening doors to a wide vocational range in later years. As with the other Experimental Sciences a total of seven periods weekly is envisaged at least for the Higher Level.

Should a candidate choose the three Experimental Sciences at Higher Level, pass his mathematical comprehension test and take Language A at Subsidiary Level, and History also, he would still have to meet a heavy schedule—at least 30 periods weekly—in the penultimate year—possibly 24 in the examination year. In comparison, a student taking Language A, History and Mathematics at the Higher Level would find he had a total of 27 periods the penultimate year and 19 in his examination year. There would be heavier research homework responsibilities resting on the second student, thus neither possibility appears impossible—at least in terms of classroom periods.

In Biology some 82 obligatory subjects divided into the following sections: Unity among Living Things, Diversity, Physiology of Life, Continuity and Communities; for the Higher Level compares favorably with the 134 equivalent Physics topics and less favorably with the 61 Chemistry items. But in contrast to Physics and Chemistry there are no optional items. Thus the total load is considerably reduced as compared at least to Physics. At the Subsidiary Level 75 topics are similarly listed, dividing into sections dealing with: Variety of Life, Unity, Organisms, Continuity, Heredity, Evolution and Community. This number is greater than the 61 presumably listed for subsidiary Chemistry and the 25 for Physics. On first glance it would appear that the differential between higher-level Biology and its subsidiary level is not sufficiently marked, but as Chemistry is unformulated at this level, and

Physics covers too wide a spectrum it is difficult to judge accurately.

In any case, the formula for Biological examinations at Higher Level presents a new pattern. The first paper is a $1\frac{1}{2}$-hour short-answer examination, while the second is a 3-hour written essay type. Each student keeps a work book which, when examined, could be used to prevent him sitting the examination at Higher Level (which constitutes a new negative factor given to classwork). The subsidiary examination is very similar to the higher-level examination, consisting of a 2-hour short-answer and a $2\frac{1}{2}$-hour essay type. Again the pattern seems oddly unstructured; it may be that the biological examinations are more useful to all the Experimental Sciences than they appear at first glance. Obviously their validity as such should be tested in a panel meeting with their peers. The overall impression which the Experimental Sciences give is that they are about as well structured as the Study of Man group. It should be recalled that they share the third place on the IB listing of subjects—one of them being required at Higher or Subsidiary Level. They also appear as second and third Sciences in the optional sixth grouping, thus they exceed any subject in the Study of Man as regarding their flexibility in being used in combination with other subjects.

There has been some consideration of preparing a combined General Science paper which would suit the francophone candidates, as being in line with current French procedures. The arguments for and against are similar to those for a combined History–Geography syllabus, except that as the Experimental Sciences appear both as third and sixth subjects, the addition of a composite paper would not so greatly compete with the more traditional Science subjects. Certainly no one of the separate Experimental Science disciplines appeared to be too eager for the joint effort. If a new international approach, similar to that possibly hoped for from Economics, could be found for a general paper, its acceptability would be greater.

Mathematics is the eleventh discipline which was presented at Sèvres. In some ways it has the hardest road to travel as the mathematical world is obviously in great upheaval. Strangely enough the final product has been described as essentially on the conservative side. Certainly no ringing statement of the value of Mathematics teaching internationally serves as a prologue to the proposed syllabus. At the Higher Level 18 compulsory topics were listed, divided into: Relations, Functions, Elementary Algebra, Plane Systems, Line, Circle, Conic Sections, Trigonometry, Derivatives, Algebraic Structure, Vectors, Matrices and Rational Complex Numbers.

In the optional section 3 topics must be chosen; some 30 appear. They are grouped under the following headings: Statistics, Theory of Numbers, Pure Geometry, Descriptive Analysis, Integral Calculus, Differential Equations, Mechanics, Numerical Methods and Computors. Like Biology, Mathematics begins with a short-answer (1 hour in this case) paper—multiple choice. This is followed by a 2–3-hour essay-type paper with a possible oral to test understanding. Finally a 2-hour paper to check deductive ability is envisaged.

Interestingly, it is stated that a balance between obligatory and optional materials is to be kept off as far as the first two papers are concerned. Does this mean that only three of the obligatory topics may be treated? In any case, as mentioned earlier, the overall battery is too heavy in comparison with other subjects. The subsidiary examination consists of one 2-hour multiple-choice paper, followed by a 2–3 hour essay with a possible oral to check on comprehension (as for the Higher Level).

What puts this examination on a separate reference from its prototype is not only the suppression of a 2-hour paper for checking deductive capacity but the fact that a separate syllabus from Higher Level is envisaged. Here a compulsory section of 24 items (18 at Higher Level) is combined with an optional group of 25 (30 at Higher Level) in which five of twelve must be undertaken—six of latter subject to special regulations. In other words a rather complicated pattern is envisaged, especially as the balance between compulsory and optional sections is supposed to be maintained (as at Higher Level). Perhaps what is needed is a simplified explanation of what is required, so that the uninitiated layman gets the regulations straighter.

Finally, in turning to the mathematical comprehension test, it would appear that it will certainly find its structure in a third dimension (not as with the linguistic comprehension test) as its syllabus is totally different from the Subsidiary Level—as would seem to be only right. Here, fifteen items divided into sets: Numerical Functions, Geometry and Probability, appear. They would seem to relate closely to the new Mathematics as suggested for the primary school by ISA. Nothing has been developed on the subject of Applied Mathematics, which appears among the optional subjects under point six of the IB. Regular Mathematics (at three levels) composes point five of the general schema. As in the case of a Geography candidate being refused the option of Physical Geography, probably the Mathematics candidate would be refused Applied Mathematics, though this point is not made clear anywhere. It might be useful for the mathematicians to be included in the joint Experimental Sciences panel, as listing of topics appears common to all four branches. In any case a joint Science–Mathematics statement regarding their approach to internationalism would be welcome, as the Humanities are usually the subjects which take initiative in making generalizations.

It should be pointed out that the Fine Arts (like Classics) listed under group six subjects were not too well spoken of at Sèvres, though ISES still plans to go ahead with examinations at Higher and Subsidiary Level in the Plastic Arts and in Music. Both lend themselves to international and contrasting Occident–Orient treatment. Their inclusion also opens to serious study those areas of human creativity which tend to be pushed aside in traditional educational approaches. As said earlier, inclusion of an international Sports program, though not discussed, would seem to round out the educational pattern. Sports, in this case, would constitute still another of the sixth grouping of options (its ninth or tenth).

Despite the anomolies and unevenness pointed out here, the ISES syllabuses presented an impressive and ingenious approach to international education and were so received at Sèvres. Admittedly the two work papers prepared for Commission A and Commission B were intended to shed light on principle and to give general guidance on the way the program should evolve. But had there been real doubt about the competence of the subject syllabuses, that hesitation would have been expressed. It was probably impressive to read that 148 educators had been involved in the production of the eleven syllabuses, 108 of whom were teachers in international schools (or their equivalent); 40 were university or Department of Education level. It should be pointed out that 36 of the schools men were associated with the International School of Geneva.

The IB syllabuses with the introductory brochure and two work papers were presented at Sèvres (as has been pointed out) to get general approval of them and to serve as a basis of examining 500 experimental candidates between 1970 and 1976, when it is hoped the theoretical value and practical utility of the IB program will have won it wide acceptance. This was generally agreed, though of course the participants were not official governmental delegates and could go no further than to agree to use their not inconsiderable influence in promoting the program.

Not only was the setting up of an Examination Board dealt with but also the question of marking the papers and qualifying oral examinations. To expedite this, a scale of seven points was adopted as follows:

1. Very poor.
2. Poor.

3. Mediocre.
4. Satisfactory.
5. Good.
6. Very good.
7. Excellent.

It was approved that candidates at Higher Level should get a 4 at least in their three main subjects. However, a 3 could be compensated in one subject by a 5 or 6 in another. But the total should not fall below 12 points. At Subsidiary Level an average of 4 was again recommended but two 3's or one 2 could be compensated for, provided the grand total of points did not fall below 24. Candidates preparing seven or eight subjects might have their unsatisfactory grade overlooked if it was not in a required subject. It was interesting that the Sèvres Conference agreed that neither linguistic aptitude should be counted for compensation, nor mathematical comprehension. However, a proposition was made that in borderline cases the Theory of Knowledge should be considered.

Thus it would seem that the pattern for the two final years of secondary international education has won general approval inasmuch as such approbation could be sought. Some ten schools—international and internationally minded—had to be selected and begin training up their selected candidates as early as the autumn of 1968. Meanwhile ISES will have to set up a research unit to test its program at every turn.

Some hesitation was expressed at Sèvres over the exclusiveness and high standards to be exacted. And although no formal decision was taken to issue a certificate of entry (and failure) in the program, it was agreed that profiles of accomplishment by all participants in the IB experiment would be kept, and results made available for students who might use a portion of their results for admission to junior colleges, art and technical schools, etc. Obviously, the IB program is not intended for such (strictly speaking) non-academic admission. But it is not intended as a penalty to any candidate.

Some interest has been expressed in having three levels of accomplishment—*cum laude* for automatic placement: baccalaureate for normal competitive university placement and certificate of non-academic (European) level, which might be useful in other parts of the world where higher education is not so severely restricted. Obviously, failure below still another level would not prove profitable at all to the candidate. However, evolution along these lines in holding a plumbline to national and other educational certificates lies well ahead in the future.

Subsequent to the Sèvres Conference, but still during 1967, eleven subject panel meetings were held. One of the most important of these was the November Conference (also held at Sèvres) dealing with Language A (Language of Instruction). At this point two more papers were added in effect, that is German for German-speaking students, and German as a subsidiary examination in German-speaking schools. No doubt this pattern of catering for other languages of instruction is possible to envisage—but it raises the question of translating the syllabuses and examinations into other languages than English or French. Such will increase the labor and cost of the IB operation immensely.

Already the teachers' guide for Language A had appeared and served as an introduction to its consideration. It was decided that study of set texts should be reduced from three to two, but that preparation of characteristic works would be increased from four to seven authors. Finally, appreciation of a literary period of a set text or specified author would be omitted in favor of widening the approach to the period and works of the seven authors specified. It was agreed that a total of fifteen literary figures in each of the three literatures should form an established list from which to draw the specified seven in any one year. As for the World Literature in Translation section it still suffers from its too Occidental outlook—Europe now appearing in five historical periods, and a "hope" expressed that this would be balanced against five other areas of the world. No teachers' guide has yet appeared covering this subject (though integrally a part of Language A). It is illuminating that of the eight authors suggested for the English section of World Literature in Translation, all were nineteenth–twentieth- century Europeans (from French, Norwegian, Swedish, Russian and German backgrounds).

The French section of World Literature in Translation produced three names only (from Russian, Norwegian and Swedish backgrounds.) Somewhat better was the German list of authors for World Literature, consisting of eleven authors; two Ancient Greek, one sixteenth-century Spaniard, another sixteenth-century Englishman and seven more or less contemporary Europeans (English, French, Russian and Norwegian). Obviously there is a long way to go before the three European languages can detach themselves from their continental ethnocentricity.

In turning to the pattern of the higher-level examination it is interesting to observe that 4 hours' written work was unquestioningly upheld, as was essentially the 1-hour oral. However, the panel did come to grips with the dichotomy of English and French options—arriving at a flexible mixing of the two—necessary, in point of fact, as the prospect of a German option and as many more national options as could be imagined would have pushed the Language A examination to a *reductio ad absurdum*. It was agreed that according to temperament two options would be offered. The first would consist of an essay on one of three subjects—possibly literary themes, and a creative commentary on passages of unseen prose or verse. This option, in fact, gets away from the British emphasis on set texts. The second option calls for an essay on a general subject (not a literary theme) or a creative commentary (of $2\frac{1}{2}$ hours) on an unseen passage of prose or verse, and an essay (of $1\frac{1}{2}$ hours) dealing with a prescribed text. Here, the traditional British approach is linked to the traditional French outlook—at least in the second version of the option. It was also agreed that an extended research paper dealing with one of the seven prescribed authors be submitted in advance as a guide for the examiner in the oral. This procedure falls in line with History and would seem to be a sensible proposition.

Similarly, in dealing with subsidiary papers, progress toward an international outlook was achieved. There it was decided that since the clientele for the' courses (English, French and German) would be either scientifically oriented or not of the language of instruction, four or five rather than seven set authors would be offered. In the examination the "dissertation" was dropped in favor of a passage indicating comprehension, or a creative commentary. In other words alternatives are maintained, but temperament again rather than national training should determine choice.

Despite progress, the result strikes me as typically European rather than international (despite a list of American authors in the English listing). It is, of course, more difficult to find German literature outside Germany. Notwithstanding, the results appear to be only a first step toward the international orientation and *formation d'esprit* which should take precedence over all national or regional content in a sound International Baccalaureate. Before leaving Language A it is well to observe that its interchangeability with Language B appears to have been improved—but quite unconsciously!

When the Philosophy panel reconvened in May it decided to leave the A-level syllabus and examination in this subject till other panels could meet to discuss Psychology and Sociology, both subjects to be included in the Philosophy option when it is finally formulated (spring 1968). Meanwhile it was decided at Subsidiary Level such subjects as Consciousness, Freedom of Choice, Individual and Society, Existence and Subsistence, Human Equality, Race, Stable Peace, Law, Justice and International Law would constitute the basic subject matter. Fundamentally what is desired is to educate young people to read classics in the general field with perception. The examination is envisaged as being composed of a $1\frac{1}{2}$-

hour commentary on a philosophical text in the field, and an essay of 2½ hours on (presumably) the basic data with which the course deals. In addition, an oral (time not specified) dealing with the Theory of Knowledge is given 20 per cent of the grade.

Whereas sympathy may be evoked by the notion of dealing philosophically with the sphere of interests which was once the province of the eighteenth-century French *philosophes*, three factors make this proposed subsidiary syllabus disappointing. First, nothing is said to indicate that students will be taught to analyze the national mythologies from which they have emerged. Second, nothing is said of classical philosophy or philosophers as such. And third, nothing justifies the extent of the examination—4 hours plus an oral which are equal to Language A at Higher Level. Surely this needs rethinking! What emerges is a pale class in international civics—and too seriously examined for both itself and the pattern of an IB—already overburdened with examinations. Finally, what has happened to the assurance given at Sèvres that the Theory of Knowledge would be taught as part of the Study of Man, but not examined? Neither is there any indication how the Theory of Knowledge is to be time-tabled when not associated directly with a Philosophy course.

As far as the Theory of Knowledge course is concerned it is envisaged as dealing with: Mathematical or Pure Logic; Scientific Measurement; Historical Theory; "I–Thou" Concepts; Ethics; Esthetics, and Metaphysics, or Role of Religion These are indeed a very stimulating assortment of concepts— and, if appropriately and skilfully used in delineating how we truly know as opposed to imposed authoritarian attitudes, may indeed serve as a key course in the IB program. Naturally the breadth of vision of the teacher will determine the effectiveness of this key course. But, of course, that is a truism applicable more or less to all teaching. In any case Philosophy has come a long way from the "wooden" cartesian model proposed at Sèvres.

In May the Economics panel gathered to sketch in the pattern for that alternative as one of the Study of Man. Only the higher-level syllabus was envisaged, and in an abbreviated manner. Like Geography there is a marked lack of structure. For instance no content whatsoever is given to the two 2-hour written papers, nor to a 20-minute oral. The syllabus notes four main headings: Process of Creating Wealth; Process of Sharing and Exchanging Wealth; Utilization of Wealth; and Economic Policy. Some thirty topics are listed under these four main headings, much as was done in the Experimental Sciences, though no effort is made to differentiate the importance of these. They give the impression of being so put as not to embarrass any traditional economic system, "socialist" or "capitalist". The basic approach appears to be sound, but more work needs to be carried out before this subject can be examined.

In June a joint History–Geography panel met to consider a Study of Cities course, which had earlier been mooted, but now met surprisingly with very general acceptance. It was agreed that the local city, plus one each of three types—one historical, one industrial, one emergent city—would serve as the basis of the two higher-level examinations, each of 2 hours duration. An oral dealing principally with an original research paper was likewise envisaged. At Subsidiary Level one $2\frac{1}{2}$-hour paper plus a smaller oral on a smaller research project were envisaged. The subsidiary examination would be limited to the home city and one other—neither treated in depth. Six cities of each of the three categories were thereupon named. Notwithstanding, a tremendous job of "programming" each city yet needs doing. Brief outlines of Alexandria in Egypt and Geneva, Switzerland, as a "historic" city and a "home" city respectively were worked up—in both cases by the author of this book. Thus, the course remains a purely academic exercise, waiting for special subsidy to cover the basic groundwork involved.

In December an Anthropological panel gathered to discuss

the configuration of a higher and subsidiary examination in that subject. The report of this panel is not to hand, but it would appear that the participants tended to get caught between the dilemma which is presented by a subject which has worked up its "lingo" to such an extent that it becomes incomprehensible except to its initiates on one hand, and on the other find that the "city" has been pre-empted as a field of investigation. Obviously our contemporary world has become a world of cities for the first time since the Hellenistic–Roman period of time. To limit oneself to primitive cultures is probably somewhat "precious" in the pattern of the IB. Possibly the answer will be to combine Anthropology with the "Cities" course. In any case, however superficially attractive it is to adventure into subjects usually limited to university work, care must be taken lest the options in the Study of Man become top heavy, particularly in comparison with those offered by the Experimental Sciences.

When the Physics panel gathered in October it spent its time in analyzing its first run of examinations held at Atlantic College, and planning for the teachers' guide in that subject. Though not explicitly stated, it would appear that only the higher level examination had been tried, although in point of fact a short-answer paper had been experimented with. The oral was utilized, but not for the candidates notebook—rather upon the short-answer paper and in identifying appropriate Physics apparatus. This was found to be valuable. On the other hand the written papers were felt to be too long. It was agreed that one 3-hour written and one 1-hour objective short-answer paper was sufficient with the oral as recast. It would appear that the Nuffield Project findings in Physics had been used pragmatically to modify the original examination pattern. Nothing was said of the encyclopedic nature of the original Physics syllabus, nor its exaggerated claims to its own importance. Both aspects appear to have been quietly shelved. The impression given is that, without saying so, the Physics program is settling into a viable performance within the IB framework.

In April a joint Physics–Chemistry panel was held to develop a subsidiary paper which would meet the needs of students desirous of some capability in both these disciplines. In the final syllabus as worked out, six areas were listed including; the Statistical Nature of Phenomena, Nature of Matter, Energy in Natural Processes, Homeostasis, Transmission of Life and The Organism and its Environment. Some thirty topics are listed under these headings. The examination is envisaged to last 3 hours, with an oral offered to judge marginal candidates. Obviously this paper has enlarged its mandate, and in fact involves biological data to advantage. Though not to hand the report of a second December panel will probably produce the structure of the higher-level examination, thus allowing Arts majors still another comprehensive alternative when working out their program. In this case the results have certainly measured up to the highest expectations possible regarding them.

It is also too early to have the results of the December panel in Biology to hand. It will be recalled that the biologists had waited nearly 3 years for this second gathering. Very probably a number of adjustments needed to be made. Certainly, work on the teachers' guide was a pressing problem. In any case the Biology syllabus was better structured than its peers in the Experimental Sciences previous to the December meeting.

In October the mathematicians convened themselves again, and agreed essentially to keep the syllabus as it was elaborated, but to revise the examination structure. If anything, the exigencies are increased so that a total of not 5 but 7 hours is considered possible at Higher Level. The materials to be examined by papers two and three are more carefully related to the syllabus. The insertion of optional topics is envisaged and the procedure for doing so outlined. At Subsidiary Level the pattern of examination is preserved, while, as at Higher Level, the written examination is specifically tied to the syllabus.

The effect of this tie-up is to increase rather than decrease the problem of understanding what is required—at least from the uninitiated. And to complete their work, the mathematicians strongly recommended that IBO employ a full-time mathematician to produce not a teachers' guide but a complete mathematics textbook. Obviously such a favorable arrangement would suit every discipline. Perhaps the importance of creating an internationally viable system of education such as this would represent will elicit sufficient subsidy for such work. Short of that, the mathematicians will have to "make do", as must other subjects. Is it unfair to suggest that in question of hours for examining candidates they should accept similar limitiations, as do all the other disciplines? Perhaps a totally new group of mathematicians should examine the proposals made to date, with an explicit mandate to bring this subject in line with the others.

This leaves only the Fine Arts panel (of those held in 1967) to be considered. Music has been reserved for future treatment, so that, in fact, only the Plastic Arts were involved. However, it was agreed that a general short course in the Arts (Plastic, Musical or Dramatic) should take its place alongside the Theory of Knowledge course for all participants in the IB course—though no practical suggestion was made as to how this could be done. It was further agreed that only a subsidiary course could be envisaged in Plastic Arts for the moment, and that this course should involve both creative (two- or three-dimensional) work as well as analytical approaches. Here, interpenetration of cultures was considered important. It was felt that creative work could only be evaluated by the visit of an IBO co-ordinator, while analytical judgement could be examined in a more traditional fashion. No final examination proposals were put forward at this time.

Despite some disappointments, the momentum achieved at Sèvres has continued. More solid bases for IB work appear across the spectrum at a happily increasing ratio. Credit for this rests with Mr. Peterson who manages, in his own words, to remain "a professional amateur" at the business of both constructing a worldwide pattern of syllabuses and finding the necessary finance to see it through. At the same time he is prevented from anglicizing the program (quite unconsciously, it should be said) by Mr. Renaud, whose cartesian mind is sufficiently broad to allow him to work effectively in a situation in which the French language and culture are not dominant.

There still remains the question of setting up a Bureau of Research and Analysis by which the usefulness of the IB program is constantly checked. This chapter has been prepared in one sense as a first step in that direction. As the Chairman of the now disbanded Technical Committee of ISES I felt a certain responsibility to analyze the program of the IB which I have had as much to do as any one. Particularly I feel this responsibility as I no longer sit on any of the directing organs of IBO.

CHAPTER 5

ORGANIZATIONS ENGAGED IN SOME FORM OF UNILATERAL OR BILATERAL INTERNATIONALISM IN THE FIELD OF EDUCATION

In turning from the field of multilateral international education to attempt to checklist educational activities of a less complete international character is, in effect, to move from consideration of the microcosm to the macrocosm. I think it is impossible for any one person to prepare a truly complete checklist. Notwithstanding, some effort should be made in this direction in the hope that as interest in the field grows many of these agencies may be transformed into bodies which serve mankind more impartially and whose management may be placed under the control of groupings representing more widely the human race.

To start with, it is interesting to note how slowly governments have accepted the notion that education could be freed of political considerations. A century ago an international Congress of Anthropologists (1866) first met to discuss prehistory. Seven years later, a similar grouping of orientalists met. Apparently, the long distant past, particularly in Asia, was safe for international consideration. Only in 1898 was a Congress of Historical Science held. The next year (1899) an International Congress of Psychology was attempted. Meanwhile, at the Philadelphia Centennial Exposition of 1876, a conference on education had been arranged, followed by one of the primary school, gathering in Brussels 4 years later

(1880). It must be pointed out that these were the result of private initiative almost entirely British–American in character and certainly not other than occidental. It is illuminating that History led the way, as would prove to be the case for the International Baccalaureate.

After the First World War in 1919, an International Research Council was formed as a world-wide information center for scientific unions. But in 1920 the nascent League of Nations declared that education was the "exclusive province of each government or of private initiative". Interestingly, it was the francophone world which proved itself most dissatisfied with the League's pronouncements, so that in 1921 they created an International Council for Intellectual Co-operation and chose Henri Bergson as its first President. Then, in 1923, the World Federation of Educational Associations was set up as the international organ of teaching professions. By 1924, the French Government had agreed to pay the budget of the International Co-operation body (which they finally got the League to adopt in 1931).

The French were interested also in the League adopting the International Bureau of Education started in Geneva privately in 1925. Unfortunately, this organization became an information center for national Ministries of Education rather than fostering genuine educational projects. With the onset of the Second World War, the British became convinced that international intellectual co-operation was vital, and so sponsored the creation of UNESCO (1942). Two years later the United States agreed in principle to underwrite educational reconstruction on a world-wide basis. In spite of this, the education section of UNESCO was nearly dispensed with at the San Francisco Conference of 1945 but did remain as a part of that organ after all. But once again the national pattern has taken priority, so that tentative efforts in the field of international understanding never got far in proposing the substance of an International Baccalaureate. The appearance of the IB had to travel by the uncertain route of the unsupported international school. Given the slowness of government to move, it is not so surprising that multilateral international education has evolved as tardily as it has. It is instructive that the 1965 edition of the *Encyclopaedia Brittanica* describes international education as consisting of the exchange of students from one country to another.

UNESCO has, of course, devoted the major portion of its educational interest to combating illiteracy, though its International Project for the Evaluation of International Achievement (IEA) in Hamburg has currently undertaken a significant project in studying the performance internationally of a group of 13-year-old pupils, particulary in Mathematics. The project started in 1958 in twelve countries (nearly 10,000 pupils). Later it was extended to 133,000 pupils and 19,000 school officials. Obviously, the scientific results of international experimentation on this scale offer guidelines for courses when they are developed for ninth grades (or third form).

The Hamburg project, in turn, was made possible by the development of the Council for Cultural Co-operation of the Council of Europe which has undertaken yeoman service in collating school syllabuses among the eighteen member countries. Dr. Halls, Chairman of the Examination Board of IBO, has been the key figure in this work. It began its activities, however, only in 1962, 4 years after the Hamburg project got under way. This body has held five pan-European conferences and has one more already more or less carefully programmed at this point. Its superior council consists of the Ministers of Education of the member countries. Naturally, the Council of Europe is regional rather than world-wide in character (as is the case of UNESCO) but its studies in comparative curricula will prove of great value to the wider field of education. Closely associated with the Council of Europe is to be found the educational work of the European Economic Community (Common Market) whose six European schools (1956) are oriented toward the European Baccalaureate (first candidates sat this in 1959). These schools are somewhat divided by a quatrolingual pattern which is further complicated by an Arts, Sciences and Languages specialization. Finally, in the field of the Study of Man, its academic work is European in orientation.

In addition to the European schools, which cover primary and secondary training, some twenty-two university institutes have been founded with specific inter-European orientation, and, as well, fifteen other graduate research bodies of a similar nature. Most of these are controlled by educational institutions which are juridically national in basic legal structure. They do, however, sharpen the new international dimension which pervades post-1945 Europe. The following list of their locations is more or less inclusive of this grouping:

1945	Frankfurt, Germany
1947	Brussels, Belgium
1949	Bruges, Belgium
1950	Nancy, France
	Mainz, Germany
	Vienna, Austria
1951	Strasbourg, France
	Saarbrücken, Germany
1952	Turin, Italy
	Edinburgh, Scotland
1953	Rome, Italy
1955	Bologna, Italy
1957	Lausanne, Switzerland
	Paris, France
1958	Fontainebleau, France
	Leiden, Holland
	Cologne, Germany
	Luxembourg, Luxembourg
1959	Louvain, Belgium
1960	Amsterdam, Holland
	Tübingen, Germany
1961	London, England

1962   Liège, Belgium
       Freiburg, Germany
1963   Geneva, Switzerland

Some few international institutes, such as that associated with the University of Geneva, antedate the Second World War. Altogether they account for the interest in nine or ten countries but do not include Scandinavia, Iberia, central or eastern Europe. They are the cultural obverse of the Common Market coinage, which President de Gaulle of France is eager to see make progress cautiously.

Most of these higher-studies programs offer courses of 1 or 2 years or supplement normal university work. In addition a vast number of summer institutes of an international character are held each year. There are also a large group of inter-European centers for information and documentation, some of which carry on very substantial studies. Notable among these are the Textbook Institute of Brunswick in Germany and the European Cultural Centre of Geneva, Switzerland.

Attention might be drawn at this point to the existence of a dozen or so pan-European professional associations, all of which have developed in the so-called "cold war" period. One of these serves the interests of the university institutes (1949) cited above, another is, in fact, the Association of European Universities (1955). At least one foundation, that known as the European Cultural Foundation (1952), with its seat in Amsterdam, is devoted specifically to promoting pan-European understanding. In fact, the ECF works very closely with the Council of Europe to supplement its formal governmental budget.

One of the more useful activities of the Council of Europe aided by the European Cultural Foundation was a series of six pan-European History conferences held between 1953 and 1958 devoted to specific European History topics, the results of which were published in the *Index des Références*, which serves as a strong corrective to national bias. Unfortunately, this activity has ceased, as the European schools have taken on the responsibilities for issuing pan-European manuals in History, and the Council of Europe has engaged itself to prepare a History of Europe. More consistently active is the Association of European School Teachers (1956), which unfortunately is grouped into national departments. Not a little attention has been put by this Association and other interested bodies in the notion of creating a common European Civics course. Consideration of the possibilities of European federalism are closely associated with this program.

In the field of the Experimental Sciences the development of the European Centre for Nuclear Radioactivity near Geneva (1955) marked an important multilateral international enterprise. In 1964, similarly, the European Centre for Spacial Research opened in Paris. It is possible that the international schools in these two cities may gear their Science programs more closely with these international scientific institutes. In contrast with the subsidies made available for USA-centered or USSR-centered international studies and activities, the European effort indeed appears modest. But in comparison with its development 20 years ago, the proportions today would have been almost inconceivable. Notwithstanding, not much has been done to create genuine multilateral educational institutions.

Discussions on the creation of a pan-European university have never got beyond that stage. It is specifically the nationalism of European universities which is the self-evidently contradictory condition which must be transformed if the European potential is to be realized.

It must be said, however, that the experiments in European-based education more nearly approach the ideal of multilateral internationalism than those promoted by the USA and the USSR. Obviously there is a vast difference between the aims and methods of the unilateral and bilateral experiments of the two colossi in the field of education. But they have one common trait in the fact that neither great power has yet come to recognize the multilateral pattern as worthy of genuine support. Note their hesitancy in promoting UNESCO for instance, though ironically the rise of a China which has no interest in the UN nor in UNESCO tends to lessen USA–USSR reservations. Europe comprises mainly a group of near-equal partners. For Europe to experiment with multilateralism is therefore quite natural. Europeans must therefore help the two great powers understand its values.

Of all European powers the British and the French are probably best equipped to do this. The Benelux powers naturally pioneered in creating the European Economic Community (Common Market) but it is French and, hopefully, British participation in the EEC which will bring the "old" continent back as a great power. A parallel is to be found in Delaware, ratifying the USA constitution as a pioneer. The success of the American Government depended rather on Massachusetts, New York, Pennsylvania and Virginia joining in. Similarly in the case of the International Baccalaureate, Bulgaria follows the example of Delaware but acceptance depends upon Great Britain and France.

Both the USA and the USSR have undergone recent experiment in multilateralization in the political sphere, which may well account for their willingness to go forward with multilateral international education. The transmutation of the British and French Empires into the British Commonwealth of Nations and the French Community of Nations probably allows for delayed-action effects in the notoriously conservative field of education. No two systems of education (however diverse they may be from each other) are the object of such wholesale domestic criticism as are the British GCE set-up and the parallel French Baccalaureate. Each in its own way is antedeluvian. The British overspecialize and, despite the boasted independence of the universities and examination boards, are faced with a too narrow preparation and the tyranny of the all-powerful terminal examination. The French similarly are handicapped, though their university entrants must become encyclopedists rather than specialists.

What is even more absurd, if one bears in mind the political evolution of empire, is to observe that in the respective international communities' association with each ex-colonial power the educational systems continue slavishly to copy the more conservative aspects of the GCE or the baccalaureate. Even more startling, in the Republic of the Cameroons the two systems continue side by side according to which part of the country was anglophone and which was francophone in the past. The *Year Book of Education for 1964*, which is published jointly by London and Columbia Universities, contains a remarkable collection of essays contributed mostly by British educators supplemented by a few French and American colleagues. Its sub-title, *Education and International Life*, allows for wide variety among its thirty-five chapters. What is missing, however, is any realistic analysis of the stranglehold traditional national patterns of education maintain against any genuine multilateralization (a term not specifically understood). Only one chapter takes account of international schools as such, and that I wrote myself. The support of the IB program which the Pedagogical Centre at Sèvres maintains is in large measure because of association their directors have made with ISA and ISES personnel. The same generalization may be affirmed as regards the initial foundation subsidy obtained for the IB program. Fortunately, the interest of Bulgaria and Poland in ISES helps balance what could tend to be an overwhelming transatlantic influence.

An analysis of the "international" experiments undertaken by the USA and the USSR in education might next be examined to throw more light on the post-war situation. It will be recalled that the USA agreed to finance educational reconstruction in 1944, that is at the time that the Second World War appeared to be drawing to its conclusion. Probably at no time in man's history was such generous unqualified giving undertaken by any government. By the nature of things, however, rather naturally, wherever Americans themselves got involved they brought with them their optimistic unquestioned belief in the values of pragmatic approaches and the progressively improving nature of the world. Often in situations in which survival was the best to be hoped for, the American outlook battered everything before it. This is particularly true of the "Far East" where Philippino, Japanese, Korean, Formosan and Vietnamese cultures came to identify internationalism with American procedures. In Europe the influence tended to be limited to military enclaves and their schools, even though American owned, run and programmed private schools had the effect of pushing other national overseas schools into defensive postures and of inhibiting the development of multi-lateral international schools. Already, for several decades, expatriate American schools were well known in Latin America. In some cases attempts were seriously undertaken to make these binational in management and character, but the essential control rested with citizens in the great northern republic.

At the same time the Orient and Europe were penetrated by a massive program of exchange of students undertaken bilaterally chiefly between American schools and those who were willing for their students to risk a year which might well prove useless as far as university entrance examinations were concerned. At university level the numbers of students brought to American colleges was legion. In 1946 the Fulbright Act allowed for a multitude of Americans to study elsewhere and when the Peace Corps was created the US Government proved it could embrace the work-camp psychology for its more idealistic youth who wished to combine international understanding with grass-roots technical competency. The foundation world, particularly the Ford Foundation, extended its generosity across the face of the globe. American controls were not exacted in return for foundation largess. On the other hand, the ideal of creating multilateral international consortia to administer generous gifts was probably not considered.

In any one year in the 1960's the US foreign student exchange involves well over 100,000 persons, of whom perhaps 15 percent are teachers. The cost to the US Federal Government of the 20-year experiment was about $50 million while a much larger sum—$300 million—was given by the private sector. These are figures released by Francis Keppel, then US Commissioner for Education.

In Merle Curti's definitive study (1963) on *American Philanthropy Abroad*, only 50 of the 650 pages are devoted to education, about which Professor Curti says: "American aid to overseas education, however broadly defined, was not solely or even chiefly inspired by a conscious desire to promote international understanding, although in a vague sense it was often implied." Specifically, most American educational efforts up till 1945 were undertaken to introduce "Western learning" in connection with Christian (Protestant) missions. As early as 1819 Hawai was reached, followed by Greece in 1830 and by Thailand in 1878. At least one prominent American sociologist, Bronislaw Malinowski, described such paternalistic educational activities as "blight" rather than genuine aid (1945). Certainly the American Universities of Beirut and Tangier trace their origins to such early missionary effort.

It is extraordinarily difficult for Americans to approach other cultures on the basis of equality. The United States is composed of people whose ancestors rejected other cultures to take their part in the pragmatic new world. That they gained more than they cost is incontestable. Consequently, though they may have curiosity to go back to seek out origins, cousins, and perhaps develop appreciation for the older ethnic grouping, they usually return to the basic assumption that America is superior—as it is in certain fields, without doubt. As some wit once said "America had her revolution". She has no need of what the Communist–Socialist revolutionaries promise still backward peoples (technically speaking). The Marxist approach regarding class conflict is obviously arrant nonsense as regards the mobile affluent society America has created. It must become, then, only a subterfuge by which power-hungry murdering dictators enslave the unsuspecting. Americans therefore assume the responsibility for saving others and themselves from falling prey to such sub-human devils. This mentality (not much understood outside the States) further inhibits the American from accepting (on the basis of equality) other cultures, which at best do not "comprehend" the Communist danger, and at worst promote it. Not all Americans accept the Communist devil stereotype, but it is sufficiently current to prevent much genuine multilateral experimentation—at least at government level.

On the other hand, the Communist elite know well enough that what they assume regarding changing human nature itself by providing the "perfect" Socialist environment is a very risky projection indeed. The mass support they get comes pragmatically from improved conditions. But violent seizure of power always occurs, contrary to what Marx himself postulated, only in backward areas (or militarily defeated "developed" states such as Czechoslovakia). Improved conditions evolve only slowly. Therefore, terrorism must be applied, at least until conditions do improve, to insure that the unconverted masses will not choose a more humanly appealing form of petty capitalism.

Once fairly optimum conditions are established, the immense appeal of the American mobile affluent society makes itself all too evident. Thus the communist state is even less willing to experiment with multilateral international activities than are the Americans—that is, unless the multilateralization of the communist world, which has gone forward progressively since 1948, allows for some smaller states to participate as a sign perhaps of genuine autonomy. Even the Soviet Union is now reaching out in ways which would have seemed inconceivable a generation ago. This does not mean that the convinced Communist does not believe that the basic problems of the developing world do not require revolution, nor that even the Americans would not profit from the nationalization of the basic American economy. That the American Government undertakes to prevent the spread of this "necessary" (and inevitable to them) revolution is proof that it is controlled by diabolical exploiters who twist out of recognition the native goodwill of the tremendously technologically gifted American people. Both mentalities prevent the mass of Americans and Russians (not to mention Chinese and several other nationalities) from trusting multilateral international experimentation except in small and unimportant situations. Thus the possibilities and advantages of Western and Eastern Europe venturing into genuinely free multilateral arrangements offers a tremendously useful method by which new dimensions may be introduced alongside the giant protagonists. From this vantage point the International Baccalaureate offers a most helpful non-political accommodation.

In 1956 the International Schools Association decided to form a taxfree body in New York to help channel money to genuine international schools. This body was called the International Schools Foundation. It was composed of a board of trustees, all but one of whom were Americans. It secured the services of an enterprising American headmaster as its President. The program then hit upon was to supply services to American schools overseas, including American staff and materials. Its budget was met by matching grants from the US State Department and the Ford Foundation—very reasonable grants they were indeed. Thus the ISF undertook the work of unilateral internationalism, for which a strong case could be made. Originally the mandate was to go outside the American continents, but in 1962 the older service organization devoted to Latin America was placed under the care of ISF (which then changed its name to the International Schools Services). Relatively efficient care was extended to the hundred or so American-run overseas schools. Also an attempt was made to extend its services to Africa. But it did not act as the American agency of ISA. If not hostile to international schools, the ISF (ISS) certainly did not promote multilateral internationalism.

Obviously the root of the trouble was the lack of foresight on the part of ISA in not assuring that it had juridical control of ISF, even if American laws make it difficult for the majority of trustees to be other than American citizens. Should an equivalent body be set up in the Soviet Union, a similar observation would be pertinent.

The ISF held at least one of its annual conferences in Rome. Later it encouraged the formation of a loose association of schools in Europe serving Americans. By 1966 this grouping was formally constituted as the Council of Overseas Schools (COS), filling a long-felt legitimate need. Fortunately the misused word "international" was dropped. COS will no doubt work in close collaboration with the Office of Overseas Schools of the US State Department. Obviously there is need of American schools abroad, as there is of British, French, German, Italian, Greek, Turkish and Russian. Notwithstanding, the existence of a handful of struggling nationally run and oriented schools in each capital of the world is inefficient and a denial, at the level at which children may break down prejudice most easily, of the essential unity of mankind (proclaimed in the UN Charter). How much greater would be the contribution of Americans (the largest expatriate grouping) if their governmental and private sector energies were devoted to creating multilateral international schools in which they would prove their disinterest by subsidizing institutions in which the basic control would be shared with people interested in education from other nations!

There are segments of both public and private opinion which move in this direction. Perhaps the most encouraging public action was the formulation in 1966 of an International Education Act calling for a total of $70 million to be devoted to strengthening educational bodies which promote international understanding, specifically to encourage all teachers in the United States to be able to include some foreign educational experience as part of their normal training. Significantly, the Act indicated that no control whatsoever would be exacted by the Government or by its officials over the institutions to which the money should be granted. President Johnson, who was once a schoolteacher, is still personally deeply interested in this Act. Mrs. Johnson on one occasion in 1966 spoke with the women of the press in Washington about the possibility of the development of a genuine international school in Washington.

The appointment of Charles Frankel as Assistant Secretary of State for Educational and Cultural Affairs has been indicative of the evolution of American thinking in government circles. His sub-department's publication entitled *Exchange*, which first appeared in the summer of 1965, shows clearly that Mr. Frankel understands the distinctions which are made in this book between and among unilateral, bilateral and multilateral types of internationalism. Unfortunately, the anxieties associated with the terrible Vietnamese war have held up implementation of the International Education Act. What could be a tremendous instrument in helping transform American involvement in multilateral internationalism is shelved—let us hope only temporarily. But one straw in the wind was the invitation extended to ISES to send a spokesman for multilateral internationalism to the Airlie House Conference, called by the Educational and Cultural Affairs division of the State Department in April 1966. The White House saw fit to send two of its most influential advisers to this gathering.

At the present time it is difficult to weave one's way through the labyrinth of organization which administers American involvement in international exchange at the national level. The Conference Board of Associated Research Councils does this co-ordinating work through its Committee on International Exchange of Persons. Its newsletter, *American Studies News*, gives clue to the breadth of vision here encountered. For instance, in August 1965, the European Association for American Studies (a member organization) arranged for a conference in Denmark at which 119 scholars from nineteen countries discussed the differences between European and

American universities; obviously, at university level, Americans are instinctively feeling after multilateralism. They are only at the opening of a dialogue. Notwithstanding, the notion of working out an interchangeable bachelor of arts degree appears not to have been raised.

The creation of the East–West Center in Honolulu (HEW), which was established in 1960, is important to demonstrate that US involvement in the Orient required mutual conditioning. Good work has been carried out, though it calls to mind the departments of Oriental Studies in British universities. In both instances the host country maintains control: English is the language used: and no fundamental neutral zone is established in which the cross-fertilization takes place. One has the impression that such institutes were better situated on the soil of a smaller Oriental power, and administered in such a way that neither the English-speaking power nor the host nation would have essential control. John Gardner, Secretary of HEW, when testifying on the International Education Act on 30 March 1966 said, in part:

> Why must we consider international education at home and educational relations with other peoples as matters of high national interest? The reason becomes plain when we think about the enemy we seek to conquer. The enemy is ignorance, inadequate skills, parochialism and lack of sensitivity as to why people of different cultures react and behave differently.

This ideal should be universal enough to be universally endorsed.

One American organization, called the Council for the Study of Mankind, located in Santa Monica, California (1958), has been responsible for a number of publications and, in co-operation with the Johnson Foundation, has held conferences in which a number of imaginative "old-world" ideas have been promoted. Its shortcoming, as that of the East–West Center, is that it is an American body operating within the American scene. It has, however, close contacts with a similar Dutch organization and one in Britain which have roughly the same orientation. Often such bodies must operate on crippling budgets and suffer from dispersal of effort. At worst they trail off into a twilight of eccentricity, which reveals they were set up to promote individual idiosyncrasies. The problem of dealing with them is their kaleidoscopic range and over-brief life-span.

The proponent of international understanding needs a life-time of inquiry and analysis to sift out those which have a real vocation and categorical imperative. The United World Federalists offer ostensibly reasonable conclusions regarding national sovereignty for example. But they are patently unable to bring about any real achievements given the actual power structure. Other organizations, such as the World Law Fund, publish more sophisticated studies regarding what interim ar-rangements are both possible and advantageous. The alert tea-cher, especially in secondary sections in international schools, can test such propositions in class against a relatively knowledgable student population. World reform organizations do not usually propose syllabus reform as such, but are certainly favorable to it.

The Twentieth-Century Fund may be cited as one of the more imaginative Foundations, which has subsidized impor-tant technological studies in the developing parts of the globe. Significantly, it grasped first among its peers the importance of the IB program. A good number of foundations are prevent-ed by their statutes from promoting multilateral international projects. Others are simply so much a part of the "coast to coast" mentality in the States as to refuse seriously to consider financing anything outside the American universe. The Ford Foundation, on the other hand, has been outstanding in its recognition of the unity of mankind postulated by the small council at Santa Monica.

Although the proportions are smaller than its domestic generosity, the Ford Foundation has proved itself the muni-ficent handmaiden of President Roosevelt's pledge to restore education throughout the post-war world (1944). In the field of education the obvious excitement of stepping out of the familiar pragmatic environment into others, especially when there is an opportunity for independent interplay, appeals to those who feel inwardly secure. Thus in America, the private sector is able to adventure into situations in which public money must be overly cautious. Thus, at a moment's glance, the advantage of the supple affluent American economy over its Socialist rival is evident. What the Socialist economy can do is to tighten its belt to undertake massive unilateral and bilateral experimentation in education but without, of course, any private sector to experiment and help bear the burden.

Only after Stalin's death, that is about a decade after the United States got thoroughly involved in her "cultural offensive", did the Soviet Union follow suit. In both cases one obvious purpose was to glamorize the way of life involved. It is estimated that the Soviet Government spent twice as much on the 1957 Moscow Youth Festival as the United States Government put into a 20-year exchange program. In point of fact, many fewer students receive solid training in Russia than they do in the United States. In addition, the numbers of students taking part in genuine bilateral exchange is tiny when contrasted with what the States carries out.

In Moscow, one special university for foreigners, called after the Congolese leader Patrice Lumumba, has already graduated a few hundred students. Observers who originally felt that this expatriate university was devoted mainly to anticapitalist propaganda, now feel that it does more seriously attempt to give a thorough university training. As the name of the expatriate university suggests, Africa is regarded as the most useful region in which to plant socialist ideas. The Soviet Union finds itself pledged to this even more firmly today to outbid the Communist Republic of China which has undertaken parallel rival educational interest in Africa on a large scale. The visit of Chou-En-lai in 1964, throughout the continent was a prelude to greatly stepped-up exchange programs. Quite obviously the objective of winning friends and influencing the course of history is intimately bound up with such a Socialist undertaking.

But just because education is being used as the League of Nations stated in 1920 that it should be, that is for political ends primarily, does not dispose of the useful weapons which such education provides in the long run against "ignorance, inadequate skills, parochialism and [most importantly] lack of sensitivity to why people of different cultures react and behave differently", to quote John Gardner again. When genuine multilateral international education is practiced by the colossus of the West in Africa, it will be difficult for the Soviet Union and China to avoid engaging in it also.

Another aspect of the focus in Africa is the Chinese insistence on "common bonds" of color. Some visitors from Peking have even struck the somewhat absurd posture of speaking of "we black men". It would be more possible for Americans to so speak if civil rights in that country were less academic. The genuine mingling of ethnic groups on the basis of equality (however debased in itself) in the Soviet Union gives the Russians an edge in appreciating differences. The sorry story of the American Indian must be quickly forgotten at this point. It would appear that the Soviet Union has the advantage over America in constructing schools and creating institutes in the developing countries. Often, USAID money goes to create what Professor Redefer of New York University calls "American schools in cellophane", for Americans or others who wish later an American college education. Obviously, developing countries need massive capital investment, particularly in education.

Parallel to investment in education, European Socialist countries have been tremendously active in attracting tourists— following the example of Yugoslavia. This has had the effect of creating a business sufficiently lucrative to pay for educational investment elsewhere. But it also has the effect of heightening the immense attraction which the affluent society has for the Socialist countries. Pan-European solidarity is rapidly being recreated. Multilateralization of Socialist countries is likewise on the increase, to say nothing of what the polarization of Moscow and Peking means everywhere.

Testimony from Adrian Jaffe, an American exchange professor, who spent the academic year 1964–5 in Bucharest, is as follows:

> I found the Roumanian extremely liberal in the sense that without in any manner rejecting Marxism or his Socialist view of the world, he was willing to admit that there were other ways of looking at things... that what it represented... was a statement that the Communist world and the world of the West are different ... that we all in our own world have made certain choices, but there is no need to conclude as a result that everything on the other side is bad or good.

Such thinking characterizes the present ecumenical dialogue and forms the essential background for what this book pleads. Naturally, some prudence is required lest the educational venture serve essentially as a front organization for the Soviet spy apparatus and in the same token for the CIA. But the odds are in favour of believing that intelligent confidence and goodwill are the best instruments with which man is equipped for the redemption of evil.

Equally important to finding a *modus vivendi* between giant antagonists is the development of genuine acceptance of less "client" cultures as worthy of equal consideration. Not only must the Russians accept an American way, but a Roumanian way of life. Americans, by the same token, must not only accommodate themselves to the Russian differences but to those of Canada. In closing this chapter, I would like to draw attention to an article by Robin Winks of Yale University, published in the State Department's *Exchange* magazine, in which he points out why American shibboleths regarding the success of frontier procedures in American life are an inapplicable analogy to discovering the way of life of a (theoretically) bi-lingual, non-melting-pot monarchy, which is the largest nation in North America. Because the State Department is concerned to know and respect the true Canada, there is reason to rejoice. The world watches Russian attitudes toward Roumania with as great interest.

CHAPTER 6

THE INTERNATIONAL SCHOOL IN THE WORLD

PROBABLY no more difficult task may be set before the educationalist than to attempt a delineation of international schools in this world. One can start with the list of members of the International Schools Association, but that is obviously very incomplete. Then the problem rises as to where to draw boundaries. If the most inclusive definition is attempted the problem is of encyclopedic proportions. There are well over a hundred capital cities. These, plus fifty others, offer some form of school serving international clientele. An analysis of 150 cities is obviously impossible—even if the material were to hand. In point of fact, each month the ISA learns of another potential international school. Some of these prove to have been "going concerns" for some years. In addition, others prove to be schools seeking reorientation in an international direction.

Certain generalizations can be made, however. Probably two-fifths of the overseas schools population of our world are American in origin—that is, three-fifths clearly speak with some form of the English language. The other two-fifths involve the overseas French *lycées,* the overseas German *Gymnasiums,* the overseas Russian preparatory schools, a handful of other overseas national schools and the few ISA schools which can point to an international origin. The easiest list of overseas schools to come by is the American grouping. A good number of them think of themselves as international. Obviously one wants to escape dealing only with American types of overseas schools, but it is difficult to find lists of others to make the picture more varied. It is this very American prevalence which makes the growth of the genuine international school so vital.

The Food and Agricultural Organization of the United Nations puts out an annual calendar giving information (in English) "on non-Italian schools in Rome used by the non-Italian community". What is first striking about this list is the fact that the host nationality is clearly considered to be "outside" the international community. In point of fact Italian children are allowed into the schools listed but apparently Italian nationals do not serve on their boards of Management. There are a good number of Italian-owned and run private schools in Rome catering to foreigners, but these schools are clearly understood to be something else than "international". In Switzerland, Swiss-owned schools of a similar type often appropriate the descriptive phrase "international school"—an action rather naturally resented by the genuinely multilateral international school.

In Rome, however, the title is used by only two of the eleven schools listed—both of these are American-run and owned—in fact by American Roman Catholic Church teaching orders. The Overseas School of Rome, one-time member of ISA, now totally American and the second largest (and most expensive) school in the grouping, makes no pretence of being international. An American Episcopal boarding school looks after the needs of Americans whose parents are posted in out-of-the-way corners of the world educationally speaking. A similar American Roman Catholic boarding school shares in this activity. Neither pretends to be other than church related. These five American overseas schools handle a total of 1900 pupils.

In turning to the British community one finds two overseas schools serving a total of 600 pupils. Obviously, more British send their children home to boarding schools than do the Americans, but the existence of these two schools may be traced in the main to the exclusive American educational policy of the overseas school. In any case, 2500 students in Rome study in the English language.

The largest non-Italian school is the official French government-supported Lycée with 1100 students paying the smallest fees of the eleven schools listed. The German School, similarly supported by the West German Government, caters to about half as many as the Lycée. In addition, there are small Swiss (German-speaking) and Spanish schools. About 950 students attend these non-English-speaking "overseas" institutions. No mention is made of a Russian School, though it probably exists for Soviet diplomatic children—and might raise the total to 1100 non-English speaking overseas children. In other words probably some 4700 foreign children receive varieties of non-Italian managed education in Rome. If English–French bilingualism were assumed as natural, some 3600 of the total would already have one of these languages. Despite other legitimate considerations, there would seem to be a "market" for a school offering the International Baccalaureate in the eternal city. The pattern in Rome is repeated in a number of capitals—at least in the European scene. In the autumn of 1967 there was revived interest in FAO circles to establish a genuine international school in Rome.

A few years ago the UN Technical Assistance Board in Baghdad reported that that city boasted ten non-Iraqian schools, but that not one of these offered any secondary educational opportunities. About 300 students were all that the schools could expect as clientele unless wealthy Iraqians got interested. There were two American, three British, one each Arab, German, Iranian, French and Russian schools in this Middle Eastern capital. Such a situation obviously borders on absurdity. Only too often, capitals in developing areas show similar patterns. The unwillingness of national expatriates to pull together, and when together to find substantial subsidy for inter-cultural schools, has driven the Americans *faute de mieux* to seek massive subsidy from USAID and, when granted this, undertake the pledge that their American clients are prepared only for American universities. On the other extremity of this spectrum there are to be found the Russian schools created for their diplomatic personnel. They studiously avoid contamination with all other systems—being, as it were, content with reaching page 106 the same day it is studied in Leningrad.

Part of the problem is that the means and will-power to formulate an analysis of what is feasible for international education in a given city or area is missing. Occasionally they are prepared. One such, of admirable character, was produced in 1966 regarding the children of CERN officials in Geneva, Switzerland. CERN is located at the opposite side of the canton from the International School of Geneva so that the problem parents face is not unlike that of potential expatriate clients whose housing is to be found on the extremities of great urban complexes the world over. The CERN study begins with a consideration of what the local Swiss schools offer, bearing in mind the importance of "convertibility". Attention is then drawn to the Common Market European Baccalaureate, and to the project of the International Baccalaureate. Consideration of the French educational system next follows (CERN borders France), private schools in the neighbourhood are thereupon listed and five kindergartens are noted, one at CERN itself, another being that affiliated with ISA. Six primary schools receive attention (including three affiliated to ISA). Secondary schools include six using French and three English (Ecolint is listed twice at this point and the Lycée des Nations once as it curiously enough offers instruction only in English (member of ISA)). The shortcoming of the study consists in absence of figures both as regards size of schools and potential numbers of CERN students. On the other hand it enumerates the possibilities in the Geneva area. There is no reference whatsoever to the flourishing Russian School in Geneva. Even in such a well-constructed report some invisibility may be encountered.

There are certain figures which can be postulated as indicating the present potential expatriate student population in cer-

STR 11

tain areas of the world. If one uses the figures issued for American schools there is a roughly reliable tally to be made. Starting with Latin America we find the approximate statistics as shown in Table 1:

TABLE 1

Schools	American children	Total attendance at expatriate schools
Argentina	700	2,000
Brazil	1,450	2,700
Chile	200	1,400
Bolivia	300	1,800
Colombia	350	1,850
Paraguay	100	200
Peru	700	2,500
Venezuela	600	1,050
Ecuador	400	2,700
Costa Rica	100	500
El Salvador	200	850
Guatemala	100	800
Honduras	150	550
Mexico	1,700	3,000
Nicaragua	300	600
Santo Domingo	200	400
Total	7,550	22,900

Very probably half of the non-American group are native Latin Americans who consider that they can advance faster if educated at least partially in English. Thus the figures probably read 7550 Americans and 14,350 expatriates, of whom 7100 are non-American expatriates. As far as North America is concerned the number of expatriates is difficult to discover. Ottawa, New York and Washington contain the really large agglomerations. Possibly 4000 would cover the area, of whom scarcely 200 would be American citizens. At least double that number of Americans are enrolled in the three ISA schools in the area. The new International School in Washington produced a feasibility study which envisaged the creation of a trilingual international school in that city.

The figures for Asia run pretty much as Table 2:

TABLE 2

Schools	Americans	Total attendance at expatriate schools
Japan	2,000	3,800
Korea	200	300
Laos	150	200
Malaysia	100	100
Philippines	1,700	1,800
Singapore	300	700
Formosa	2,000	2,200
Thailand	1,600	2,000
Afghanistan	200	700
Ceylon	200	500
India	1,100	2,500
Pakistan	1,200	1,500
Iran	1,200	2,000
Israel	100	800
Kuwait	100	300
Iraq	100	300
Hong Kong	200	1,000
Lebanon	600	1,600
Turkey	100	1,500
Saudi Arabia	300	400
Total	13,450	24,200

In this case the number of native nationalities is very small, at least in comparison to Latin America. There are probably 10,000 expatriates other than Americans in these schools.

11*

The African picture (Table 3) is even less American.

TABLE 3

Nation	Americans	Total attendance at expatriate schools
Congo	200	650
Ghana	100	1,500
Kenya	250	700
Morocco	100	1,500
Nigeria	350	600
Senegal	100	1,100
Rhodesia	150	200
Tripoli	100	400
Ethiopia	400	1,600
Total	1,750	8,150

There the total expatriate (non-American) population runs to about 6000. Somewhat similar figures exist for Europe (Table 4).

At least 5000 of the European attenders are natives of the countries in which the schools are located. Thus the non-American expatriate grouping runs to about 16,000. The following totals appear to be reasonably near the mark: 33,000 American children in overseas schools (omitting an equal number in American military dependent schools) and 48,000 non-American expatriates similarly enrolled. In addition, probably 19,000 "natives" attend such schools, bringing the total student population to 100,000. The irreversible effects of jet aircraft travel, of Common Market expansion and world governmental agencies activity will probably triple this figure in the next decade. If we divide them into twelve grades, about 2500 will complete their studies each year. Half of these

Table 4

Nation	Americans	Total attendance at expatriate schools
Austria	300	1,200
Belgium	600	1,500
Denmark	100	800
France	1,000	4,000
Germany	700	2,500
Greece	1,200	1,700
Italy	2,200	6,300
Netherlands	250	1,500
Portugal	150	600
Spain	700	1,500
Switzerland	1,200	4,000
United Kingdom	700	2,000
Luxembourg	100	1,500
Yugoslavia	100	700
Poland	100	200
USSR	100	300
Total	9,500	30,300

should be able to pass the International Baccalaureate. It is thus possible to envisage a solid core of international school students whose orientation is clearly towards the IB. No doubt an even larger (probably double) number of candidates will be presented by internationally minded schools. It is not inconceivable that by 1977, one year after the ISES experimental period has passed, 7500 candidates will be using the IB successfully each year. Naturally a good many of the expatriate schools will continue to pursue national and ideological curricula. But the prospect still proves interesting and significant for the field of International Education.

In order to give a broad picture of schools of essentially

expatriate and international orientation I am appending a checklist of such schools. It is admittedly partial, and far short of the actual list one could make. Notwithstanding, it tends to substantiate some of the figures just cited. (It does include the members of the Council of Internationally Minded Schools but does not include a much larger grouping of schools belonging to associations for the United Nations or national commissions for UNESCO.)

These run to a total of 85 schools. The grand total of schools in this listing is 372, probably a third of those which actually do exist. The total number of students cared for by these schools may well run to 300,000—or three times the figure suggested by listing expatriate schools. Still another and still larger criterion may be established by examining the school systems throughout the world.

Between 1958 and 1966 UNESCO published a four-volume *World Survey of Education* running to 4500 pages and based upon reports submitted by Ministries of Education of most of the countries of the world and their dependencies. A rapid perusal of the four volumes gives indication that central interest was focused on public education, but that in some cases independent schools were covered. At no point was international education nor even the expatriate school seriously considered—except for a report on Tangier in which the American School in that place was described both juridically and organizationally speaking. Notwithstanding this, and despite the fact that most data is from 7 to 15 years out of date, certain impressions may be formed which help picture the magnitude of expatriate education and give some guidelines as to the acceptability of integral international education.

First of all there is an educational legacy left by the dominance of Europe for 400 years from 1560 to 1960. The first great portion of this may be described as Roman Catholic education, which preceded the secular public school and occupies the most prominent position among the private schools in a number of countries. Latin America, in general,

LIST OF SCHOOLS WITH SOME INTERNATIONAL ASSOCIATION

EUROPE

		Category*
Austria		
English Speaking School of Vienna	GB	D
American International School (Vienna)	USA	C
Lycée Français (Vienna)	Fr.	B
Russian School (Vienna)	USSR	C
Belgium		
Antwerp International School	USA	D
International School of Brussels	USA	C
European School (Brussels)	CM	B
Russian School (Brussels)	USSR	D
European School (Antwerp)	CM	C
Bulgaria		
Anglo–American School	GB	D
Denmark		
Katedralskolen (Arhus)	Dk.	C
Copenhagen International High School	USA	D
Bernadotteskolen (Copenhagen)	Dk.	D
Bjørnsskolen (Copenhagen)	Dk.	D
International Folk High School (Elsinore)	Dk.	C
France		
Lycée Internationale (Fontainebleau)	Fr.	C
Lycée Internationale (St. Germain-en-Laye)	Fr.	B
Lycée de Sèvres (Paris)	Fr.	A
American School (Paris)	USA	C
International School (Paris)	Fr.	C
German School (Paris)	WG	C
UN Nursery School (Paris)	ISA	D
Russian School (Paris)	USSR	C
Marymount International School (Paris)	USA	D

* Student enrolment:
   A, 1500 up
   B, 1000–1500
   C, 500–1000
   D, 0–500

		Category
English School of Paris	GB	D
Cours Maintenon (Cannes)	Fr.	D
Collège Cevenol	Fr.	C
Germany		
International School of Munich	USA	D
International School of Hamburg	GB	C
Frankfurt International School	USA	C
J. F. Kennedy School (Berlin)	USA	C
French Academy (Berlin)	Fr.	A
Lycée (Saarbrücken)	Fr.	B
European School (Karlsruhe)	CM	C
International School (Dusseldorf)	ISA	D
Anna-Schmidt Schule (Frankfurt)	WG	C
Salem School (Konstantz)	WG	B
Verband Deutcher Privatschulen (Bad Soden)	WG	C
Schiller Gymnasium (Hamelin)	WG	B
Waldschulheim Breuer (Bad Aachen)	WG	C
Goethe Gymnasium (Frankfurt)	WG	B
Russian School (Berlin)	EG	A
Greece		
American Community School of Athens	USA	B
Pinewood Schools of Thessalonika	USA	D
Anatolia College	USA	B
Athens College	USA	B
British School of Athens	GB	D
Lycée Français	Fr.	B
Hungary		
British Embassy School	GB	D
Italy		
International School of Milan	It.	D
American Community School of Milan	USA	D
Overseas School of Rome	USA	C
Marymount International School (Rome)	USA	D
American School of Torino	USA	D
Swiss School of Torino	CH	D
Notre Dame International School (Rome)	USA	D
International School of Trieste	CM	D
St. Georges English School (Rome)	GB	C

		Category
St. Stephens School (Rome)	USA	D
Junior English School (Rome)	GB	D
Lycée Chateaubriand (Rome)	Fr.	B
Lycée Français (Naples)	Fr.	B
Swiss School (Rome)	CH	D
Liceo Español (Rome)	Sp.	D
German School (Rome)	WG	C
Russian School (Rome)	USSR	D
St. Francis School (Rome)	USA	D
European School (Varese)	CM	B
International School of Genoa	USA	D
Luxembourg		
European School	CM	A
American School	USA	D
Poland		
American School (Warsaw)	USA	D
Portugal		
St. Colombans School	USA	D
St. Christophers School	GB	D
Switzerland		
International School of Geneva	ISA	A
English School of Geneva	GB	D
Collège du Leman (Geneva)	CH	C
UN Nursery & Primary School (Geneva)	ISA	D
Lycée des Nations (Geneva)	ISA	D
Aiglon College (Villars)	CH	D
Villa St. Jean School (Fribourg)	USA	D
Chateau Brillantmont (Lausanne)	CH	D
Lycée Jaccard (Lausanne)	CH	D
American School (Lugano)	USA	D
Commonwealth–American School (Lausanne)	GB	D
American International (Zurich)	USA	D
Intercommunity School (Zurich)	GB	D
Institut Montana (Zugerberg)	CH	C
Pestalozzi Kinderdorf (Trogen)	CH	C
Institut International (Le Rosey)	CH	C
CERN Nursery School (Geneva)	ISA	D
German School (Geneva)	WG	C

		Category
Institut Florimont (Geneva)	CH	C
Pensional Marie-Thérèse (Geneva)	Fr.	C
Institut Notre-Dame (Geneva)	Fr.	D
Bon Séjour (Geneva)	Fr.	D
École d'Humanité (Goldern)	CH	C
Institut Moser (Geneva)	CH	D
Yugoslavia		
Russian School	USSR	B
International School (Belgrade)	USA	D
Great Britain		
Ackworth School (Pontefract)	GB	B
Badminton School (Bristol)	GB	C
Bedales School (Petersfield)	GB	B
Box Hill School (Mickleham)	GB	C
Calday Grange Grammar (W. Kirby)	GB	B
Collegiate (Bristol)	GB	C
Don Valley (Doncaster)	GB	D
Gordonstoun (Elgin)	GB	B
Hall School (Wincanton)	GB	C
Leighton Park (Reading)	GB	C
Queen Annes School (Caversham)	GB	C
Queenswood (Hatfield)	GB	D
Richmond Lodge (Belfast)	GB	C
St. Christophers (Letchworth)	GB	B
St. Matthias (Bristol)	GB	C
Strathern School (Belfast)	GB	C
Whitgift Foundation (Croydon)	GB	C
American School (London)	USA	D
French Lycée (London)	Fr.	A
Atlantic College (South Wales)	GB	D
Marymount International (London)	USA	D
Sevenoaks	GB	B
Dover College	GB	B
Netherlands		
International School (Hague)	Ne.	D
International Quaker School (Werrhoven)	Ne.	D
European School (Amsterdam)	CM	C
American International (Rotterdam)	USA	C
Biltoven Kindergarten	Ne.	D

		Category
American School (Hague)	USA	D
German School (Hague)	WG	D
English School (Hague)	GB	D
International School (Amsterdam)	USA	D
International School (Eerde)	Ne.	D
Lyceum (Amersfoort)	Ne.	B
Da Costa Kweek School (Blokmandael)	Ne.	C
Lyceum (Overveln)	Ne.	B
Harlem Schools	Ne.	A
Spain		
British Institute School	GB	B
Marymount International (Barcelona)	USA	D
American School (Barcelona)	USA	D
North American (Madrid)	USA	D
Baleares International (Palma)	USA	D
American School (Madrid)	USA	C
Lycée Français (Madrid)	Fr.	B
German School (Madrid)	WG	C
La Plana Kindergarten	USA	D
Sweden		
Vigebyholmskolen (Stockholm)	Sw.	B
Anglo–American (Stockholm)	GB	C
USSR		
Anglo–American School (Moscow)	USA	D
Czechoslovakia		
English Speaking School (Prague)	USA	D

Of the total of 151 schools listed more than half are "national" schools with formal international outreach. This type of school is commoner in Europe than elsewhere.

AFRICA

		Category
Algeria		
English Speaking School of Algiers	GB	D
Angola		
English Speaking School of Luanda	GB	D
Cameroons		
Man o' War Bilingual School	GB	C
Alexandra College at Younde	Br.	C
International School of Younde	Br.	D
Congo (South)		
American School of Leopoldville	USA	D
Congo (North)		
Lycée Savorgman de Brazza	Fr.	C
International School of Brazzaville	GB	D
Ghana		
Achimota Primary School	GB	D
Christ The King School	GB	B
Achimota School	GB	C
International School (Accra)	GB	C
Tema International School	GB	D
Ridge Church of Accra	GB	D
Kenya		
Rift Valley Academy	GB	D
Hospital Hill School	GB	C
Nairobi Russian School	USSR	D
Libya		
Benghazi English School	GB	D
Morocco		
American School of Tangier	USA	D
Tangier Lycée	Fr.	C
Tangier Spanish School	Sp.	C
Casablanca Lycée	Fr.	B
Nigeria		
International School of Ibadan	GB	D
Hillcrest School at Cos	GB	D
American International School of Lagos	USA	D
Corona Trust of Kano	GB	D
Kaduna School	GB	D
Senegal		
Dakar Academy	GB	C

		Category
Somaliland		
American School of Mogadiscio	USA	D
Russian School of Mogadiscio	USSR	D
Sudan		
American School of Khartoum	USA	D
UAR		
American School of Alexandria (Suspended)	USA	D
Swiss School of Alexandria	CH	D
Russian School in Cairo	USSR	C
American School in Cairo (Suspended)	USA	D
Swiss School in Cairo	CH	D
Rhodesia		
Marymount College at Umtali	USA	D
Sierra Leone		
International School of Freetown	GB	D
Liberia		
Lamco International School	Sw.	D
American School of Monrovia	USA	D
Tanzania		
American International College (Keresin)	USA	D
International School of Dar-es-Salaam	GB	C
Lushoto School	GB	D
Tripoli		
American School (Benghazi)	USA	D
American School of Tripoli	USA	D
Central African Republic		
Libreville International School	GB	D
Bangui Lycée	GB	C
Ethiopia		
Wingate School	GB	B
American School of Addis Ababa	USA	C
English School of Addis Ababa	GB	D
Lycée Français of Addis Ababa	Fr.	C
German School of Addis Ababa	WG	D
Swedish School of Addis Ababa	Sw.	D
Italian School of Addis Ababa	It.	B
Good Shepherd International School	USA	D
Italian School (Asmara)	It.	B

		Category
Swaziland		
Mbabane Waterfield School	GB	C
French Somalia		
Lycée of Djibouti	Fr.	C
Zambia		
International School of Lusaka	GB	D
Madagascar		
Lycée Français	Fr.	B

ASIA

Vietnam		
Lycée de Saigon	Fr.	B
Lycée de Hanoi	Fr.	B
Turkey		
Community School at Robert College	USA	D
Lycée Français of Istanbul	Fr.	C
German School of Istanbul	WG	B
British School of Istanbul	GB	B
Cyprus		
English School of Nicosia	GB	C
Lebanon		
Brummana College	GB	C
International College of Beirut	USA	B
American School	USA	C
Jordan		
American Community School	USA	D
Bishops School (Amman)	GB	D
Syria		
Damascus Community School	USA	D
Russian School of Damascus	USSR	C
Iraq		
French Sisters School	Fr.	D
American Community School	USA	D
German School	WG	D
Iranian School	Ir.	D

		Category
Russian School	USSR	D
Mansour School	GB	D
English Language School	GB	D
British Council Kindergarten	GB	D
Tarrants Primary School	GB	D
Kuwait		
International School	USA	D
Israel		
St. Georges of Jerusalem	GB	C
Convent of Nazareth	GB	C
Baptist Center High School (Petach)	USA	D
American School of Tel Aviv	USA	D
Saudi Arabia		
Dharan Academy	USA	D
Iran		
British School of Tehran	GB	D
Community School of Tehran	GB	C
American School of Tehran	USA	C
Community School (Abadan)	GB	D
Lycée Français of Tehran	Fr.	C
German School of Tehran	WG	C
Afghanistan		
American International School of Kabul	USA	D
Russian School of Kabul	USSR	C
German School of Kabul	WG	D
Turkish School of Kabul	Tur.	D
Ceylon		
Overseas School of Colombo	GB	D
India		
International School of Pondicherry	Fr.	B
American International School of Delhi	USA	C
Rodiganal School	USA	C
Woodstock School of Mussorie	GB	C
Wynberg-Allen School of Mussorie	GB	C
American International School of Calcutta	USA	D
Nepal		
Lincoln School of Katmandu	USA	D
Hong Kong		
American International School	USA	D

		Category
St. Josephs School	GB	C
Japan		
Marist Brothers (Kobe)	USA	D
Canadian Academy	Can.	D
American School (Tokyo)	USA	B
Christian Academy	USA	D
Sacred Heart (Tokyo)	USA	C
St. Marys International (Tokyo)	USA	C
St. Josephs (Yokohama)	USA	C
International School of Yokohama	GB	D
Nacoya International School	USA	D
Korea		
Seoul Foreign	USA	D
Christian (Taejon)	USA	D
Laos		
American School of Vientiane	USA	D
Malaysia		
International School of Kuala Lumpur	GB	D
Pakistan		
Farm View School (Dacca)	GB	D
Karachi American School	USA	D
Dacca American School	USA	D
Karachi Grammar School	GB	B
Lahore American School	USA	D
Mangla International School	USA	D
Murree Christian School	USA	D
Cathedral of Lahore	GB	C
Philippines		
Brent School (Baguio)	USA	D
American School (Manila)	USA	A
Singapore		
American School	USA	D
Thailand		
International School of Bangkok	USA	A
Taiwan		
Morison Academy	USA	D
Taipei American School	USA	A

This list, it will be observed, includes 76 schools. There follows a list of schools in the Americas.

THE AMERICAS

		Category
Argentina		
American Community	USA	C
Collegio Ward	GB	C
Lycée Français	Fr.	C
Italian School	It.	D
German School	WG	D
Arguello Academy (Cordoba)	GB	D
St. Andrews (Buenos Aires)	GB	C
Bolivia		
American Institute (Cochabamba)	USA	B
American Co-operative (La Paz)	USA	D
Collegio Anglo–Americano	GB	C
Santa Cruz Co-operative	USA	D
Brazil		
St. Georges of Bahia	GB	C
American Co-operative at Curitiba	USA	D
American School of Recife	USA	D
British School of Rio de Janeiro	GB	C
American School of Rio de Janeiro	USA	C
Our Lady of Mercy (Rio de Janeiro)	USA	D
British School of St. Paolo	GB	C
American School of St. Paolo	USA	C
American School (Brasilia)	USA	D
Lycée Français (St. Paolo)	Fr.	A
Chile		
St. Johns (Conception)	GB	D
Collegio Nido de Aguilas	GB	D
Grange School (Santiago)	GB	C
Santiago College at Braemar	GB	B
British School (Punta Arenas)	GB	C
Colombia		
American School (Carta Cena)	USA	D
Marymount of Barranquilla	USA	D
Abraham Lincoln (Bogota)	GB	D
Estados Unidos	USA	D
Collegio Bolivar Cal	USA	C
Colombus Medellin	USA	D

		Category
Paraguay		
American School (Asuncion)	USA	D
Peru		
Markham College of Lima	GB	C
American School of Lima	USA	B
Collegio Villa Maria	P.	B
St. Silvetre	GB	D
American School of Asuncion	USA	D
Venezuela		
British School of Caracas	GB	C
La Castellana (Caracas)	USA	D
Las Delicias of Maracay	USA	D
International School of Valencia	USA	D
Santo Dominica		
Carol Morgan School	USA	D
Collegio Santo Domingo	GB	C
Ecuador		
American School of Guayaquil	USA	C
American School of Quito	USA	B
Alliance Academy (Quito)	USA	D
Cotopaxi (Quito)	USA	D
El Salvador		
American School	USA	C
French Guiana		
Cayenne Lycée	Fr.	C
Guatemala		
American School	USA	C
Honduras		
American School	USA	C
Mexico		
American School (Durango)	USA	D
American School (Guadalajara)	USA	C
American School (Monterrey)	USA	C
American School (Mexico)	USA	A
J. F. Kennedy (Queretaro)	USA	D
American School (Torreon)	USA	C
International School of Sampedrano	USA	D
Aruba		
Seroe Colorado	USA	D

		Category
Nicaragua		
American School	USA	C
Neptune	USA	D
Canada		
French Speaking School (Toronto)	Can.	D
USA		
UN International School (New York)	ISA	C
Phillips Academy (Andover)	USA	A
Washington Primary	USA	D
Allen Stevenson (New York)	USA	C
Chatham Hall (Va.)	USA	C
Colorado Academy	USA	C
Colorado Rocky Mt.	USA	C
Cottingham (Fla.)	USA	C
Fountain Valley (Colo.)	USA	D
Graland (Colo.)	USA	D
Hawken (Ohio)	USA	D
Ken (Colo.)	USA	D
Nat. Cath. (Washington)	USA	B
Nightingale Bamford (New York)	USA	C
Park (Mass.)	USA	B
Park (Md.)	USA	C
St. Timothys (Md.)	USA	D
Stoneleigh (Mass.)	USA	C
Williston (Mass.)	USA	C
Northfield (Mass.)	USA	A
Haiti		
Union School (Port-au-Prince)	GB	C
Uruguay		
Uruguayan American School (Mercedes)	USA	D
British School of Montevideo	GB	B

fits into this picture, with notable exceptions—Cuba and Mexico. Ironically, what could be a mighty force for internationalism is corroded by three tendencies: zenophobic military dictatorship, inflexible social feudalism and obscurantist pious intolerance. The extent to which widespread illiteracy and grinding poverty flourish in a region naturally rich gives clue to the backwardness of this education in practice. Spain and, to a lesser extent, Portugal reveal similar shortcomings. The Portuguese Empire in Africa and Asia and the Spanish Empire in Africa reflect this situation as well. In Italy, in which fascism proved temporary, similarly in Austria as in the Congo and in Belgium particularly, a far more "up-to-date" catholicism has great influence in education. In Ireland the four centuries of protestant domination have left a peculiar vacuum and sense of inferiority which has similarly affected catholicism in the United States. In Poland the continuance of foreign domination over two centuries has driven Catholic education in that state into a militantly defensive posture. Despite such a package of shortcomings the present *Ajournimento* of the Catholic Church gives clue to a remarkable capacity for renewal, and ability to measure up to the international and interfaith challenge which is the world's today.

The second tradition stemming from Europe springs from militant puritan protestantism. This approach, particularly in its nineteenth-century evangelical outreach, has dominated the Anglo–American world, and that of the Dutch Empire. Its orientation has clearly been rooted in the uplifting of men—but by God's self-conscious chosen elect. The notion of the white, protestant and English-speaking elite carrying what was known as the "white man's burden" has been the touchstone of the educational approach. Among the Dutch Calvinists of South Africa it receives its final shape in "apartheid".

Fortunately such education has postulated man as a democratic political animal. At its best Puritan education offers clarity of vision as to practical ways in which to arrange international affairs. Canada (except Quebec), the USA, the

British West Indies, British Africa, British Asia, Australia and New Zealand are the areas, along with, of course, the British Isles and the Netherlands (and even Switzerland), which may be considered particularly receptive to this outlook. In Germany there is half-openness, as there is in France, but for totally differing reasons.

It is only fair to state that the Anglican approach to education, particularly after it accepted the Quaker gloss regarding toleration has produced an urbane educational influence which at its best has never been won over to the "do-goodism" of the Puritans. Although it maintained a high sense of vocation as regards duty, fair-play and honesty, it hardly escaped the spirit of dominant nationalism evident in the past four centuries. The so-called "public school" and its parallel in the USA as well as in the white dominions is probably as capable of becoming internationally international as any in the world.

The Lutheran influence in education has been largely limited to Scandinavia, though it has contended with puritanism in Germany. The approach was eminently common-sensible, as is revealed in its later manifestation as creator of the folk-school tradition. It is perhaps significant that the Scandinavian school systems first got together to rewrite history which would be commonly satisfactory to them. The basic honesty of Scandinavia in front of the taboos created or reinforced by Puritan approaches is further evidence of the down-to-earth character of Lutheran education. Internationalism is second nature to this approach.

The most important European approach to education comes through reacting against its earlier Christian orientation. This is implicit in Scandinavia—note Ibsen—but reached a totally secular godfather in Rousseau. France has been the first nation to take education away from the church and, in consequence, to build a public-school system. The clarity of the French language, the psychologically satisfying logic (to Frenchmen) of Descartes, allowed for the construction of a system of education whose admirable qualities can only be matched by its tendencies toward ossification.

This system is to be found in francophone Africa and the Middle East, Madagascar and Indo-China, as well as in the French West Indies. In fighting off puritanism, the cartesian system of education has adopted its superiority complex. It is interesting in contrast to observe that secularism in Britain brought utilitarianism in its train, while in America, secularism took the form of pragmatism, leading, in fact, to progressive education. In Germany secularism moved in a wide orbit, from Kant's categorical imperative to Hitler's *Mein Kampf*.

But, of course, the greatest gloss on secularism in education was made by Marxist Leninism in Russia. There, a parody of Hegel's dialectic appealed to minds drugged by the opiate of Christian orthodoxy till they had become nihilistic. Once Stalin united the universalist appeal of Marx to the secret, sacred destiny of Holy Russia, an educational system emerged which proved itself to be the ultimate in ethnocentricity. It may be that as the Eastern European countries free themselves from Soviet domination, even Soviet education may learn the value of comparative judgments.

The Soviet educational system is, of course, excellent in two regards. It requires the once illiterate masses to read and write, and it builds a superior technological force. The Soviet educational evolution is not unlike that of Roman Catholicism. Both are self-authenticating systems now just beginning to explore their Yin-shadows for the first time. Both are finding that it is not enough to be condescendingly superior when, in certain areas, they have, in fact, not even examined the data. One great disadvantage with the Soviet system is the abolition of the private school (some Polish and East German private kindergartens survive). This is done in the name of equality. But obviously a reasonably responsible private sector is invaluable in trying out experiments which, when proven worthwhile, may be adopted by the state system.

The Russian school system is practically identical with that in the other twenty-five constituent republics and in the six "satellite" states. That in Roumania is now moving into what might be called "national communism", while Albania takes her cue from Soviet China. And China has not yet "jelled" educationally speaking. It will, no doubt, finally adopt a Marxist system conditioned by confucianist–taoist–buddhist psychologies. Meanwhile, the Chinese are going through a period of educational chauvinism, in which international co-operation is as impossible as it was for the Soviets before Stalin's death. And it is fascinating to discover in Mexico that Marx, Plato, Buddha and Christ have found mutual accommodation in promoting a secular-religious synthesis which is as challenging as it is generally unknown.

One other main influence springs from Islam, bringing an approach to bear upon schools from Mauritania to Indonesia. It would be unwise to ignore the current attempt of certain leaders in Arab states to identify exclusive Arab nationalism with Islam, in fact with the Islamic Holy War psychology. Such an activity flies in the face of Mohammed's early ministry, the development of the universalist Abbasid Caliphate and the Turkish acceptance of the Koran. The magnificent Islamic Empire of Medieval and Renaissance times was marked as the great tolerant international society in which not only Christians and Jews were protected but Zoroastrians as well. That caricatures of this urbanity have appeared in contemporary developing nations is understandable.

More disquieting is the ideological influence inherited from ancient Persia in which each particularism is allowed to go its own way. In seeking national identity even this tradition now tends to disappear—notably in Egypt. In its place a true international internationalism should be created, if only to protect Egyptian expatriates the world over. But to do this the notion must capture the poetic imagination of the Middle Easterner. Here is a task for the truly gifted educationalist. Fortunately there is a great medieval Islam heritage upon which to build —for those who have ears to hear.

In the great sub-continent of India–Pakistan–Burma–Ceylon– the substratum is not as evident as in "Islamia". But here the cultivation of superhuman mysticism in educational procedures should open every sort of aid to genuine international education. Only the Japanese Zen Buddhist *cum* Shinto adept is able to give more in paradoxical insights into reality of the most profound order. And then there is the challengingly simple hedonism of the Polynesian yet to be appreciated, be he on Fiji or in the Malagasy Republic. Finally, the African is to be discovered as profoundly capable of objective goodness, and instinctive instantaneous procedures to effect justice.

These approaches obviously do not exhaust the fascinating spectroscope of educational variety which our world offers. The seven deadly sins beset all men in all social situations. Man is a material–spiritual animal for whom each advance is matched by the reappearance of the aboriginal temptations in new and ever more sophisticated garb. The world may be only a button-push away from nuclear destruction and faced with mass starvation from overpopulation in a generation or so—but it offers a most exciting variety of challenge to the creative spirit. At last man is capable of seeing himself as a single entity, of communicating instantaneously everywhere. Thus the work of the educator is clear—to create an influential group which can move instinctively through all situations, capable of communicating such a creative universal internationalism. Bilingual English–French linguistic skill which balances biblical prophetic utterance with hellenic rationalism offers as practical a method for communization as one can imagine. An English garden is man's idea of what nature would do if she were right minded. A French garden is decorative art carried out in live materials. What does this augur for capacity to perceive other ways and to construct an educational system in which the best of every way of life is emphasized?

LIST OF COUNTRIES ACCORDING TO PATTERNS OF EDUCATION

Roman Catholic (Orthodox-Coptic)

Andorra	Guatemala	Philippines
Angola	Guinea	Portugal
Argentina	Honduras	Quebec
Austria	Ireland	Salvador
Belgium	Italy	San Marino
Bolivia	Lebanon	Santo Domingo
Brazil	Liechtenstein	Sao Tomé
Burundi	Luxembourg	Spain
Cape Verde Islands	Macao	Spanish Guinea
Ceuta	Madiera	Spanish West Africa
Chile	Malta	Timor
Columbia	Monaco	Uruguay
Costa Rica	Mozambique	Urundi
Cyprus	Nicaragua	Vaticano
Ecuador	Panama	Venezuela
Ethiopia	Paraguay	
Greece	Peru	

Calvinist (Jewish)

Canada	North Ireland	South-West Africa
Dutch Antilles	Scotland	Surinam
Israel	South Africa	Wales
Netherlands		

Anglican

Aden	Gibraltar	Rhodesia
Anguilla	Gilbert Islands	St. Helena
Asceusion	Guiana	St. Kitts
Australia	Honduras	Seychelles
Bahamas	Hong Kong	Sierra Leone
Barbados	Jamaica	Singapore
Basutoland	Kenya	Soloman Islands
Bechuanaland	Malaysia	Swaziland
Bermuda	Man	Tanzania
British Virgin Islands	Mauritius	Tonga
Channel Islands	Montserrat	Trinidad and Tobago
Cook Islands	Nevis	Tristan da Cunha
England	New Guinea	Uganda
Falkland Islands	New Zealand	Western Samoa
Fiji	Nigeria	Zambia
Gambia	Papua	
Ghana	Pitcairn	

LIST OF COUNTRIES ACCORDING TO PATTERNS OF EDUCATION *(cont.)*

Lutheran

Denmark	Greenland	Sweden
Faroe Islands	Iceland	West Berlin
Finland	Norway	West Germany

Western Non-religious (Pragmatic)

American Samoa	Pacific Islands	Turkey
Guam	Panama Zone	United States
Liberia	Puerto Rico	Virgin Islands
Mexico	Ryuku	

Western Non-religious (Cartesian)

Algeria	Guadeloupe	New Hebrides
Cambodia	Guiana	Niger
Cameroons	Haiti	Oceania
Camoro	Ivory Coast	Polynesia
Central Africa	Laos	Réunion
Chad	Lebanon	St. Pierre and Miquelon
Congo (Brazzaville)	Malagasy	Senegal
Dahomey	Martinique	Syria
Djibouti	Mauritania	Switzerland
France	Morocco	Tunisia
Gabon	New Caledonia	Vietnam

Eastern Non-religious (Marxist)

Albania	Georgia	Poland
Armenia	Hungary	Roumania
Azerbaijan	Kazakhstan	Russia
Bulgaria	Latvia	Tadzhikistan
Byelorussia	Lithuania	Turkmenistan
China	Moldavia	Ukraine
Cuba	Mongolia	Uzbekistan
Czechoslovakia	North Korea	Yugoslavia
Estonia	North Vietnam	

Eastern Religious (Oriental)

Bhutan	Indonesia	Sikkim
Burma	Japan	South Korea
Ceylon	Nepal	Thailand
India		

Eastern Religious (Islam)

Afghanistan	Jordan	Qatar
Bahrain	Kuwait	Saudi Arabia
Egypt	Libya	Sudan
Iran	Muscat and Oman	Trucial Oman
Iraq	Pakistan	Yemen

Obviously, such a list gives evidence of arbitrary allocation —but at least the world picture is somewhat clearer by virtue of making such a list.

In concluding this chapter it is interesting to inquire as to what extent the creation of an international university has been considered. According to Michael Zweig's *Idea of a World University* at least a thousand proposals have been promulgated since the First World War. Only one of these, the International University of Brussels, actually came into being, and then only till the outbreak of the Second World War (1919–39). How genuinely international this institution was is not known to me. Probably it was dominated by Belgian board members. In any case no revival was attempted at undergraduate level after the Second World War, though a graduate institute (dominated by Belgians) appeared at Bruges as earlier indicated.

The nearest thing to an international university are six intergovernmental technical institutes: CERN, founded in Geneva in 1954, the UN International Atomic Energy Agency created in Vienna in 1957, the UN Institute for Training and Research set up in New York in 1963, the UN International Centre for Study of Theoretical Physics formed in Trieste in 1964, the International Computations Centre, organized in Rome in 1964 and the ILO Technical Training Institute, which got under way in 1965. All six of these deal with Laboratory Sciences, in which international co-operation is essential for success. Yet it is the political area which causes difficulties, and no attempt has been undertaken to bring the arts subjects, particularly studies of History and Government, into similar international focus. The nearest exception to this statement comes from the creation in 1963 of the European Centre for Co-ordination of Research and Development in the Social Sciences—with its seat in Vienna. It is interesting that Geneva is most frequently suggested as the possible site of a world university. However, the university, whose roots go back to Calvin, and its Institute for studying international affairs (1927), seem to have pre-empted any such institution.

Such a state of affairs would seem to indicate that an international university should be formed in a state, for instance Malta, which has no indigenous university tradition. It would also seem the course of wisdom for half a dozen key professors from different nations representing a wide spectrum of curricula, to set up a summer school under the aegis of UNESCO, grant certificates, and then seek financial support from foundations—that is from the private sector. Probably the government whose state would be chosen for the location of the world university would grant land if not some buildings—and probably a regular subsidy. It would then be time to form a board of trustees drawn from the lists of outstanding educators and statesmen representative of the major systems of education. The final choice would be left to the original participating professors, some of whom would no doubt elect to join the permanent faculty. This teaching staff would elect one of their number a Vice-chancellor to assure independence. UNESCO national commissions would be asked to choose students to be enrolled in the university, and to ensure that scholarship aid would be forthcoming and that upon receiving his degree the university student would be guaranteed the exercise of the profession in which he qualified himself—be it ever so sticky as medicine. Interestingly, such an outline of forming a world international university was elaborated at the Conference of Internationally Minded Schools, held at Chichester, England, in the summer of 1967. All that is needed is the same faith and technique which brought the International Baccalaureate into existence.

CHAPTER 7

THE IDEAL INTERNATIONAL SCHOOL

Ever since the advent of Plato's *Republic*, the inventive mind
has had a go at one or another type of Utopia. Most of these
dreams have had to be radically revised before any part of
them proved very useful. Notwithstanding, the formulation
of hypotheses constitutes perhaps the most creative element
in any scientific formulation. Much of this book has, of necessity, been devoted to pointing out shortcomings in the field
of international schools. It is time now to draw some blue-
prints for what could be created. In undertaking this I have
had the collaboration of some of my colleagues in Geneva.
In fact the plans were drawn in preparation for the alumni
organization work in which I was involved for 6 months in
1966. Naturally we had the Geneva International School in
mind, but most of what we discussed has wide potential application.

First, the legal entity which represents any given international school should be considered. In most countries a limited
non-profit-making company (corporation) is appropriate for
safeguarding both the institution and its potential donors.
This legal entity should be so constituted that its trustees
cannot be dominated by any one government or nationality.
Preferably some form of retirement from the board should be
envisaged after a maximum period of service. The board should
engage the services of an internationally recognized auditing
firm to assure that the highest level of accounting is maintained. It should seek subsidy from local, national host and international governmental bodies. The trustees of the school can

point out to all potential patrons that a sound international school is the first fundamental requirement of all international bodies recruiting staff with families. It is therefore in return for primordial international service that the school seeks financial recognition from those who benefit from it. Education is expensive. Most schools in this world are governmentally subsidized.

Until such time as international law allows for the incorporation of international schools under extraterritoriality arrangements similar to the post offices, customs houses and mints of most nations, it is unrealistic to ask from UN agencies more than token support. Once, however, some form of world federal government is set up, it would seem only wise for it to adopt a chain of international schools as the nucleus of its own world system of education. Meanwhile, a genuine international school should be an active member of the International Schools Association and should prepare at least those who are academically capable to take the International Baccalaureate.

It would appear that a viable international primary school caters best to a student body numbering from 300 to 600 students, while the secondary section (which may contain a boarding department) is most efficient at double those figures. Certainly where both exist together a single director-general is indicated to oversee both primary school and secondary school headmasters. If possible, each of these should represent the dominant linguistic groups in the school (preferably Englis andh French). If this is the case the director-general might well derive from a neutral (non-English, non-French, non-host country) nationality. Care should be taken to assure that all three directors are concerned to promote multilateral internationalism, and are essentially bilingual.

Similar controls should be exercised by the headmasters in employing staff—all of whom should be given in-service training, at least during the fortnight before assuming teaching responsibilities. Naturally, care should be taken to employ imaginative people who are adjustable and, if possible, prepared to cut loose from national cultures. Some sort of balance between and among the major cultures of the world should be undertaken in implementing employment of staff, though obviously technical competence must play a decisive role. In any case the headmasters should provide explicit guidance through spoken and written directives in promoting genuine balance. It should be understood that a successful staff member would be expected once in a 10-year period to exchange posts with his equivalent in another international school. After a decade's service a year's sabbatical would have been earned —with salary.

In addition to full-time staff each international school should consciously seek to serve as a laboratory for outstanding-practice teachers from leading university schools of education from all over the world. In addition, care should be taken whenever a given school experiments in "programming" a subject (or an academic year in one subject) to bring into the school representatives of outstanding national academies in given subjects, and also library and audiovisual technicians from the more developed agencies to assure that the highest common denominator possible is achieved. Probably the best method of financing such efforts would be for schools to draft possible work plans for ISA to present to the foundation world. Once well established and proved successful, a single international school would be encouraged to seek local government subsidy for the maintenance and continuance of such programs.

In any case, I would envisage the typical international school as being so set up that teaching loads would encourage program experimentation, and each school would find itself frequently host to distinguished educators from outside. Only by such cross-fertilization can the schools achieve the fulness of originality which is envisaged for them. In fact the prospect is as exciting for the tough-minded intellectual as was the founding of Aristotle's Academy, or of President Kennedy's New

Frontier. There is even the possibility that frightening international tensions might be reduced by such procedures.

I would also envisage the genuine international school as an institution which would expect a life-long interest on the part of its graduates. Obviously, students who spend only a few primary school years would not be expected to show the same commitment as those who might spend an equivalent amount of time in secondary school. Notwithstanding, Mme Indira Gandhi (who falls in the first category as far as the International School of Geneva is concerned) recently wrote of how great an impact the experience brought to her life.

If the international school has risen to its true vocation its "old boys and girls" will want to keep in touch with its most recent developments. In other words, instead of spawning "alumni" who reverence each hedge and custom as it was, they will be so acclimatized to the notion of dynamic change that they will be eager to participate in each validated insight as it occurs. To facilitate this participation I would envisage the construction of an alumni house, or better, a wing attached to the boarding department which would afford pilgrim accommodation to visitors, particularly alumni. Imagine how useful a Sunday evening boarding house discussion on Contemporary India could be, with Mme Gandhi sitting in! Obviously, lesser figures would be free for such extra-curricular activity. But their range of interests would be as vast as the concerns of men. In any case, participants in the programming of courses, along with visiting parents, would be afforded the opportunity of appreciating the dimension which the students themselves would offer.

Lest, however, the student body, particularly those boarding, be drawn only from privileged backgrounds, I would suggest that half those living at the school come on scholarship from developing nations. An ordinary international secondary boarding school section should, it would appear, allow for from 150 to 300 students, chosen by national UNESCO commissions of ninety nations, which might wish to benefit from this arrangement, and would allow for from one to three gifted students from each of these countries to attend any one international school offering such a program. No doubt there would be headaches. But the confrontation of developed by developing and by ethnic groups of every sort; of capitalist consumerists by socialist communists; by religions of all kinds or none—in such a boarding house the bilingual concept would go far to undo the image and reality of the boarding as a convenient shelf upon which the *mondaine* world deposits its hardly wanted offspring. In fact such a boarding house as is proposed here might go far to redeem the exercise in fashionable snobbishness which besets too many schools in which the patrons children "live in".

Naturally, the cost of paying for half the boarding school through scholarship is immense. It is to be hoped that the foundation world might first glimpse the reality that such schemes represent. Later, governments might be willing to engage in such subsidy. When one reflects upon the magnitude of the efforts both the USA and the USSR have undertaken already to attract capable people in the developing world to their way of life, it is not impossible to envisage a more modest effort which would at last bring comprehension of each other in a world in which both begin to see that as valuable. If such boarding departments build lasting friendships—one has only to realize what fruit the post-Second World War education offered Germans in the USA has brought to present US–German relations—it might even be worth allocating the cost of a super bombing fortress which might otherwise go down in flames in some "localized" conflict, possibly in an obscure jungle or desert.

It is not impossible that the creation of a truly international boarding department might offer exactly the kind of matrix in which the true values of multilateral internationalism may be best appreciated. The creation of such a boarding department may be the decisive element in persuading other capital ventures that it is worthwhile creating the model international school.

STR 13

I should add hastily at this point that I conceive of the major portion of this boarding department as coterminous with the British sixth-form college, that is of the 2 final years in which the International Baccalaureate is intentionally studied. Obviously preparation, particularly in Languages and in Laboratory Sciences for students from developing countries, may require a 4- or 5-year residence to guarantee success. It is as important for the recipient of a scholarship that he keep in close touch with his *milieu* as it is for the non-scholarship student. Obviously, great care in guidance work on the part of the school is required. Care must be given that culture conflict is approached intelligently and concern for universally valid solutions undertaken. Here, the participation of sociologists who have achieved really creative accommodation in conflict situations must be drawn upon. Imagine once again the interest generated by a panel discussion held with staff and boarding students in which Vinobe Bhave and Danielo Dolci exchanged ideas.

In order for sound evaluation to be made regarding subsequent experience, and since international schools alumni are relatively few in number, it might be useful for a single alumni organization to operate, thus drawing people of similar experience together throughout the world. Obviously the tradition of entering into a life-long financial commitment to one's *alma mater*, which is generally accepted in the United States and Canada, should be fostered. It is necessary to generalize upon this concept if international schools are to enlist substantial foundation and government support. The essential rallying point for alumni is the fact that they have actively participated in an educational experience, which, if sufficiently increased, could transform the basis upon which world problems are approached.

In turning from the personnel involved in international schools to the educational program of the genuine multilateral international institution we come to what should be the most revolutionary and pedagogically exciting consideration.

First as regards the primary school, it should in most cases occupy separate quarters and grounds from the secondary school, though it might well share in the focal facilities offered by the latter. As useful a way as any to allow for this arrangement would be for the central buildings to serve as the division point on the campus, one side of which would be normally secondary territory, the other primary.

It would be important for each primary school classroom to be sufficiently large as to serve as part-time laboratory, assembly room and library with direct access to a play area. There should be in addition a combination gymnasium–assembly hall–theatre, with fixtures suitable for small children and large enough to accommodate all six grades or, if impossible, each group of three grades. Equipment for audio–visual aids should, of course, be maximum throughout—and sufficient laboratory equipment to allow for projects in all subjects. In addition, access to music and art rooms is invaluable—and, of course, to that portion of the library set aside for young children. Naturally, some rooms of the cafeteria would likewise be available. The staff notice room would be similarly situated where access would be easy, though a primary staff room or two would allow for relaxation and informal consultation.

Perhaps the most striking innovation would be the boarding department, which, with alumni wing or house, would lie on the secondary side of the campus, preferably in close contact with the gymnasia and playing field. Good boarding schools usually arrange for some weekend supervision with athletic equipment including the use of swimming pools. I would envisage a more elaborate athletic set-up than most schools offer, simply to accommodate the large range of sports which exist internationally speaking. I would even go so far as to envisage a genuine international sports training to Higher Level for candidates looking forward to teaching Physical Education or even to a non-professional sports career. It might even be suggested to UNESCO national commissions that intelligent boys and girls with potential Olympic possibilities be suggested as scholarship candidates.

The boarding house itself might well be organized into groups not dissimilar to the Pine Manor Junior College quadrangles (near Boston) in which small groups of students occupy houses grouped about a courtyard, each catering to about 50 students. Thus three to six groupings would be created allowing for intramural competitions. Naturally the school would be coeducational, though not in any one quadrangle! In constructing and planning these residence halls, proximity to dining halls and cafeteria would, of course, play an important role. Architecturally, each quadrangle should represent one region of the world, though, in fact, along with the general buildings they should not clash with the cultural style associated with the region in which the school is located.

Several rather famous architects have passed through international schools. They might be encouraged to compete to produce imaginative plans which would mirror the universal confrontations which international schools imply. In any case, it is important that each quadrangle possess a distinctive common room, and that it communicate directly to the staff apartments. There is some wisdom in connecting the alumni wing (house) with the staff block, complete with committee dining rooms, staff announcement room, study rooms, games room and common room.

The dining rooms–cafeteria–kitchen complex would, with staff rooms, form one of four focal centers at the heart of the plant. The others would be the Performing Arts center, Library center and Experimental Science center. Each of these latter three would contain a complex of rooms or buildings as accessible to the primary school as the dining and staff rooms would be.

Each of the three academic centers would find its apex in its appropriate theatre. That for the Experimental Sciences would allow for dramatic public-lecture experiments not unlike those offered by General Electric at the New York

Worlds Fair. Clustered about it would be found a complex of Physics, Chemistry, Biology, Physical Geography and Mathematical laboratories, fully equipped for use of upper primary, junior and senior secondary classes. Conveniently placed technical library alcoves might well surround the central hexagonal demonstration complex.

The second academic center ranging alongside the Experimental Science concentration would be devoted to the Performing Arts. Its focus would appear in a dramatic theatre complete with workshops to prepare scenery and costumes, constructed with an orchestra pit and music wing, consisting of a number of rehearsal rooms. Parallel to the theatre would be an exhibition lounge connecting to a Fine Arts wing. There, each school term, a complete change of art exhibits could be arranged. In the wing itself activities would vary from printing to sculpture, from decorating to mobiles. Still another wing would be given over to creative writing and listening. It would be part of each year's program to invite authors, dramatists and poets to be in residence as well as offer small theatre rooms for the reading of fine literature. Attached to this would be a complex of language laboratories so placed that easy access from the primary school would be available. Obviously every international school has great need of intensive individual work with students whose vehicular language must be maintained.

Finally in this grouping would be found a Comparative Religion wing in which the atmosphere of various world religions as well as primitive, secular and agnostic atmospheres could be experienced. Obviously no one religious exercise could be expected of a student group embracing all types of thinking. It would be wrong, however, to ignore the vast complex of thinking which man has developed in relating himself to the universe. A judiciously organized program might have the effect of introducing the appropriate eschatology which a Carl Jung, a Taillard de Chardin or an Arnold Toynbee would consider exciting.

Between the theatre and the assembly hall (the latter equipped with desks, public-speaking apparatus and simultaneous translation booths (much on the order of the assembly hall at CERN) would lie a formal reception area appropriate to the ceremonial visits of distinguished personalities, complete with rotating expositions which quickly establish the effectiveness of the school in the spectrum of its activities. As the central focus area of the school it might be conceived with the adventurous quality of the Piretti Building in Milan. Parenthetically, the Science center might utilize the more inspired of Aztec wall-construction, while that center devoted to the Humanities adapt itself to modern Japanese interpretations of oriental approaches. It would be hoped that this variety of architecture could be harmonized, but in such a way that the impression would be given that the school consciously intends a synthesis of what the world has to offer.

At the opposite pole to that devoted to Laboratory Science would appear the Library complex with wings running out into the liberal arts subjects—History, Geography, Languages of Instruction, Classics, Philosophy, Anthropology. At the center there would function a multiple hexagonal series of audio–visual laboratories with back projection toward the six center screens. Above this would appear the Library proper, with extensive individual study cubicles fitted for similar audio–visual work. Within each department, as with the Science groupings, permanent installations of facilities would allow for maximal sensory appreciation of whatever is being taught.

Often, the legitimate exigencies of a given discipline interfere with truly co-operative interdisciplinary teaching. It would be hoped that with maximum facilities, with a somewhat reduced teaching time-table and with the commitment to multilateral international education to be found in a genuine international school, really imaginative programs could be developed.

The foregoing projected school should, it seems to me, contain sufficient originality and challenge to elicit the interest of foundations concerned to help unusual programs to succeed. Once operative, such a school could well be recapitulated in the major world centers. However, costs of building such a system would of necessity fall upon governments. When it is realized that 85 per cent of the immense cost of world armaments is borne by five developed nations, USA, USSR, France, China, UK and Canada, it is only good sense to ask these powers to bear the major cost of such a chain of schools, though an 85 per cent figure would be unrealistic. However, the USA might be expected to provide 40 per cent of the capital, USSR 15 per cent, France 5 per cent and UK 5 per cent. The remaining 20 per cent could be financed by the following nations, which are sufficiently developed to bear a smaller proportion of the cost: Argentina, Australia, Belgium, Canada, China, Czechoslovakia, Denmark, East Germany, Egypt, India, Indonesia, Italy, Japan, Netherlands, Norway, Pakistan, Poland, South Africa, Spain, Sweden, Switzerland and West Germany. Host nations might well be excepted to provide land and possibly buildings if financing should prove difficult.

By subsidizing a chain of such international schools, governments would, in fact, put some of their trust in supra-nationalism as a safeguard for the future of mankind. Sulwyn Lewis, in his Pergamon study entitled *Towards International Co-operation*, suggests eight basis components of modern nationalism. The first of these is "self-determination". Multilateral international education postulates basic interdependence among all ethnic groupings, especially among nations. The second of Lewis' proposals is the "super-human nature of the state". Such a characteristic is transference to mankind—and to an eventual world federal state. The third emphasizes the "virtue of struggling with other States". Surely the competition between and among the highest common denominators in a neutral environment offers the fairest arena for struggle. The fourth of Lewis's points has to do with the "need for diversity". Surely the immense variety of human experience is emphasized in the international school. The fifth point has to do with the "importance of the national language". Obviously, this must take second place to the international languages. The sixth point has to do with "racial identity", to be reinterpreted in the light of blood types, which are more important than pigmentation. The seventh point is "religious identity", which finds its reorientation in ecumenicity. And finally, Lewis suggests "educational identity", which is exactly what the international school seeks to achieve on a higher level. More important, the international school must offer a cure to that psychological maladjustment by which nations organize against others (usually with high visibility) in order to placate their own insecurity.

Attention must be given to the truly terrifying problems facing humanity: population explosion, mutual atomic overkill, contamination of water and atmosphere, the danger of exclusive self-authenticating orthodoxies and the tendency to dispose of groups of people and nations through superficial stereotypes. In fact the international school must submit to careful scrutiny by each authoritarian approach, to discover, in fact what virtues and vices are obscured by its insistence on a monopoly of truth. It is sometimes difficult for those who hold mutually exclusive ideologies to realize that they are to some degree prisoners of the approach they affirm and are often quite incapable of viewing their doctrines objectively. In fact they cannot appreciate the affirmative values of their point of view, being unable to set them against unrecognized negative aspects.

Thus, the international school challenges the more enlightened elements in any given nation to be willing to submit ethnocentric shibboleths to universal standards. The success of a chain of international schools may well be involved in the survival of man. The post-jet age must once and for all scrap the 1920 League of Nations dictum that education is a private or national prerogative.

APPENDIXES

I HAVE chosen three main topics to be placed in the appendix of this study because they illuminate three aspects of the History program of ISES (now IBO) rather than deal specifically with international education as such. They are, in fact, directly associated with the one experiment in multilateral education now in practice. The first (A) has to do with the experience of 5 years of experimental History examination. The second (B) consists of my draft for a teachers' guide in the program of the IB. The third (C) consists of a draft syllabus which I have written in collaboration with my department for a ninth class (third form) dealing with History from A.D. 550 to 1250. Only upon developing such techniques will it be possible for a genuinely viable international system to be developed.

ANALYSIS OF EXPERIMENTAL HISTORY
EXAMINATION PROGRAM 1963–7 INCLUSIVE

THE table on pages 190–1 gives a summary of numbers of questions formulated for various examinations offered in the initial 5-year period. It will be observed that in 1967 only those papers which were sat were actually prepared, in contrast to earlier years when the exampel of a complete History program was important for attracting financial subsidy. Also it is important to note that the change of program of late autumn 1966 affects the total range of subjects. When grand-total figures contain two numbers, the second indicates the real number of new questions written—the first indicates duplication of higher level and subsidiary formulation.

In 1963 only the Alpha Higher Level was taught—in a 1-year crash program. Only five selected candidates sat the two 3-hour papers, plus oral on thesis examinations, handled by the Ecolint History staff. Four passed.

In 1964 in the same program but with 2 years' preparation, three of ten candidates (not selected) qualified, with university collaboration in grading. One pre-baccalaureate (Subsidiary) selected candidate passed his single 3-hour paper graded by department members. Total, four passes.

In 1965 in the alpha Higher Level (2 years' preparation) twelve students sat, of whom six were successful, with full responsibility given to university examiners. There also qualified eleven of nineteen pre-baccalaureate (Subsidiary) candidates. In addition four selected students sat the beta higher-level examinations of whom two were qualified by the Ecolint His-

SUMMARY ON HISTORY QUESTIONS SET BY ISES

Higher Level—Alpha

	Americas	Europe–USSR	Africa–Middle East	Asia–Oceania	General	Grand total
1963	12	12	9	9	6	
1964	12	12	9	9	6	
1965	12	12	9	9	6	
1966	12	18	9	9	6	
1967	1	12	1	1	—	
Total	49	66	37	37	24	**213**

Subsidiary Level—Alpha

1965	2	2	1	2	1	
1966	2	2	2	1	1	
1967	—	12	—	—	—	
Total	4	16	3	3	2	**30 12**

Higher Level—Beta

1965	12	20	8	8	—	
1966	12	20	8	8	—	
1967	—	—	—	—	—	
Total	24	40	16	16	—	**90**

Subsidiary Level—Beta

Americas		Europe–USSR	Africa–Middle East	Asia–Oceania	General	Grand total
1964	8	8	2	6	—	
1965	9	10	2	7	—	
1966	8	10	2	8	—	
1967	—	—	—	—	—	
Total	25	28	6	21	—	**100 88**

Subsidiary Level—Gamma

		Europe–USSR		Asia–Oceania		Grand total
1965	—	18	—	6	—	
1966	—	22	—	6	—	
1967	—	22	—	6	—	
Total	—	62	—	18	—	**80 76**

tory staff. In addition, twenty-three students sat a gamma (pre-baccalaureate-subsidiary-level) examination, of whom eight were passed by the Ecolint staff.

Also, experimentally, eighteen students sat the Occident section of the alpha higher-level paper (as a "second alternative") giving subsidiary-level passes. Four of these were successful. It was also decided that a proper subsidiary paper covering the alpha syllabus be given to the French linguistic section students. Eight volunteered. Two were successful. Thus there was a total of thirty-one passes.

In 1966 this large program was reduced as an adjustment to the rest of the IB program was coming. No subsidiary examinations at all were sat (none for beta in 1965). No beta pre-baccalaureate was sat, while the alpha pre-baccalaureate was graded as an internal Ecolint examination. The beta Higher Level was taken by sixteen candidates (but without theses) and was passed by five. The alpha Higher Level was offered with an Occident paper only and thesis. It was taken by twenty-five candidates of whom seven qualified (they had only 1 year's preparation). Total, twelve passes.

In 1967 only the revised alpha higher-level papers were taken. This year a proper chief examiner for History was operative. (In 1966 all papers were handled by external examiners.) Twenty candidates presented themselves. Fourteen qualified. (One year's preparation was allowed.)

Thus, the following totals may be put forward:

	1963	1964	1965	1966	1967	Total
Subsidiary Level	—	1 1	68 25	—	—	69 26
Higher Level	5 4	10 3	16 8	41 12	20 14	92 41

Thus it may be seen that 161 candidates have presented themselves with 67 successes registered, or a proportion of a little better than 40 per cent. This may be taken as indicating probably that about 40 per cent of the graduates of the International School of Geneva are of the standard of European university training. (This figure allows for counting the 1966 candidates as Higher Level, when they might well be considered as Subsidiary, in fact.)

A further note on the preparation of examination questions and thesis topics is in order. The 1964 alpha set was effected co-operatively by Ecolint and University of Geneva men. All the 1965 alpha and gamma questions were so constructed. Ecolint worked up the beta questions and topics. In 1966 all questions and topics were effected jointly by Ecolint and Atlantic College.

The 1967 topics were written by UNIS (New York) and Atlantic College, while the chief examiner proposed the questions. He is likewise responsible, in collaboration with chairmen of departments involved, for the 1968 beta topics and questions. (No alpha candidates are foreseen, but Atlantic College will set the examinations the first time.)

Some other subjects, notably Geography and English, were sat at Ecolint in 1967, and some Modern Languages at Atlantic College. Thus the experiment is now going outside Geneva and the original discipline of History.

APPENDIX A 2

DECISIONS RELATIVE TO A COURSE IN THE STUDY OF CITIES

IN JUNE 1967 a joint History–Geography panel was called to follow up the discussion initiated in 1965 on the possibility of teaching among the Study of Man grouping a course in urban development both historical and geographical in content. Already a draft paper on Alexandria in Egypt had been prepared as constituting a location in which cultures have mingled and in which geographical considerations play a major role. At the request of the ISES (now IBO) a second more detailed paper on Geneva, Switzerland was formulated. In both cases I had a good deal to do with these papers. As they point to an interdisciplinary type of study useful internationally, they are both attached at this point.

It was decided that the cities listed in Table 5 would be offered from which the school choosing the Cities course would nor-

TABLE 5

Historic city	Industrial city	City in developing area
Vienna	Manchester	Brasilia
Istanbul	Pittsburgh	Kuwait
Alexandria	Essen	Dakar
Peking	Volgograd	Saigon
Delhi	Osaka	Nairobi
Mexico City	Johannesburg	Santiago de Chile

mally work in depth in the home city, but would then select one historical, one industrial and one developing area city for lesser treatment.

At Subsidiary Level no city would be treated in depth, but a survey of the "home" city and two others would be undertaken. It was agreed that two 2-hour written papers for Higher Level, one on home city would be undertaken—for Subsidiary Level one paper of 2½ hours. Orals would be offered at both levels. Two original research papers at Higher Level and one at Subsidiary were considered appropriate. Team teaching naturally was recommended.

CITIES PROJECT—ALEXANDRIA

Unit 1

Geography: Mediterranean, Nile Delta, harbor sites.
Archaeology: Neolithic cultures.
Anthropology: Semitic–Hamitic origins.
Economic: early cultures—Minoan connections.

Unit 2

Geography: Rhakotis.
Linguistics: growth of hieroglyphics.
Anthropology: Osiris and Serapis worship—Egyptian culture.
Literary references: Homer.

Unit 3

Biology: semi-desert and littoral ecology.
History: Alexander the Great, founding of the city.
Archaeology: Alexander's Tomb, Hellenistic sculpture.
Linguistics: Greek hieroglyphs and demotic script.

Unit 4

History: Ptolemies: 323–222 B.C.
Anthropology: marriage system.
Architecture: Pharos, Museum, Temple of Serapis.
Economic: place of Ptolemaic Empire.

Unit 5

History: Later Ptolemies—Cleopatra.
Literary references: Shakespeare, Theocritos, Plu-
tarch, PETRIE *History of Egypt*, IV.
Science: Euclid, Claudius Ptolemy, Eratosthenes,
Alexandrian Year.

Unit 6

Anthropology: Judaism, Christianity, Gnosticism,
Arianism, Desert fathers.
Archaeology: ruins of monasteries, tombs, colon-
nades.
Linguistics: Coptic.
Philosophy: Athanasius, Dioscuras, Plotinus.
History: SHARP *History of Egypt*, II.

Unit 7

History: the Arab Conquest.
Anthropology: Monophysitism—Monothelism, Islam.
Archaeology: fortress of Kaitbey, Mosque of Pro-
phet Daniel, Attarine Mosque.
Economic: economic consequences of Arab Con-
quest.

Unit 8

History: relations with Byzantine Empire, Belisarius
Crusades, Saladin, St. Louis.
Economic: position of medieval Egypt.
Anthropology: development of Arab civilization.

Unit 9

Archaeology: medieval walls.
Sociology: removal of the body of St. Mark.
History: sack by Cypriots, Turkish Conquest.
Anthropology: the Turks.

Unit 10

History: Napoleon, Mohammed Ali, Western imperialism.
Linguistics: Rosetta Stone, development of Egypto-
logy.
City planning: present structure.

Unit 11

Ethnic: expulsion of foreigners, Arab nationalism.
History: the Second World War.
Religious: variety of faiths.
Economic: Suez Canal.

STUDY OUTLINE FOR GENEVA

Based on a 12—week block of periods—five periods per week
(including one double period) for field study and laboratory
work.

14*

Unit 1

History: Palaeolithic and neolithic periods—visit to *Musée d'Histoire*. Appearance and local effect of copper, bronze and iron. Arrival of the Allobrogenes. Connections with Greek colonies in the Mediterranean.

Geography: Initial study of local topographical maps. Construction of base maps for future use during the course. Structure of Geneva—its buildings, origins of the lake, character of the rocks. How the region "mirrors" Switzerland physically, up "Le Salève".

Unit 2

History: Classical period first century B.C.–fourth century A.D. Roman Conquest: imperial structure: Geneva—Nyon—Avanches. Appearance of christianity. Establishment of bishopric 379. Early architecture—visit to "Roman" town of Geneva.

Geography: Foundation and siting of city: recording it on base map. Topography of the region: results of glaciation, drainage patterns, local stream study. Local water supply—visit to town waterworks.

Unit 3

History: Collapse of the Burgundian Kingdom A.D. 534. Position as Gunthrum's capital city. "Dark Ages" of Geneva. Origins of the city state in the new Burgundian Kingdom. Influence of Charlemagne and Frederick Barbarossa, etc. Medieval fairs. The Combourgeoisie. Bishop *vs.* town.

Geography: Growth of the city, fourth–fifteenth centuries—location of markets. Climatic studies—recording of local weather, analysis of Geneva's climate, analysis of Swiss weather charts—visit to meteorological center at the airport. Linguistic patterns in Geneva?—in Switzerland.

Unit 4

History: Sixteenth and seventeenth centuries. Impact of protestantism in Geneva; its European influence. Calvinism and capitalism: the development of Geneva as a banking center. Savoyard problems. Arrival of the Huguenots. Visit to archives for document study.

Geography: Growth of the town during the sixteenth and seventeenth centuries. Soils and vegetation: soil testing and analysis sample vegetation. Agriculture: pattern in canton markets. Land use survey or local farm study. Agriculture on Swiss plateau.

Unit 5

History: Eighteenth and nineteenth centuries. Influence of Rousseau and Voltaire, etc. French Revolution and Napoleonic period. Unification of Switzerland: confederation, federal system. Political parties in Geneva. Refugees, for example Mazzini, Lenin, Garibaldi. Red Cross.

Geography: City's form in the eighteenth and nineteenth centuries: emphasis on architectural changes during the period. Boundaries: political geography of the canton. Transport: railway network, lake transport, road pattern, survey of present traffic and problems.

Unit 6

History: Twentieth-century impact of First and Second World Wars. Establishment of League of Nations and ILO—European office of the United Nations. Visit to a session of the United Nations. Specialized agencies of the United Nations. Specialized organizations in Geneva. *Ad hoc* conferences.

Geography: Final form of the city—delineation of functional areas within the city. Industry in Geneva—Geneva as a commercial center. Visit and study of a local industrial establishment.

INTERNATIONAL SCHOOLS EXAMINATION SYNDICATE — INTERNATIONAL BACCALAUREATE

TEACHERS' GUIDE

History

PREFACE

The syllabuses put forward by ISES as a basis for the experimental testing of the International Baccalaureate provide a framework the substance and interpretation of which calls for comments and concrete examples. It is far from the intention of ISES to dictate to teachers, many of whom have years of experience behind them, how they ought to arouse the interest of their pupils. Indeed, it would rather warn young teachers not to be tempted to seek in a guide the secret of success: the quality of the instruction given must always depend on the caliber of the teacher, and freedom for the latter is an extremely important element which must at all times be fully respected.

While not wishing to impose ideas or to direct efforts, however, ISES must seek a certain harmony. The International Baccalaureate is an experiment, and that calls for testwork. Each of the proposed guides is both a conclusion and an introduction—a conclusion in that it sums up and reflects the trends which, over a number of years, have gradually crystallized what may be called "the philosophy of the International Baccalaureate"; an introduction in that it leads up to the exchanges of views which must be developed as the experiment proceeds.

The teachers who took part in the working panels gradually discovered horizons and methods which were perhaps unfamiliar to them from their own training. The syllabuses which were finally drawn up are neither definitive nor perfect, but even in their present form they have at least the advantage of being a synthesis of systems which were often widely disparate. The necessary improvements can be made only in the light of their practical application.

If the experiment is to be useful and significant, every teacher required to use these syllabuses will have to make a certain effort of adaptation, possibly following lines that differ considerably from his traditional methods. In other words, every one concerned must give them a fair trial. The effort will be worthwhile if each one appreciates the dual purpose of the experimental baccalaureate: (1) to reconcile the present divergences in syllabuses and examinations as between national systems and thus be of service to schools with an international and floating population; (2) to serve as an instrument of pedagogical research into the best criteria for assessing ripeness for university study.

Each guide attempts to give the necessary explanations for its particular subject. There are, however, certain general lines which must be followed in developing the International Baccalaureate.

ISES makes no claim to be producing completely new ideas on education. There exist already a number of converging trends on which a large measure of agreement has been reached. These are reflected in a number of current phrases: to train the mind rather than to impart information; to learn how to learn; knowledge of the world rather than just knowledge, etc. Every teacher is conscious of the dangers of mere accumulation of facts or of premature specialization.

It may nevertheless be desirable to recall certain important points.

One is tempted to say that the teacher must above all resist the temptation to instruct. His aim should be to let the pupils *discover* and not to communicate to them his discoveries. He must, of course, stimulate their thinking, but experience shows that he cannot do this all the time, not being in the privileged position of a visiting lecturer. He must appreciate the joy a pupil derives from discovering things for himself: an ingot discovered by someone else cannot compare with a nugget found by oneself.

This links up with a second principle, that of *motivation*. It is a mistake to think that the substance of a course has value in itself. Everyone knows from experience that even the most engrossing subject can fall flat; the element of interest or lack of interest is often an imponderable and can change considerably from one group of pupils to another. There is no golden rule in this field. The point to stress is that a lesson can often be made vivid by the use of material aids which are available at little cost. A 30-minute film, a visit to a chemical factory or attendance at a theatrical performance may often produce results far in excess of those that can be obtained by a mere study of the same subject in the classroom.

Finally, one of the essential aims of the course is to instill a *method of work*. The teacher must constantly bear in mind that he must pass on his pupils to a colleague in a higher class and that the best service he can render his colleague is not to gorge the pupil prematurely with undigested facts but to develop on sound lines the pupil's working tools. This holds good equally for the lowest grade and for the immediate pre-university class.

Present-day educators will no doubt be prepared to accept these general principles, but more than that, will be required to ensure co-ordination of syllabuses. The purpose of the guides is to define the scope of the syllabuses and the standards which may reasonably be expected in the examination; examples are given, especially in the case of innovations, such as the courses in World Literature, Theory of Knowledge or Anthropology. The ISES co-ordinators and the chief examiners will act as advisers, and it would be well for the teachers handling the same courses in different schools to consult together.

The most important, and no doubt also the most difficult point will be the fixing of criteria for judging the pupils' work. The juries responsible for correcting the texts will have to determine those criteria for the papers submitted to them, but it is clear that the marking done by the teachers during the school year must be guided by the same principles; otherwise the pupils will not be adequately prepared. One of the aims of the experiment over the period of 6 years, in co-operation with the Research Centre, will be precisely to get away from the individual empirical approach and draw up criteria of assessment based on rational, scientific principles.

This first edition of the guides is merely a starting point. As soon as the first year of experiment is over, adjustments will have to be made. All teachers concerned will be asked to contribute suggestions and comments in the light of their experience with their own classes.

INTRODUCTION

The Teaching of History

The teaching of History offers the gifted teacher the widest possible opportunity of engaging in fruitful international dialogue. Most teachers and students now two-thirds of the way through the twentieth century are the products of unilingual national cultures at a time when intelligent people are generally in agreement that mutual accommodation between and among ethnic groups is essential for the survival of man. Historians cannot pretend that their subject offers the best means of achieving the necessary accommodation. Even in as limited a field of experimentation as is offered by the International Baccalaureate, the Study of Knowledge and World Literature occupy considerably stronger positions than does History (as one of the Studies of Man). Notwithstanding, History is the only subject to be allowed two full-scale options.

This is unquestionably due to the wide recognition of the immense inter-cultural potentialities in the subject; considerations which swayed the thinking of those responsible for the development of the ISES program toward giving History a unique position within the International Baccalaureate syllabus arrangements. It is hoped that many students will feel drawn to one of the three History courses which will be provided, if only to achieve depth perception regarding the major dilemmas facing man.

Oddly enough at first glance, the alpha and beta History streams deal with progressively earlier stages in human development. The gamma stream, which has been abandoned and has to do with the study of medievalism (600–1300 B.C.) would probably appeal to relatively few. But those few would be concerned to appreciate the true inwardness of the birth and early stages of many of the social institutions which determine the nature of our world. Some gamma candidates would, no doubt, be among the more gifted students—certainly those with a genuine penchant for "History" as an objective discipline. No student deeply steeped in either Occidental or Oriental medievalism is likely to be deceived by the self-serving propaganda of any nationalism, since he should be capable of living in that universe which existed before nations were. Even the student who might enter the gamma stream at Subsidiary Level cannot escape, for instance, the truism that Christianity and Islam are two sides of one coin, or that Hinayana and Mahayana Buddhism bind together such two dissimilar peoples as the Indians and the Chinese.

The beta stream, which starts at mid-eighteenth century and stops perhaps short of the contemporary moment—at the discretion of the teacher—approaches a world which is enormously more complicated than the medieval scene; one in which Occident and Orient were logical divisions. (Perhaps ISES should offer a fourth Renaissance paper, 1300–1750, in which a compromise between the two medieval and four modern eras could be presented.) In any case the modern paper allows for concentration on the Americas; or Africa–Middle East; or Europe–Russia; or Asia–Oceania. It can be maintained that after the exuberant Renaissance period, the growth of science and technology and the rapid crystallization of nations as we know them have created the modern world. Perhaps most students of History will prefer this beta alternative not because they lack curiosity about origins or wish to avoid emotional involvement about what happens today, but simply because the last two centuries have demonstrated a universalization hitherto unknown in the history of man. At Higher Level there is every opportunity, no matter which of the four areas is chosen, to appreciate the dynamics of colonialism, the appeal of totalitarian egalitarianism, the impact of shortening travel span and the industrial imperative of precise interchangeable parts. At Subsidiary Level the impact of the American Revolution, of English industrialization or of the Turkish political vacuum can hardly be escaped. In any case, whatever news dominates the written word or appears on the television screen will not be wholly unexpected.

The alpha stream, which concentrates on the last half-century, lacks, of course, the comfort which open archives offer to historical judgment, but neither do the statesmen and demagogues who make history have this comfort. There is a growing group of students whose potential political sense seeks cultivation. They need as full a factual background as can be given to guide their incipient involvement. For such students the alpha higher-level course is vital. As in the beta stream, the same four-way emphasis presents itself. It is instructive, however, that the American youth cannot escape knowing Canadian history, nor may the French girl remain ignorant of the NEP in Russia. The Ghanaian boy is not unaware of what forces brought Israel into existence, while the Australian youth must understand why Kashmir plagues Pakistan. At Subsidiary Level two world wars, a universal depression and a frustrated Security Council make a not unsatisfactory list of items upon which to build some understanding of the contemporary world. So much for the content of the courses.

History in the International Baccalaureate programs is, however, conceived not only as dealing with a world outlook, but is so constructed as to involve the students in historical procedures. As the syllabus for the International Baccalaureate points out, more is expected than routine lecturing on the part of the teacher.

First it must be admitted that to teach "biological" segments of the history of the world—medieval, modern or contemporary—requires an omniscience worthy of the *Encyclopaedia Britannica*. Obviously every teacher will quickly come to the frontiers of his own knowledge; what he should know is where to turn to help guide an eager young mind into exhaustive research in any one corner of knowledge. It is the intention of ISES to supply teachers with annotated bibliographies for each major division of teaching. In addition, some key books will be suggested in connection with lists of special subjects. Rapid leafing-through of suggested source material will give the alert teacher some sense of what scope each text offers. Obviously he will want to read others in order to be fully conversant with different points of view.

Fortunately the teacher is not required to be equally competent in the Occidental and Oriental sections of any one of the three syllabus options. In point of fact he need be fully conversant with only one area. The selected topics can be prepared on short notice. He may even suggest what these might be. Special topics require a wider range of knowledge. But it is quite possible to develop competence in consultation with the individual student as his final year progresses. There is no rule of thumb regarding how much time should be devoted to the major area in contrast to that allocated to the selected and special topics, but any one year given to each would seem to constitute a reasonable balance.

Obviously the teacher must be a counsellor. But he must also be a dramatist. Dull lecturing must not be replaced by duller lexicography. The teacher must be able to bring alive a series of associated events in such a way that their interrelationships become organic. Some complexes of historical data dramatize more effectively through group oral techniques—formal debate, round table discussion, simulated inquest, reading of answers to examination questions (sat under examination conditions), etc. The teacher must be flexible in being open to those techniques which most effectively recreate conditions, so that they are really absorbed by the class. One general counsel which has proved its worth is to ask students in formal oral presentation to defend positions which are strange to them personally, or to attack those which normally they would defend. In areas of sensitivity the teacher should develop the point of view which is obliquely different from a conventional outlook, particularly from his own. A categorical imperative is placed upon the teacher to the end that he question every accepted view, and progressively to the extent that it holds itself to be sacrosanct. Such activity is important where religious, racial, ideological or political orthodoxy is normally expected. Such attitudes will win respect from the ablest students, who will realize that they must think everything through —that they will not be given conventional reassurance for closed opinions, however respectable they may appear at first glance.

In such a program of critical inquiry every national orientation naturally comes under question. Since political history is largely the account of what happens to political entities, one cannot escape discussing them. They can, however, be dissected to advantage, and weighed in whatever universal scales the teacher may find immediately useful. Here the quick wits of the teacher in interplay with perhaps even sharper young intellects will allow for imaginative presentation of data to substantiate positions. Surrealism (if understood as such), humor, unexpected withdrawal from advanced positions and genuine humility before the more complex issues will win respect and guarantee the genuine involvement of the student in the subject.

It has been envisaged that five periods a week (plus two given over to guided research) should constitute the higher-level time-table, over a period of 2 years. These break down in the final analysis to ten 6-week teaching units each allowing for thirty lessons. There are other times available, but these are, roughly speaking, absorbed by the mechanics of handling materials, by revision and by periodic examination. Some are absorbed by unforseen schedule clashes, teacher illness, etc. In other words there are 150 lessons clearly available for teaching the main area, and an equal number for revision and organizing the selected and special topics, if equal weight is given to the two groupings. If a similar budgeting is allowed for Subsidiary Level the total number of full-time teaching periods runs to ninety lessons each for 2 years.

It will be observed that candidates at Subsidiary Level are to be examined on some documents in a range of thirty recommended items. Obviously these will appear in modern English and French, that is in translation, if written more than two centuries ago or if appearing originally in another language. This requirement raises the question of what might be called the "historical method" aspect of the International Baccalaureate Historical program. Obviously History consists of both the primordial events in themselves and the first-, second-, third- and fourth-hand accounts we may have of given historical events. It is vital for History students to learn to judge the validity of any given historical account by exercising judgment regarding the internal evidence which any given document can reveal about its origins and basic orientation. It is not enough to cite classic example of the "Donation of Constantine" to illustrate historical forgery. The laboratory scientists have long been rightly scornful of the unscientific methods and faulty conclusions drawn by historians (not to mention other fellow travellers in the Study of Man series). The special paper should be so planned as to allow for exercise of judgment in historical documentation. But at least one such exercise should be engaged upon during each 6-week unit during each year. Naturally the writing of critical essays should allow for such activity. But it may mean that a series of original documents should be collated either in a group oral exercise or by students who write *précis* or similar compositions on the data offered them. The use of a number of textbooks and of printed documentary material in itself offers an impression of variety of interpretation. A brief exposition of propaganda analysis might well be given at the outset of the course. What should be achieved is a clear understanding of what constitutes sound historical method.

Finally this introduction would not be complete without indicating that an imperative is laid upon History teachers in the ISES experiment to "program" their courses to the best of their abilities. By this word "program" is meant the bringing to bear upon the teaching of History of all the auxiliary audio–visual techniques which are available. The syllabus outline indicates that the social, cultural, scientific and intellectual aspects of any given section of historical instruction must not be neglected. The study of Plastic Arts, of Music, of urbaniza-tion and of fine literature of a given age and culture can best be demonstrated by audio–visual techniques. It is, of course, another matter to catch the essence of the audio–visual data in words on paper. Obviously this must be done. Otherwise the aids are as diffuse as daily commercial television. In fact the art of transmuting the essence of a truly imaginative History program into tightly disciplined prose is one of the most useful activities on such a course.

Thus it may be understood that History in the International Baccalaureate program is far more an art by which a way of dealing with complex material is developed than the storing away of encyclopedic data. Naturally, the student is expected to know his field of History, but that knowledge is clearly secondary to the systematic use to which it may be put.

STANDARDS OF WORK EXPECTED AT HIGHER AND SUBSIDIARY LEVELS

History, curiously enough, occupies an underprivileged place in the major educational systems in the globe. Generally speaking in the Socialist nations, History is a subservient topic in dialectical theory. In continental countries it is often a minor subject, examined only orally and superficially, wholly over-shadowed, in fact, by the "dissertation" which allows the candidate to show his virtuosity in his native language while dealing logically and exhaustively with some literary theme. At best History teaching is Europe centered. In the United States a narrower ethnocentricity prevails. In Latin America this tendency is carried to even greater extremes. Rather naturally, the developing nations have also tended towards ethnocentricity, though sometimes an incongruous European orientation hangs on from "colonial" days. On the other hand, in Scandinavia, a serious attempt has been made to take account of each of the five versions normal in the area. Britain has possibly laid the greatest stress on History as a major subject, though traditionally the subject is as insular as only our British colleagues are capable of making it (i.e. everything right, objective and disinterested relates to the core of British character).

Generally speaking, History has been allowed a minor role in a curriculum ever more crowded by the scientific subjects. On occasion it has been united with civics to produce a poor apology for any given national mythology, on the pretence that sound citizenship is being built. Obviously the point of view of ISES is deliberately opposed to such approaches. The proponents of the International Baccalaureate program believe that the objectivity and sense of proportion with which Thucidides conceived his Peloponnesian War must be the root principle of the History program which takes its honorable place as one of the Studies of Man. Tough-minded clarity, willingness to appreciate universals and basic intellectual honesty are the ingredients expected of students taking the International Baccalaureate course. In addition they are expected to be able to marshal specific facts to support positions taken in oral examination and, more importantly, in lucid prose when composing 4 hours of examination papers.

In other words the standard for excellence more nearly resembles the British scholarship-level papers than other national examinations. Gifted students are expected to do university-level work (Junior year in most colleges in the USA); less gifted students are expected to perform at British A-level (but not so widely), similar to American advanced placement (but more narrowly). At this point the work resembles the European "dissertation" (but not so profoundly). Expectation of excellence, particularly of students from an international milieu, brings with it agreeable surprises. It must be borne in mind at all times that the International Baccalaureate is designed for gifted students who desire entry into the best universities in the world.

At Subsidiary Level the intention is to teach to the level of a good sixth form (grade twelve) class; that is roughly at the level of major subjects in European examinations, and above the rather momentary O-level of the British GCE and well above that of normal CEEB subjects.

The following questions selected from experimental ISES History papers at both levels give some clue as to the standard required. (No higher-level gamma papers have been set to date.)

Gamma (Subsidiary)

Occident

1. Why was the medieval Western empire known as Holy, Roman and German? Discuss the evolution of imperial authority. [1965.]
2. To what extent does the twelfth century cultural revival in Europe invalidate the statement "men were not at this time interested so much in living fully as dying safely"? [1965.]

Orient

1. Discuss the interpenetration of Orient and Occident brought about by Marco Polo. [1965.]
2. What cultural influences are to be found in the ruins of Ankhor Vat? [1966.]

Beta (Higher Level)

Americas

1. "In the character of the Americans a love of freedom is the predominating feature which marks and distinguishes the whole; and as an ardent is always a jealous affection, your colonies become suspicious, restive and intractable whenever they see the least attempt to wrest from them by force or shuffle from them by chicane, what they think the only advantage worth living for." (From a speech by Edmund Burke to the House of Commons in 1775.) How far does this extract explain the origins of the American Revolution? [1965.]
2. Why were the indians of South America integrated while those of North America were segregated? [1965.]

Europe–Russia

1. "It is obvious that the French and Russian Revolutions move from moderation through extremism to authoritarianism." Attack or defend this statement. [1966.]
2. "In the last analysis the basic causes of the First World War were economic." Agree or disagree with this statement. [1966.]

Africa–Middle East

1. Discuss the course of Dutch settlement in South Africa in the eighteenth century. [1965.]
2. How were the pirates of the North African coast subdued? [1965.]

Asia–Oceania

1. Analyze the following statements for their validity:

   "In India we encounter the most colossal example history affords of the successful administration by men of European blood of a thickly populated region of another continent". (Attributed to F. D. Roosevelt.)

   "I came reluctantly to the conclusion that the British connection had made India more helpless than she ever was before ... I have no doubt whatsoever that both India and the town-dwellers of India will have to answer for this crime against humanity..."

   (Attributed to M. H. Gandhi.) [1965.]
2. Why did Russia expand into the Far East? Did she succeed in doing so? [1966.]

Beta (Subsidiary)

Americas

1. Why did the Spanish–American war occur and what were its results? [1964.]
2. Why was monarchy attempted in Mexico and Brazil and why did it fail? [1965.]

Europe–Russia

1. "The industrial revolution started in England 50 years before it started on the European continent." Discuss. [1964.]
2. What similarities can be found between the Congress of Vienna and the League of Nations? [1965.]

Africa–Middle East

1. Explain the persistence of French cultural influences in the Eastern Mediterranean. [1966.]
2. Comment on the significance of the following extract from A. E. Scrivener's *Journal* (1913) regarding the policy of the Congo Free State:
   "To kill people off in the wholesale way in which it has been done in this lake district because they would not bring in sufficient quantity of rubber to satisfy the white man—and now here is an empty country and a very diminishing output of rubber as an inevitable consequence." [1965.]

Asia–Oceania

1. How did Japan emerge as a world power? [1966.]
2. What were the repercussions of the Second World War in Asia or in Oceania? [1965.]

Alpha (Higher)

Americas

1. Contrast and compare the Peron and Castro dictatorships. [1963]
2. Discuss the view that US foreign policy since 1945 has been dominated by the fear of communism. [1964.]

Europe–Russia

1. Describe the main stages in the Russian Civil War, 1917–21. [1967.]
2. In what way was Munich a decisive turning point affecting the balance of power in Europe? [1965.]

Africa–Middle East

1. Why did their African colonies become financial liabilities to the colonial powers between the two world wars? [1963.]
2. Give an account of Arab nationalism since 1952. [1964.]

Asia–Oceania

1. Discuss Japan's bid for power in China from 1915 to 1945. [1963.]
2. Discuss the growth of the socialist movement in Australia and New Zealand. [1966.]

Alpha (Subsidiary)

Americas

1. To what extent did the "New Deal" save American capitalism? [1965.]
2. How does the linguistic problem affect Canadian politics? [1966.]

Europe–Russia

1. How do you account for the rise of the Fascist and Nazi parties? [1967.]
2. Do you think the Soviet Union has really adopted a policy of coexistence since the Second World War? If so, why? [1967.]

Africa–Middle East

1. What are the political, social and economic factors determining the aspirations of contemporary black Africa towards a unitary or federal state? [1965.]
2. Why was Mustapha Kemal interested in Western methods? [1966.]

Asia–Oceania

1. Why did the communists come to power in China in 1949? [1966.]
2. Discuss the role of neutralism in Indian foreign policy. [1965.]

The foregoing have been drawn as fairly representative of the thinking of History panels in the ISES program over a period of 5 years. During this period, 102 questions on the Americas were written (5 duplicates), half of which were essentially non-political in orientation. In the Europe–Russia section 232 questions were written (8 duplicates), a third of which were non-political. Sixty-two questions dealt with Africa–Middle East (9 duplicates), half of which were non-political. A larger total of 95 questions (6 duplicates) dealt with Asia–Oceania, a third of which were non-political. Finally, 26 questions (2 duplicates) dealt with the world at large. Thus, a total of 517 questions have been formulated (30 duplicates), constituting a sufficient body of experience to allow for a certain perspective which cannot be found in the other more recently developed disciplines in the ISES program.

As there are, in fact, ten areas for which somewhat detailed outlines could be made in this teachers' guide, each constituting a possible major field of study, the size of the guide could easily get out of hand. Consequently it is our intention to present nine very abbreviated programs and one in rather full detail. The abbreviated syllabuses follow:

I. Gamma (Higher and Subsidiary Levels)

A. Occident

1. Byzantine Empire — end classical age.
2. Islam — Arab and Turkish Empires.
3. Holy Roman Empire — Papacy — Norse conquests.
4. Crusades — rise of towns — end paganism.
5. Scholasticism — Gothic architecture — universities.

B. Orient

1. End Gupta Empire — Rajput States of India.
2. Islamic Ghaznavid Empire. Slave dynasty of Delhi.
3. Tang, Five and Mongol dynasties of China.
4. Silla, Korea; Fugiwara, Japan.
5. South-east Asian States — cultural interpenetration.

II. Beta (Higher and Subsidiary Levels)

A. Americas

1. End French Empire — revolt British colonies.
2. Formation and development of United States.
3. Revolt of Latin America — formation of states there.
4. US Civil War — formation of Canada.
5. Contemporary USA and pan-America.

B. Europe–Russia

1. Enlightened despotism — French Revolution.
2. Napoleon — Congress of Vienna — Revolution of 1848.
3. Second Empire — unification Italy and Germany.
4. Imperialism — First World War — Soviet Revolution.
5. League of Nations — Second World War — Cold War period.

C. Africa–Middle East

1. Napoleonic incursion — collapse of Janissaries.
2. Suez Canal Politics—Turkey, "sick man of Europe".
3. Barbary pirates — race for African colonies.
4. Mandate system for Middle East — Israel.
5. Arab nationalism — African independence.

D. Asia–Oceania

1. British in India — Russians in Siberia.
2. Rivalry for China — open door — republic set up.
3. Colonization of Australia and New Zealand.
4. Modernization of Japan — Pacific, Second World War.
5. Independence of India, Southeast Asia — communism in China.

III. Alpha (Higher and Subsidiary Levels)

A. Americas

1. First World War — isolationism of USA.
2. US Marines — Peronist-type regimes.
3. Depression — New Deal — FDR — McKenzie-King.
4. Second World War — creation of United Nations.
5. NATO — Korean War — Vietnamese War — Cuba.

B. Europe–Russia (see below)

C. Africa–Middle East

1. Balkanization of Middle East — Arab nationalism.
2. Westernization of Turkey — Italian conquest of Ethiopia.
3. South African apartheid — effect Second World War.
4. French–British decolonization — Portuguese stand.
5. Algerian and Israeli wars — Middle East petrol.

D. Asia–Oceania

1. Washington Naval Conference — infiltration of Manchuria.
2. Far Eastern Republic — Outer Mongolia.
3. Mukden Incident — greater co-prosperity sphere.
4. India–Pakistan–Indonesia–Indo–Chinese imbroglio.
5. Communist China — Korean War — SEATO.

The following is a detailed syllabus of the **Europe–Russia** section of the alpha syllabus (Higher and Subsidiary Levels).

I. First 6-week teaching period
A. General subjects — *First World War and Peace Settlements*

1. First fortnight — *Background of First World War: Russian Revolution*
   (a) Triple Alliance *vs.* Triple Entente.
   (b) Russian *vs.* German Bosphorus interests.
   (c) Arms Race – colonial rivalry — anti -Victorian sentiment.
   (d) Sarajevo — July 1914 — Marne — Turkish involvement — Japan.
   (e) Italy — Bulgaria — Verdun, 1916 — Roumania.
   (f) Fall of Tsar — Kerensky — American entry — Brest-Litovsk — second Marne.

2. Second fortnight — *Post-war settlements*
   (a) Collapse of Central powers — Armistice — blockade.
   (b) Allied negotiations in Russia – Czech Legion.
   (c) Peace negotiations in Paris — five treaties.
   (d) League of Nations — American withdrawal.
   (e) End of Russian Civil War — allied intervention.
   (f) Nature of Lenin's Marxism and Civil War communism.

3. Third fortnight — *Post-war states*
   (a) Germany, Weimar Republic — Silesian — League settlement.

    (b) Reparations, inflation, Ruhr Dawes Plan.

    (c) Austria, Hungary, Czechoslovakia, Yugoslavia.

    (d) Turkey, Greece, Albania, Bulgaria, Roumania.

    (e) Poland, Lithuania, Latvia, Esthonia, Finland.

    (f) Belgium, France, Britain, Irish Free State.

II. Second 6-week teaching period

B. General subjects — *Two decades between two wars*

    1. First fortnight — *Normalization of relations between states*
        (a) NEP, Rapallo. Recognition of Soviet Union.
        (b) Little Entente — Locarno — Germany to League.
        (c) Stalin–Trotsky struggle — First Five Years Plan — purges.
        (d) Kellogg–Briand Pact — Litvinov protocol.
        (e) British General Strike — Zinoviev letter — Socialists to power.
        (f) French revaluation of franc — Young Plan.

    2. Second fortnight — *Rise of Fascism*
        (a) Turkish, Hungarian, Spanish and Bulgarian models.
        (b) Mussolini's Corporate State and *coup d'état*.
        (c) Portugal, Poland, Lithuania, Roumania, Albania, Yugoslavia follow.
        (d) Effect of US depression — war debt fiasco.
        (e) League failures with Japan and disarmament.
        (f) Hitler's national socialist state and its establishment.

    3. Third fortnight — *Collapse of Peace*
        (a) Austrian fascism — attempted Nazi coup.
        (b) Italian–Ethiopian War — reoccupation of Rhineland.
        (c) Spanish Civil War — Japanese–Chinese War — Greek fascism.
        (d) Annexation of Austria — Munich — Soviet Army purge — Memel.
        (e) Axis — seizure Prague and Albania — Molotov–von Ribbentrop Pact.
        (f) Invasion of Danzig and Poland — Soviet occupation — "Phony War",

III. Third 6-week teaching period

C. General subject — *Second World War and occupation of Germany*

1. First fortnight — *Establishment of Neuropa*
    (a) Finnish–Russian War — fall Scandinavia — Low Countries.
    (b) Fall France — Vichy — Russian occupation Baltic States.
    (c) Battle for Britain — Roumania, Bulgaria, Yugoslavia, Greece.
    (d) Ethiopia — Russian–German War — Atlantic Charter — Pearl Harbour.
    (e) El Alamein, Leningrad, Stalingrad, North African landings.
    (f) Sicily, Italy, Russian War, D-day, end second Finnish War.

2. Second fortnight — *Creation of United Nations*
    (a) UNRRA — Nazi barbarities — Dunbarton Oaks, etc.
    (b) Liberation Low Countries — Eastern Europe.
    (c) Collapse Fascist Italy, Germany — freeing of Scandinavia.
    (d) Casablanca, Cairo, Tehran, Yalta, San Francisco, agreements.
    (e) Division of Germany. Berlin, Austria, Vienna.
    (f) Potsdam and Hiroshima, origins of Cold War.

3. Third fortnight — *Cold War Period*
    (a) Five Small Nation treaties — Peoples' Republics.
    (b) Greek Civil War — Truman Doctrine — Marshall Plan.
    (c) Fall Czechoslovakia, Western union — NATO — Warsaw group.
    (d) Berlin blockade — evolution two Germanies — Yugoslavia.
    (e) Korean War — Council of Europe — coal–steel community.
    (f) Soviet partisans of peace movement.

IV. Fourth 6-week teaching period

D. General subject — *Post-Stalin epoch*

    1. First fortnight — *Attempt at East–West accommodation*
- (a) Creation Common Market — European *vs.* community.
- (b) Death Stalin — Malenkov *vs.* Khruschev — de-Stalinization.
- (c) Rise of Adenauer and Germany — Geneva Conferences.
- (d) First Suez War and Hungarian Rebellion — Eisenhower Doctrine.
- (e) Algerian War — creation of De Gaulle Republic.

    2. Second fortnight — *Contemporary Europe*
- (a) Decolonization French Africa — British Empire — Portugal.
- (b) USA — Cuban crisis — nuclear treaty.
- (c) Fall Khruschev — Kosygin Regime — anti-Chinese policy.
- (d) Ecumenical Trends in Roman Catholic Church — protestantism.
- (e) French bid for European leadership — Roumanian independence.
- (f) Second Suez War — diplomatic initiatives — Greek *coup d'état*.

    3. Third fortnight — *Toward a federal Europe*
- (a) European Payments Union set up.
- (b) Rome Treaty on Common Market and Euratom signed.
- (c) Strasbourg Parliament created.
- (d) GATT established.
- (e) Kennedy Round Agreements signed.
- (f) International Baccalaureate following European example.

V. Fifth 6-week teaching period

E. General subject — *Culture of contemporary Europe*

    1. First fortnight — *To the Great Depression*
- (a) Achievement of Equal Rights for Women.
- (b) Revolution in Physics–Biochemistry.

(c) Psychology — Behaviorism, Gestalt, Jung–Freud.

(d) Philosophy — Irrationalism and Logical Empiricism.

(e) Literature — Proust, Mann, Huxley, Eliot, Rilke.

(f) Music — Stravinsky, Prokofieff, Schönberg.

2. Second fortnight — *To the end of the Stalin epoch*

(a) Art — fauvism, cubism, expressionism, abstract art.

(b) Picasso, Utrillo, Rouault, Modigliani, Chagall, Matisse.

(c) Post-cubism, dadaïsm, surrealism, figurative painting.

(d) Sculpture — Brancuŝi, Pevsner, Moore, Mobiles.

(e) Architecture — Empire State, Grundvig church, Le Corbusier.

(f) Post — Second World War painting — Klee, Pollock, Buffet.

(g) Tachisme, Cobra group, Nervi school, Ponti, Niemeyer.

From 1953

3. Third fortnight — *Till today*

(a) Literature of engagement — Hemingway, etc.

(b) History — Spengler, Toynbee, Crole, Bloch.

(c) Economics — Keynes — reactions.

(d) Italian and Swedish films, theatre.

(e) Music — Shostakovich, Hindemith, post-Schönberg, Beatles.

(f) Maritain, neo-orthodox, protestantism, worker priests.

(g) Impact of America on Europe — reactions.

It will be observed that the detailed outline is made to fit a six-lesson pattern for each fortnight: that is to push the subsidiary program to its greatest possibility. Nearly double the time is left for higher-level instruction. Any one 6-week period should be sufficient for teaching a selected subject — which obviously would be tailored to the requirements of the title of that selected subject. It is clear, however, that sufficient time is allowed in three 6-week periods to cover the work required.

This leaves one 6-week period for concentration on special subject work, and this could be scattered about during the final year. The remaining 6-week period is left for revision of major and selected areas of study. Obviously not all teachers are as efficient as others. Interests will vary. Thus the patterns suggested above are not rules to live by, but pointers to possible solutions.

The special topics are selected by students from a list of some fifteen proposed by the chief examiner—in May preceding the final examination—and at the suggestion of the heads of History departments, who will be active in the International Baccalaureate experimental program. The following are some of the typical examples of subjects used during the original 5-year period (there have been none arranged for the gamma stream to date).

Beta Higher Level
1. Role of Radical parties in nineteenth-century politics. [1965.]
2. The migration of African peoples. [1966.]
3. The price revolution. [1967.]

Alpha Higher Level
1. Examination of interpenetration in the field of civil disobedience between Occident and Orient. [1963.]
2. The due process of law in emergent nations. [1964.]
3. The significance of the "absurd" in modern art. [1967.]
(A total of sixty-eight special subjects has been formulated to date.)

In the future it will be the policy of ISES to provide a short recommended bibliography with each special topic offered. There is appended at this point a brief recommended bibliography (only in the English language) applicable to the ten areas of specialization possible. In the case of alpha Europe–Russia the list is appropriately enlarged to fit in with the syllabus pattern above presented.

Gamma—Occident

KNOWLES, *Evolution of Medieval Thought*, Longmans, 1962.

LAMONTE, *World of Middle Ages*, Appleton–Century, 1949.

TREVOR ROPER, *Rise of Christian Europe*, Thames & Hudson, 1965.

Gamma—Orient

BEASLEY and PULLEYBANK, *Historians of China and Japan*, 1961.

HALL, *History of South-East Asia*, Macmillan, 1960.

MORELAND and CHATTERGEE, *Short History of India*, Longmans, 1957.

Beta—Americas

NEVINS and COMMAGER, *Short History of US*, Modern Library, 1956.

DOZER, *Latin America*, McGraw-Hill, 1962.

MASTERS, *Short History of Canada*, Anvil, 1958.

Beta—Europe–Russia

LANGER, *Rise of Modern Europe*, Harper, 1935.

SETON-WATSON, *From Lenin to Khruschev*, Prager, 1960.

TAYLOR, *Origins of Second World War*, Athenaeum, 1962.

Beta—Africa–Middle East

OLIVER and FAGE, *Short History of Africa*, Penguin, 1962.

STAVRIANOS, *Balkans Since 1453*, Reinhart, 1958.

KIRK, *Short History of Middle East*, Methuen, 1958.

Beta—Asia–Oceania

REICHAUER and FAIRBANK, *East Asia Great Tradition*, Houghton–Mifflin, 1964.

PANIKKAR, *Asia and Western Dominance*, Allen & Unwin, 1953.

PIKE, *Australia, the Quiet Continent*, Cambridge, 1962.

Alpha—Americas

GOLDMAN, *Crucial Decade and After*, Vintage, 1960.
AREVALO, *Anti-Communism in Latin America*, Stuart, 1964.
COMMAGER, *American Mind*, Paperback, 1955.

Alpha—Europe–Russia (see later)

Alpha—Africa–Middle East

CAMERON, *African Revolution*, Thames & Hudson, 1961.
HAHN, *North Africa*, Public Affairs Press, 1960.
GABRIELI, *Arab Revival*, Thames & Hudson, 1961.

Alpha—Asia–Oceania

CLUBB, *20th Century China*, Columbia, 1964.
TAYLOR, *Far-East in Modern World*, Methuen, 1956.
SCHWARTZ, *Tsars, Mandarins and Commissars*, Lippincott, 1964.

It is possible that some beta books will prove useful in the alpha course.

Alpha—Europe–Russia Fuller Bibliography

ROSTOW, *Stages of Economic Growth*, Cup, 1960.
LANDAUER, *European Socialism*, California, 1959.
HAYES, *Nationalism, a Religion*, Macmillan, 1960.
WERTH, *France 1940–1955*, Holt, 1956.
ARENDT, *Origins of Totalitarianism*, Harcourt Brace, 1951.
BULLOCK, *Hitler: A Study in Tyranny*, Odhams, 1962.
SETON-WATSON, *Eastern Europe*, Cambridge, 1946.
HUDSON, *Hard and Bitter Peace*, Pall Mall, 1966.
BOYD, *Atlas of World Affairs*, Methuen, 1957.
HUGHES, *Contemporary Europe*, Prentice-Hall, 1961.

TAAFÉ, *Atlas of Soviet Affairs*, Methuen, 1965.

KOHN, *Modern World*, Collier–Macmillan, 1963.

KOCHAN, *Making of Modern Russia*, Penguin, 1962.

KETELBY, *History of Modern Times*, Harrap, 1964.

KENNAN, *Russia and the West*, Hutchinson, 1961.

CRANKSHAW, *Khruschev's Russia*, Penguin, 1959.

Discovering Art, 20th century, Vols. 1 and 2, London, 1966.

SABINE, *History of Political Theory*, Harrap, 1964.

ISES is always receptive to constructive criticisms offered in connection with the development of its program. This is particularly true regarding the teachers' guide for History.

SYLLABUS

INTERNATIONAL SCHOOL OF GENEVA

HISTORY A.D. 550–1250 FOR CLASS NINE
1967–1968

INTRODUCTION

1. General outline of content and aim

With the collapse of the revived political power of the Roman Empire of Justinian in Western Europe, the center of gravity definitely passed to the East. The rise of Islam then introduced an area of close contact between Europe, Africa and Asia, and at the same time challenged the religious and cultural climate of christianity. Whereas the culture of Europe had been unified by the Graeco–Roman ethos, outside influences, diverse in origin, began to dominate it from the sixth century onwards. Likewise, European development became less important within the world scheme of this period than it had been during the previous eight centuries.

The syllabus for class nine recognizes this partial eclipse of Europe. The work for the first term is designed to show how the old worlds of Rome and Persia were replaced by the new, more primitive, but potentially more vital worlds of the Germanic kingdoms and the Islamic Empire; and how new social and political orders evolved out of a mingling of these old and new elements. During the second term, classes are given a chance to compare these upheavals in Europe and North Africa and the Middle East with the more stable and exclusive developments of Asia and the Americas, and the more primitive growth of sub-Saharan Africa. The sterile civilization of pre-Colombian America in particular demonstrates the need of outside stimulus and interpenetration of ideas for cultural vitality, elsewhere provided by the Arabs and eventually the Mongols. The third term is devoted to the re-emergence of Europe as a vital force under the impact both of outside stimulus and internal competition. Here, classes are brought to a point from which they can look ahead to the increasing dominance of European ideas in world affairs in the early modern period, and understand the advantages and disadvantages arising from this.

2. General advantages and outlines of teaching methods and materials

Evidently the details mentioned in the week-by-week outlines are more than can be dealt with in three 45-minute periods. This is necessary to allow each teacher to select materials to fulfil the general aims of each section according to his own judgement of the interests and abilities of his classes, from a full knowledge of what is, in fact, significant in that period. However, in any 6-week period, each group of classes will be dealing with broadly similar problems. Much of the teaching time will be used by the teacher in directly outlining developments and problems, and in leading the class to discuss the relative importances of events and situations and to be aware of reasons and consequences. However, class time will also be given to the written preparation of summaries and reports, to set discussions and debates and, in some cases with some classes, to more practical work. This is necessary because in the teaching of History it is as important to give guidance in the presentation and use of information as in the gaining of it. Where visual materials relevant to a subject are available, exposition and discussion will center round them. As a general rule each weekly group of material will include some documentation, written, visual or aural, to be used for its intrinsic value to the topic and as a regular exercise in the technique of extracting and evaluating first-hand information. Underlying the whole method of teaching is the concept that beyond ascertainable facts there is no exact answer to historical problems. Where categorical statements have been made, there has often been a non-historical purpose at work. This is not to say that the aims and methods of this syllabus are leading the student to cynically non-aligned positions, but that one of the most important parts of education is the inculcation of the desire to reach to the truth on the basis of one's own judgements.

Each weekly section of the syllabus contains a statement of aims and suggested methods, together with some exact references from which the teacher can obtain detailed information for the preparation of his lessons and for the preparation of materials for classes to use.

OCCIDENTAL SECTION II OF CLASS 9 SYLLABUS OUTLINE

First 6–Week Period of First Term of Year

Medieval Europe—Eastern Mediterranean A.D. 550–800

Aims. In general the first 6 weeks is given over to comprehending the "Dark Ages", the post-Justinian epoch, till the creation of Charlemagne's Empire in contrast to the brilliant creation of the Islamic civilization under the Ummyads,

First Week

Subject. Nature of medievalism.

Details

    I. 1. *Economic patterns* — change from city to rural economy — *manorialism*, origins in Diocletian's Reforms.
      2. Dying *classicism* culturally — Roman control of *Mare Nostrum*.
      3. Ancestors of political *feudalism* in tribal arrangements of Germanic kingdoms.
    II. 1. Notion of *Papacy* as inheritor of Western Empire.
      2. *Monasticism* — particularly Benedictines devoted to preserving classical record.
      3. *Caesaropapism* as practiced in Eastern Empire.
    III. 1. Struggle between Orthodox and *Monophysites*.
      2. Struggle between *Nestorians* and Zoroastrians in Persian Empire.
      3. Appearance of *Avars* as successors to Huns.

Materials

BERNARD and HODGES, *Readings in European History*, 63.
MUMFORD, *City in History*, chap. 9.
LAMONTE, *World of Middle Ages*, chaps. 5 and 12.
CARROLL et al., *Development of Civilization*, 186–96, 176–8 and 198–203.
OSTROGORSKY, *History of Byzantine State*, 63–78.
PREVITE-ORTON, *Shorter Cambridge Medieval History* **1**, 185–200.

Aims. To get it straight that economic medievalism was in existence in the West for three centuries before this time, that politically it would only appear in three centuries. As classicism disappeared in West, the Benedictine Order was pledged to keep it alive.

Methods. To direct students in sources to prove thesis declared above. Act out Cloister.

Second Week

Subject. Lombards — Reforms of Maurice — Persian War.
Details

- I. 1. *Italy* at end of Reconquest — *Three Chapters* — condition of Papacy.
  2. Invasion of *Lombards* — social structure of tribe — division of Italy.
  3. Visigothic reaction — collapse of *Justin II.*
- II. 1. Work of Tiberias and Maurice — reform of Army — *Ars Militaris.*
  2. Creation of *Papal State* by Gregory the Great.
  3. *Phocas* and attack of Chosroes II.
- III. 1. Rise of *Heraclius* to power.
  2. Course of Avar and *Persian Wars* to conclusion.
  3. *Religious policy* of Heraclius.

Materials

Penguin Atlas of Medieval History Maps 562, 600 and 626.
LaMonte, *World of Middle Ages* 67–73 and 117–19.
Ostrogorsky, *History of Byzantine State,* 79–98.
Previte-Orton, *Shorter Cambridge Medieval History* **1**, 201–20.
Discovering Art **2** (23) 169–76 and No. 24.

Aims. To trace the decline of the Byzantine Empire from A.D. 565 to 610, then to trace its deadly struggle with Persian Empire, noting military reform and permanent division of Italy. To prepare the ground for the Moslem erruption.

Methods. Show Byzantine Art to give clarity to culture (also Persian) debate the wisdom of Maurice and Heraclius's military and civil reforms.

Third Week

Subject. Rise of Islamic Empire — fall of Persia.
Details

- I. 1. Arabia on the eve of *Mohammed's* career. Life and influence of the prophet on his own society.

2. Condition of the *Byzantine* Empire in the Seventh century. Situation on the immediate borders of Arabia—collapse of *Ghassanid* Empire, successor to Himyrites.

II. 1. *Religious* concepts and *social* concepts of Islam, contrasted with those of Christian and Zoroastrian areas.

2. Economic and political urges to the expansion of Islam. Collapse of resistance in *Middle Eastern* Mediterranean.

3. Early period of expansion after Mohammed's death. *Four Companions* 632–61 — *communism.*

III. 1. *Spread* of Islam West and East during the Umayyad period — to about A.D. 750.

2. *Arabian Empire* — its evolution.

3. International *Abbasid Empire* to A.D. 800 — its evolution.

Materials

HITTI, *History of the Arabs.*
Penguin Atlas of Medieval History, Maps.
LAMONTE, *World of Middle Ages*, 93–108.
Historical Atlas of Muslim Peoples, 2–5.
BINGHAM, CONROY and IKLE, *History of Asia* **1,** 63–72 and 74–88.
Larousse Encyclopaedia of Medieval History, 260–5.
CARROLL *et al.*, *Development of Civilization* **1,** 227–31.

Aims. To show a key period and area of interpenetrating cultures. To establish the details of the roots of Islamic–Arab culture as a link between East and West. To examine the effect of sophisticated city cultures on an adjustable primitive religious–political ideology.

Methods. Explanation of outline development of material in each lesson. Class to make simple time chart of material. Illustration by slides and maps of distinct art forms of

Islam. Reading of comparative extracts from Koran, Bible and Zoroastrian writing. Discussion by class of differences.

Fourth Week

Subject. Collapse of Visigoths — evolution of Franks.
Details

I. 1. Development of *Visigothic* Kingdom once settled in Spain and south-west Gaul, after Half-Byzantine conquest.
   2. *Conversion* to catholicism — Civil Wars — Jewish question.
   3. Effect of *Islamic conquest* of Visigoths (711–20). (N.B. Clash of primitive Islam and primitive christianity.) Role of Mosarabs — Septimania — attack of Franks survival in Asturias.

II. 1. *Clovis Grandsons* — Brunhilde *vs.* Fredegonde — collapse of Clovis Government.
   2. Rise of *Mayors of Palace* — early period.
   3. Type of christianity adopted by Franks. Its importance to them politically. Contrast with Visigothic christianity and with imported *Irish monasticism*.

III. 1. Career of *Charles Martel* (717–41). Extinction of Merovingians.
   2. Establishment of Frankish Kingdom. *Donation of Pepin.*
   3. Repulse of Islamic penetration into France. Significance of this. Creation of *landed gentry*.
   4. Creation of Papal States. Emergence of concept of papacy — extinction of *exarchate of Ravenna* and Lombard Kingdom.

Materials

Penguin Atlas of Medieval History, Maps.

LaMonte, *World of Middle Ages*, 152–5.

Larousse Encyclopaedia of Medieval History, 248–51 and 267–9.

Steinburg, *Historical Tables*, 9–13.

Aims. To show why one political society succeeds in a crisis when another fails. To emphasize the historical importance of geographical position, personal opportunism and chance in historical development. To indicate the degree of cultural vacuum left in Western Europe by the Roman decline. To show the setting in which the Papacy began to emerge as a world force. To contrast with the impact of Islam on Eastern Europe. To show the development of the self-sufficient Frankish economy in contrast to the previous open economy.

Methods. Outline of material in each lesson. Concentration on personalities involved leading to a debate. Drawing of annotated map to show reasons for relative success and failure. Discussion of differences between closed and open economies.

Fifth Week

Subject. Anglo–Saxon–Celtic evolution.

Details.

> I. 1. *Arthur* and traditional merging of two *heptarchies*.
> 2. Christianizing of *Pictland*.
> 3. South Saxon and Jutish leadership — *catholicism* introduced.
> II. 1. Rivalry with *Essex* and *Northumbria*.
> 2. Council of *Whitby* — rise of pagan Mercia.
> 3. Work of *Theodore of Tarsus*.
> III. 1. *Irish missionary* work on continent.
> 2. *Venerable Bede* — Book of Kells.
> 3. Emergence of *Wessex*.

Materials

SAYLES, *Medieval Foundations of England*.

WILSON, *Anglo Saxons*, chaps. 1 (29–36), 2 (54–60), 3 (71–100), and 4.

DE PAOR, *Xtian Ireland*, chaps. 1 and 2.

CHADWICK, *Celtic Britain*, chaps. 1–4, 7 and 8,

Aims. To trace disappearance of one completely paganized area at fall of Ancient Rome — to note rivalry of Celtic and Roman faiths not only in England but on continent. To produce insight into pre-Viking–Norman Britain.

Methods. To assign essay on some aspect of the religious problem from pelagianism onward to illustrate unusual character of island civilization.

Sixth Week

Subject. Avars, Khazars and Magyars.
Details

> I. 1. Appearance of *Avars* — problem for Byzantines into Persian wars.
> 2. Effect on *Frankish realm.*
> 3. Creation of *ring* — destruction by Charlemagne.
> II. 1. *Khazars* — allies of Byzantium — conversion to Judaism.
> 2. Movement of lesser *Bulgars* to Danube region. Rise of Khanate.
> 3. *Georgia,* remnants of Goths' other neighbours.
> III. 1. Origins of *Magyars.*
> 2. Conquest of *Hungary.*
> 3. Post-Carolingian *land piracy.*

Materials

VERNADSKY, *Origins of Russia.*
SINOR, *Hungary,* 17–18, chaps 2 and 3.

Aims. To note character of nomads coming into contract with settled civilizations, and more universal religious bodies—role in dark ages.

Methods. Draw maps showing wanderings of major groups.

ORIENTAL SECTION OF CLASS 9

Second 6-Week Period of First Term of Year

Medieval Europe—Eastern Mediterranean A.D. 800–1000

Aims. In general, the second 6 weeks is given over to the second or darker of the dark ages in the West from Charlemagne to Otto III. The Norse threat is met, while the Western Church begins to revive. The Abbasid Empire goes into decline as Islam multilateralizes.

First week (three teaching periods throughout).

First week

Subject. Charlemagne's Empire.

Details

- I. 1. Inheritance from *Pepin I*.
  - 2. *Character*, education, reputation.
  - 3. Wars and *Imperial Coronation* — end Avars.
- II. 1. Imperial organization of government — *Missi Dominici* — capitularies — field of May.
  - 2. Role of clergy — relationship with Eastern Empire — *Carolingian Renaissance*.
  - 3. Succession by *Louis Pious*.
- III. 1. Grandsons — divisions — Strasbourg oath — *Verdun*.
  - 2. Evolution *Lothairs Empire*.
  - 3. Carolingian successors — Capotian succession in light of *Viking* and *Moslem* invasions.

Materials

LaMonte, *World of Middle Ages*, 155–69.

Penguin Atlas, 771, 830 and 888.

Previte-Orton, *Shorter Cambridge Medieval History* **1**, 303–60.

CARROLL et al., *Development of Civilization* **1**, 256.

PIRENNE, *Mohammed and Charlemagne*.

BERNARD and HODGES, *Readings in European History*, chap. 8.

Aims. To place Charlemagne in his proper role as Frankish chieftain, inciter of Norse raids and founder of ephemeral empire.

Methods. Map-making to note size of empire, tribes incorporated, numbers of campaigns.

Second Week

Subject. Abbasid Caliphate and its successors.

Details

    I. 1. Achlabid Emirate — Crete — Alid Emirate (emergence of *Shiites*).

       2. Idrisid Caliphate — Tulunid and Ishkidid emirates. *Abd-ar-Rahman III* and Ommiad Caliphate.

    II. 1. *Fatimid* Caliphate and *Al-Hakim* — Qarmatians.

      2. Tahirid, Samanid and *Chaznavid* emirates. Rise of ex-Buddhist Buwahids.

    III. 1. Successor emirates in Caspian area as *Buwahids* declined.

       2. *Hamdanids* — appearance of Saljuk Turks Tuchril Beg.

       3. Artistic and scientific *contributions*.

Materials

KIRK, *Short History of Middle East*.

HITTI, *History of Arabs*, 288–428.

Historical Atlas of Muslim Peoples, Maps 6–11.

NUTTING, *Arabs*.

LAMONTE, *World of Middle Ages*, 109–16.

TREVOR-ROPER, *Rise of Christian Europe*, 71–100.

PREVITE-ORTON, *Shorter Cambridge Medieval History* **1**, 238–44.

Aims. To develop notion of richness of Islamic civilization with two main branches and decentralized state of Islamic peoples—to note Arabic *vs.* Turkish rivalry, and inter-penetration with Europe and sub-continent.

Methods. Individual projects on cultures of various Muslim regions.

Third Week

Subject. Byzantines into Macedonian Dynasty.

Details

I. 1. Constans II and Arab invasion — Constantine IV. Justinian II and *collapse of Heraclian Dynasty.*
  2. Leo III and *Iconoclastic* controversy.
  3. Constantine V and *Bulgarian wars.*
II. 1. Leo IV, Constantine VI, *Irene* and Iconodule reaction.
  2. Reforms of Nicepohorus I, *Leo V* (the Amorian and Iconoclastic reaction).
  3. Michael II (Amorian dynasty) Theophilus and Incondule conclusion under *St. Theodora.*
III. 1. Michael III and *Golden Age of Byzantium.*
  2. *Basil I* and founding of Macedonian Dynasty.
  3. *Leo VI* and growth of absolutism.

Aims. To comprehend the Iconoclast–Iconodule controversy as parallel to similar Islamic movement — to appreciate regenerative powers of greatest Christian power of the day, and restore it to its rightful place in European history.

Materials

OSTROGORSKY, *History of Byzantine State*, 98–231.
CARROLL *et al.*, *Development of Civilization* **1**, 209–22.
Penguin Atlas, Maps 830, 888, 923 and 998.
PREVITE-ORTON, *Shorter Cambridge Medieval History* **1**, 210–24, 245–64.

Methods. Debate on importance of Iconoclastic controversy. Diagram of different ideas.

Fourth Week

Subject. Norse invasions West and East.

Details

- I. 1. Nature of *Norse* civilization — reasons for raids.
  2. *Raids* and settlements in British Isles — effect on Celtic and Anglo-Saxon peoples.
  3. Raids on Continent — settlement of *Normandy*.
- II. 1. Varangian raids—settlement to *Kiev—Tmutorkakan.*
  2. Evolution of Russian state — *christianity.*
  3. Development of "Nations" in *Scandinavia* — growth of christianity.
- III. 1. Settlement *Iceland,* Greenland, Vineland.
  2. *Alfred the Great* and his successors.
  3. *Vitality* of Norsemen as compared with Germans.

Materials

RICE, *Scythians.*

LaMONTE, *World of Middle Ages,* 147–52, 166–70 and 196–206.

Alfred the Great.

VERNADSKY, *History of Russia,* 29–35.

PREVITE-ORTON, *Shorter Cambridge Medieval History* **1,** 264–8, 360–8, 379–94.

VERNADSKY, *Origins of Russia,* 174–316.

Aims. To grasp the extent of Scandinavian civilization in its spread from America to Asia — its specific impact in Western Europe and development in Russia. To comprehend the immense vitality this influx contributed in contrapuntal effect with Islam.

Methods. Debate as to whether or not the christianizing of the Norsemen robbed them of their essential birthright. Map possible.

Fifth Week

Subject. Creation of feudalism.

Details

- I. 1. *Roots of feudalism* in Germanic and Roman institutions — causes for appearance.
  2. *Benefice vs. Fief* — relationship of Church and nobility in a contractual society.
  3. Survival of *fee simple* in Britain, Scandinavia, central and eastern Europe.
- II. 1. Capitulary of *Lewis the Stammerer* — centralized feudalism in Normandy.
  2. Oath-taking ceremonies — substance of oaths in legal practice — *subinfeudation.*
  3. Evolution of castles from fortified villas *Donjon keeps* to elaborate medieval structures.
- III. 1. Life of lords and ladies and other dwellers in *castles.*
  2. Importance of hunting — *tournaments* — peace and truce of God.
  3. *Courts of Love* — chivalry.

Materials

CARROLL *et al.*, *Development of Civilization* **1** (71).
TREVOR-ROPER, *Rise of Christian Europe*, chap. 3.
LAMONTE, *World of Middle Ages*, 206–25, 376–91.
PREVITE-ORTON, *Shorter Cambridge Medieval History* **1**, 418–26.
HEER, *Medieval World.*

Aims. To comprehend *ad hoc* political society made necessary by collapse of Central Government. To see its relation to a closed economic economy — and to the civilizing influences of the Church and Islam.

Methods. To write an imaginative defense of any one medieval personage caught in the complications of breaking fealty by nature of contradictions involved in subfeudation.

Sixth Week

Subject. Cluniac Order and revival of Church.

Details

    I. 1. Nature of *estates*—duality of First Estate—condition of Papacy at collapse of Frankish Empire.
       2. Weakening of *Benedictine order* in face of Irish monasticism and tripartite non-Christian maurauders.
       3. Purpose of *Cluniac Order.*
   II. 1. Effect on Church of *Ottonian Revolution.*
       2. *Parades* of saints' bones.
       3. Birth of Crusading idea—*Romanesque churches.*
  III. 1. Origins of *Investiture controversy.*
       2. Creation of *College of Cardinals.*
       3. *Filioque* separation from orthodoxy.

Materials

Discovering Art **4** (40).

PREVITE-ORTON, *Shorter Cambridge Medieval History* **1**, 471–84.

LAMONTE, *World of Middle Ages*, 170–8.

Aims. To get across the abysmal level to which the Western Church had fallen, and the essential contradiction of the Holy Roman Empire and the Cluniac reform making a marriage of convenience. To note the rejection of democracy in favor of an oligarchical set-up.

Methods. Chart of a typical Cluniac monastery to make the life of the regular clergy comprehensible.

ORIENTAL–OCCIDENTAL SECTION OF CLASS 9

SYLLABUS OUTLINE

Third 6-Week Period of Second Term of Year

Medieval Asia A.D. 550–1250

Aims. In contrast to the West, which is treated in more detail, Asia is given a seven-century survey. At the time, India was divided and half conquered by Islam, and China, though united under the Tang and Sung dynasties, went down under the Mongols. South-east Asia, Korea and Japan meanwhile developed basic patterns.

Specifically—First week (3 periods throughout).

First Week

Subject. Chalyukas, Pallavas, Harsha.

Details

    I. 1. *Background* of Hinduism, Buddhism, Jainism.
       2. Role of *Krishna* from Gita to Purana.
       3. Importance of *Ramayana* to family life.
   II. 1. Revival of *Guptas* under Harsha.
       2. Cave culture of Hindu *Chalyukyas*.
       3. Rivalry of Temple *Pallavas*.
  III. 1. Settlement of *Ceylon*.
       2. Evolution of *Theravada* Buddhism.
       3. Cult of *Shiva*.

Materials

BALLOU, *World Bible:* 65, General duties of man; 66, of associates; 68, Karma; 69, Duty to children; Sumati instructs his father; 72, Creation of castes; 144, Asvachosha's doctrine of suchness.

CARROLL *et al.*, *Development of Civilization* **1,** 478, Worship of God in many forms; 480, Ideal of family life; 484, Indian sub-continent in historical perspective.

Discovering Art, **1** (36), 177–81 (for introduction pp. 168–76 of No. 35, parallel to social and historical background).

AUBOYER, *Life in Ancient India*, 233–90.

Aims. To make Hindu revival as opposed to Buddhist and Jainist revisions of Indian way of life vivid by concentrating on two outstanding states in Deccan in contrast to short-lived revival of Gupta syncretism undertaken by Harsha.

Methods. Use of texts, perhaps through *précis*. Showing of art pictures to make styles vivid.

Second Week

Subject. Palas and Muslim Conquest to Ghaznavids.

Details

    I. 1. Summary of Hindu–Muslim *clash.*
       2. Conquests of *Sindh* by Ommiads.
       3. Buddhist *Bengal* State of Palas.
    II. 1. Saffirid reconquest of *Sindh*—Samanids.
      2. *Ghaznavid* rise and Hindustan conquests.
      3. *Ghurid* conquests into Bengal.
    III. 1. *Slave dynasty* of Delhi.
       2. Empire of *Ilutmish.*
       3. Mongol raid on *Delhi.*

Materials

Historical Atlas of Muslim Peoples IV, VII–X, XIV, XV and XX.

Discovering Art **1** (37), 193–5 (vol. 39 for background).

BINGHAM, CONROY and IKLE, *History of Asia* **1,** 200–16.

Aims. To relate the first stages of Muslim conquest of India (Pakistan particularly) to Arab, Turk and Mongol intrusions. To explain the disappearance of Buddhism from its homeland and to note how sub-continent affected Muslim art forms.

Methods. Study of comparative maps. Essay on why Hindu–Muslim conflict was so severe.

Third Week
Subject. Prataharas, Rashtrakutas, Cholas, Senas.

Details

I. 1. Hunnish state of *Prataharas*—Nygabhata II.
   2. Ellora Cave State of *Rashtrakutas.*
   3. Revival of *Chalkuyas* Dynasty.
II. 1. Revival of *Cholas* Empire in Tamiland.
   2. Great Indian *Naval Empire.*
   3. *Conquest Chalkuyas* and collapse.
III. 1. *Vishnu* worshipping Bengal State of Senas.
   2. Evolution of *Mahayana Buddhism.*
   3. *Art forms*—Hindu, Buddhist, Islamic.

Materials

Discovering Art **1** (36), 182–92.
MORELAND, *Short History of India.*
RAWLINSON, *History of India.*

Aims. To trace rivalries of principal Rajput dynasties in Deccan, Tamiland and Ceylon, with special emphasis on rise of second great Indian naval empire (Cholas). To note Islamization of Bengal and Buddhism of Ceylon.

Methods. Showing of art pictures to make styles vivid. Preparation of map on area.

Fourth Week
Subject. Tang, Five Dynasties, Sung, Chin Dynasties.

Details

I. 1. Summary *post-Han* feudalism—three kingdoms.
   2. Attempts to unify *Mahayana Buddhism*—Taoism.
   3. Hinayana, Amida and Pure-land influences—*Tantrism.*

II. 1. *Sui* Dynasty—imperial confucianism.
   2. *Tang* Dynasty—Moslem contacts.
   3. *Five small* dynasties.
III. 1. Sung Dynasty—revolution *Wang an Shih*.
    2. Kitans, Mongols, conquest *Ghenchiz Khan*.
    3. Mongol Dynasty—conquest *Sung* China.

Materials

FITZGERALD, *China: A Short Cultural History*, 249–454.
CARROLL *et al.*, *Development of Civilization* **1**, 504, Ascendancy of Buddhism; 506, Confucian revival; 508, Wang an Shih.
BALLOU, *World Bible*, 147, Elegant sayings of the Lamas; 500, Book of filial piety; 523–45, Chuang Tze.
Discovering Art **6** (26), 27–33; Nos. 27 and 28.

Aims. To capture the second and third universal empires of China (Tang and Sung) with contrasts to three kingdoms and the dynasties periods—noting Chin and Mongol eruptions.

Methods. Showing of art pictures to make styles vivid. *Précis* of document dealing with period.

Fifth Week

Subject. Silla, Koryo, Asuka, Nara, Heian, Fugiwara periods.

Details

  I. 1. *Korean* background—*Han* colonization.
    2. Great Silla and *Koryo–Asuka* kingdoms.
    3. Conquest by *Mongols*.
 II. 1. Japanese background—*Asuka–Nara* period.
    2. Rise of Fugiwara family—*Shinto*.
    3. *Heian period*—Ichijo, Sanjo and Kampaku.
III. 1. *Fugiwara Period*—Zen Buddhism.
    2. *Kamakura period*—Taira *vs.* Minimoto.
    3. *Hojo family*—Samurai, Bakufu.

Materials

SANSON, *Japan: A Short Cultural History*, 1–311.
Discovering Art 6 (31); (32), 113–23; (30) 90–94.
CARROLL *et al.*, *Development of Civilization* 1, 514, Prince Shotoku's constitution; 517, Arrival of Buddhism; 519, Cult of beauty; 521, Kitabatake Chikafusa; 522, Hojo Code; 526, Zen and Amida.

Aims. To trace development of Chinese civilization in Korea and Japan—and in latter case to note role of Shinto and Zen in creation of unique Shocunate government.

Methods. Showing of art pictures to catch essence of difference. Essay on state of Japan in any given year.

Sixth Week

Subject. Sailendra, Srivijaja, Ankhor, Burma, Thailand, Champa (medieval south-east Asia).

Details

    I. 1. *Background* Chinese–Indian interpenetration.
       2. *Sailendra* and *Srivavaja* empires in Java and Borneo.
       3. *Cholas* imperialism and arrival of Muslims.
    II. 1. First Empire of *Ankhor* in Cambodia.
      2. Rise of *Burma*.
      3. Second Empire of Ankhor—*Thailand* succession.
    III. 1. Empires of *Champa* and *Annam*—anti-Chinese policies.
      2. Struggles with *Khmers*—Mahayana–Hinayana struggles.
      3. Conquest by *Mongols*.

Materials

BUTWELL, *Southeast Asia Today and Tomorrow*.
Discovering Art 3 (38), 209–10 and 215–23.
Historical Atlas of Muslim Peoples XXIV.

Aims. To make real the interplay of Indian (Hindu–Hinayana Buddhist) and Chinese (Taoist–Mahayana Buddhist) influences in South-east Asia, to note great art work achieved, especially in Cambodia.

Methods. Sketch plans for Ankhor Vat or Ankhor Thom. Note pictures of area.

Seventh Week

1. Review of India.
2. Review of China and neighboring states.
3. Examination.

ORIENTAL – OCCIDENTAL SECTION OF CLASS 9

SYLLABUS OUTLINE

Fourth 6-Week Period of Second-Third Terms of Year

Medieval America and Africa—and Return to Europe 1000–1250

Aims. To follow out Medieval Asia with consideration of America and Africa in the 700 years under consideration, and to return to Europe–Eastern Mediterranean considerations from 1000 onwards. This allows for comparison between and among relatively isolated cultures and those at the heart of human development at the time when Europe takes the initiative.

Specifically—First week (three teaching periods throughout).

First Week

Subject. Fall Mayas—evolution Colombia and Peru (A.D. 550–1250).

Details

    I. 1. Background of *classical* Mexican cultures—religion, architecture, major centers.

        2. Conquest by *Toltecs* of Nayarit, Teotihuacan, Tajin, Uxmal (Mayans) and Zapotecs—rise of *Tula.*

        3. Mayapan culture—rise of *Chicimecs*—especially Chichen-Itza in Yucatan.

    II. 1. Rise of *Eskimo* cultures—Old Bering Sea—four Canadian groups.

        2. Evolution of *mound builder* culture—impact of Norsemen.

        3. *Chibchan* culture of Columbia.

    III. 1. *Mochica* (coast) and *Nasca* (interior) give way to *Tiahuanaco* culture (Peru).

        2. *Chimu* city-state period.

        3. Religious, architectural and cultural *comparison* with Mexico.

Materials

    Discovering Art, Primitive Art, Nos. 1–9 inclusive.

    WALLBANK and TAYLOR, *Civilization Past* and *Present* **1,** 537.

    Isotype Film Strip On Pre-colombian America.

    Sound Recordings of early American dances.

Aims. To note the high level of technical excellence achieved by the Toltecs (First Universal Amerind Empire) in contrast to more isolated cultures. To impress students with wealth of detail usually overlooked.

Methods. Use of illustrative lectures to present data. Students to prepare time charts to appreciate data.

Second Week

Subject. Trans-Saharan penetration—Murabit Empire.

Details

    I. 1. Theories of *penetration* of African continent—Polynesian, Berber, Negroid—Ethopia—Nubia *(Dongola).*

    2. Jewish influence on Empire of *Ghana*.

    3. Muslim penetration of East Coast—Zanzibar—*Zens*.

II. 1. Jewish influence on Empire of *Chad*.

    2. Rise of *Hausa* State in Nigeria—arrival of Islam.

    3. Rise of Empire of *Mali—Bornu*.

    4. *Murabit* Empire conquers Mediterranean coastline.

III. 1. Rise of *Muwahid* Caliphate.

    2. Rise of independent *Songhai* Empire.

    3. Berber penetration of *Rhodesia—Zimbabwe*.

Materials

WALLBANK and TAYLOR, *Civilization Past and Present* **1**, 540–6.

WILLIAMS, *Portrait of World History* **2**, 28–42.

OLIVER and FAGE, *Short History of Africa*, chaps. 5–9.

Muslim Historical Atlas, 16–17. Historical Atlas of Muslim Peoples.

PREVITE-ORTON, *Shorter Cambridge Medieval History* **1**, 278–82.

DAVIDSON, *African Past*.

OLIVER and FAGE, *Atlas of African History*.

GABRIELI, *Arab Revival*, 12–19.

Aims. To dispell notion that Africa had no civilizations (except in north), to note what connection existed with other centers, and to spell out unique African approaches.

Methods. To use eye-witness accounts to give authenticity to lectures. To have maps made showing areas of empires and movements of peoples.

Third Week

Subject. Fatimid—Buwayhid—Saljuk evolution.

Details

    I. 1. Collapse of Spanish *Ommiads*—successor states.

    2. Peak of *Fatimid* power—Hakim—Jebel Druse.

    3. Peak of Buwayhid power—fall of Abbasids—Al-Dowlah.

II. 1. *Tughril Beg* and rise of Saljuk Turks—assassins.
   2. *Alp Arslan* and Battle of Manzikirt, conquest Asia Minor.
   3. *Iconium, Danishmond,* Eastern emirates.
III. 1. Zangid Empire—*Nurradin.*
   2. *Khwarwismian Turks*—revival of *Abbasids.*
   3. Culture of Islam during Medieval age 1000–1250.

Materials

Penguin Atlas of Medieval History, Maps 54–76 inclusive.
Historical Atlas of Muslim Peoples.
HITTI, *Arabs.*
LAMONTE, *World of Middle Ages.*

Aims. To show that though religiously and politically divided, Islam had a common culture. To stress, however, the alien incursion of the Turks and to set the background for the Crusades and reconquests.

Methods. To have research essays written to evaluate the importance of Turkish appearance in Middle East. To use maps to trace growth of various Islamic states.

Fourth Week

Subject. Holy Roman Empire—Poland—Hungary—Empire of North.

Details

I. 1. Empire annexes Burgundy—loses out in Italy—work of *Barbarossa*—end of Investiture controversy.
   2. Rise of *Venice,* Pisa and Genoa.
   3. *Rivalry* with Sicily, Church and Byzantium.
II. 1. Emergence of *Poland*—its problems, evolution.
   2. Emergence of *Hungary*—its problems, evolution.
   3. Rise of *Serbian* and *Croatian* principalities.
III. 1. Breakdown of Principality of *Kiev*—Cuman incursion.
   2. *Canute's* Great Empire—christianity to North.
   3. Evolution of *Scandinavia,* 1050–1250,

Materials

HMV History of Music in Sound, Record **1**, Vol. 2.

Filmstrips of MSS in Bodleian Library.

LaMonte, *World of Middle Ages.*

Previte-Orton, *Shorter Cambridge Medieval History* **1**, 295–417 and 420–60.

Wallbank and Taylor, *Civilization Past and Present* **1**, 336–41.

Aims. To show how it was Empire could not gather power of vital Europe to its own use, and to trace the expansion of civilization and christianity into Middle, Eastern and Northern Europe.

Methods. Written and visual source material used to aid in exposition of basic material. Debate on some aspect of Church–State controversy.

Fifth Week

Subject. Normans of England, Sicily, Antioch, Crusades.

Details

I. 1. *French Normandy — Edward the Confessor — William the Conqueror.*
   2. *Evolution*, especially Henry I.
   3. Scotland, Celtic and Norse *fringe.*

II. 1. *Tancred de Hauteville, Robert Guiscard.*
   2. Evolution, especially *Roger I* and *William I.*
   3. Greater Sicily under *Constance* and *Henry VI.*

III. 1. Causes of *First Crusade* — evolution.
   2. Principality of Antioch — *Bohemund.*
   3. Founding Kingdom of *Jerusalem.*

Materials

Filmstrips on Crusades and Norman England.

Power, *Medieval People.*

Coulton, *Medieval Panorama*, **1.**

LaMonte, *World of Middle Ages.*

PREVITE-ORTON, *Shorter Cambridge Medieval History* **1**, 507–43, 562–77 and 583–99.

Aims. To whow vital force of Western Christian Norse settlers in turning both feudalism and Islamic naval supremacy to their own use in hitting back in the First idealistic Crusade.

Methods. Utilize drama of first "International" movement of Western Europe — probably by means of reporting on events from point of view of various participants.

Sixth Week

Subject. Revival of trade-growth of Third Estate.

Details

   I. 1. Evolution of *town* on river and sea routes from closed manor economy.
      2. Development of *Craft* and *Merchant* guilds — purchases of town liberties.
      3. Growth of *fairs* — of *banking* — insistance on repre-sentetion of *estates généraux*.
  II. 1. *Population Explosion* — Cistercian Order — Premonstratensian Canons.
      2. Introduction of window glass, *Carpets*. Varied diet.
      3. Development of *fortifications*, chivalry.
 III. 1. Development of Chronicles — history writing.
      2. Growth of *vernacular*.
      3. *Medieval Latin*, poetry, *Giolardic* verse.

Materials

MUMFORD, *City in History*.

PIRENNE, *Medieval Cities*.

GARROLL et al., *Development of Civilization*, **1**.

PREVITE-ORTON, *Shorter Cambridge Medieval History* **1**, 544–54.

Aims. To show importance of revival of trade, implied by Crusades, especially in recreating the beginnings of urban culture and all which that implied.

Methods. Chart growth of typical town and its institutions. Study of original documents to illuminate trends—essay to analyze such.

OCCIDENTAL SECTION III OF CLASS 9

SYLLABUS OUTLINE

Fifth 6-Week Period of Third Term of Year

Medieval Europe 1000–1250

Aims. To complete consideration of high medievalism in Europe from 1000 to 1250, noting political, cultural and artistic achievements up to time of Mongol invasions.

Specifically—First week (three teaching periods throughout).

First Week

Subject. Second through Sixth Crusades—Orders.

Details

    I. 1. Evolution of *Kingdom of Jerusalem*—Second and Third Crusades.
       2. Evolution of *Byzantium*—Fourth Crusade.
       3. Evolution of *Islamic* States—Fifth Crusade.
   II. 1. Development of Templars—Hospitallers—*Cyprus.*
       2. Crusading Orders in Spain—*Las Novas de Talosa.*
       3. *Albigensian* and Teutonic Crusades.
  III. 1. *Sixth Crusade*—Khwarzimian Turks.
       2. *Latin States* in Byzantine area.
       3. Rivalry of *Venice* and *Genoa.*

Materials

TREVOR-ROPER, *Rise of Christian Europe*, 101–30.
BRENTAND, *Early Middle Ages*, 291–306.
LYON, *High Middle Ages*, 118–30 and 239–48.
LaMONTE, *World of Middle Ages.*

Aims. To discuss the decreasingly idealistic notion of crusading —with consequence for Middle East, for the Baltic region and the Occident itself, above all the smashing of Byzantium takes a central place.

Methods. Debate on function and value of the crusading orders.

Second Week

Subject. Rise of feudal France and Medieval papacy.

Details

- I. 1. *Feudal France*—effect Norman Conquest of England.
  2. Louis VI, Louis VII, escheatment of *Philip Augustus.*
  3. *University of Paris*, Gothic style, scholasticism.
- II. 1. *St. Louis* and reputation of Crown—place of France.
  2. *Innocent III* and the Papal Monarchy—inquisition.
  3. Lateran Council and *Waldensians.*
- III. 1. Rivalry with Stupor Mundi—Council of *Lyon.*
  2. *Dominicans* and *Franciscan* friars.
  3. Contacts with *Nestorians* in Asia.

Materials

LaMonte, *World of Middle Ages.*

Previte-Orton, *Shorter Cambridge Medieval History* **1.**

Aims. To note the rise of medieval France with its great University as third element to Empire and Papacy, and to observe how the pretensions of latter body were promoted by punitive and exhortatory mechanisms.

Methods. Essay on some aspect of the thirteenth century Church to complete material presented.

Third Week

Subject. Plantagenet England—Spanish Reconquest.

Details

- I. 1. Formation of Empire of *Henry II.*
  2. John and Magna Charta, Papal overlordship.
  3. Simon de Montfort and Henry III.

II. 1. Kingdoms of *Asturias* (Navarre) and *Galacia* (Leon).
   2. Kingdom of *Aragon*, County of *Barcelona*.
   3. Evolution of *Portugal* and separate *Navarre*.
III. 1. Transmission of Islamic culture.
   2. Role of *Jews*.
   3. Emirate of *Granada*.

Materials

LaMonte, *World of Middle Ages*.
Previte-Orton, *Shorter Cambridge Medieval History*, 2.

Aims. To show common-law England as contrasted to Continent, and to trace evolution of crusading states in Spain, to note their particularism in church-oriented organization.

Methods. To draw series of maps illustrating changes of territorial control effected by English and Spanish as peripheral to main European areas.

Fourth Week

Subject. Stupor Mundi—Mongol Invasion.

Details

I. 1. Background, personality of *Frederick II*.
   2. Struggles for control of Germany—*Otto III*.
   3. International Battle of *Bouvines*.
II. 1. Involvement with *Middle East*.
   2. Constitutional work—constitutions of *Melfi*.
   3. Collapse of *Empire*.
III. 1. Mongol attack on *Russia*—Khanate Golden Horde.
   2. Penetration to *Baltic* and *Adriatic*—effect on Hungary.
   3. Destruction of Caliphate-*Ilkhans* of Persia.

Materials

LaMonte, *World of Middle Ages*.
Penguin Atlas of Medieval History, Maps 68–76 inclusive.

Aims. To note the collapse of Empire when tangled with Sicilian aims and in conflict with the Papacy. To observe how this struggle blinded the protagonists to danger of Mongol destruction. Finally, to note nature of the Mongol State as created.

Methods. Debate the merits of the Papal–Imperial position in thirteenth-century Europe.

Fifth Week

Subject. Arts—scholasticism—Islamic encounter.

Details

   I. 1. Varieties of Romanesque and Gothic *architecture*.
     2. *Stained glass*, lesser arts.
     3. Mosaics, frescoes, *Byzantine* norms.
  II. 1. *Conceptualism*—work of Albertus Magnus.
     2. The Medieval synthesis—*Aquinas*.
     3. Roger Bacon—Spiritual Franciscans.
 III. 1. Canon of *Aristotle*.
     2. Work of *Palermo—Salerno*.
     3. Alexandria Cycle—Arthurian—German.

Material

Carroll *et al.*, *Development of Civilization*, *1*.
LaMonte, *World of Middle Ages*.

Aims. To attempt to encompass the tremendous complexity of European art forms—To show how the synthesis of Aristotle and Faith offered a unifying principle—To give Islam its due as a civilizing device.

Methods. To have essay written to develop appreciation of the relationship of art forms to the medieval outlook on life.

Sixth Week

Subject. Creation of guilds—trade, manufacturing, university.

Details

    I. 1. Comparison of *degrees* with guilds.
      2. Leagues of cities run by guilds—*Hansa.*
      3. Bologna, Paris as originators of *university* guilds.
   II. 1. *Trade routes*—staple goods.
      2. *Wool* trade—Britain, Spain, Italy.
      3. *Florentine* banking.
  III. 1. Construction of *"Cloth Halls"*.
      2. Evolution of classes in *Italian* city states.
      3. Usages of *Barcelona*—naval regulations.

Materials

    LAMONTE, *World of Middle Ages.*
    PREVITE-ORTON, *Shorter Cambridge Medieval History*, **1.**

Aims. To give a full picture of thirteenth-century economic life in the European Eastern Mediterranean scene.

Methods. Draw maps of main trade routes 1028 and 1212, to analyze development during two centuries.

BIBLIOGRAPHY

BLABER, D. and CERYCH, L., College of Europe, an institution of higher education, *Yearbook of Education, 1964*, London, Evans Brothers.

BRIDEL, F. Rejouissants progrès de l'UNESCO, *Tribune de Genève*, 25 November 1964.

BRITISH COUNCIL, *Handbook*, 1967.

CERN, *Study of the Problems Posed by Education of the Children of CERN Staff Members*, Geneva, 1966.

CENTRE EUROPÉEN DE LA CULTURE, *Bilan des Activités Culturelles au Service de l'Europe 1949–1964*, Vol. 11, Nos. 3 and 4, Spring, 1966.

COLE-BAKER, J. D., Towards an international university Entrance examination, *Comparative Education*, Vol. 2 (1), November 1965.

COMMITTEE ON AMERICAN STUDIES, *American Studies News* 1 (2), December 1965.

CONFERENCE OF INTERNATIONALLY MINDED SCHOOLS, *Member Schools*, 1966.

CURTI, M., *American Philanthrophy Abroad*, New Brunswick, Rutgers Press, 1963, 650 pp. (quotation, p. 312).

FALK, R. and MENDLOVITZ, S., *Strategy of World Order*, New York, World Law Fund, n. p.

FAO, *Cooperative Calendar of Nations and Schools of Rome*, 1966.

FRANKEL, C., Cultural affairs officer, US Advisory Commission on International Educational and Cultural Affairs, *Exchange* 1 (4), Winter, 1966.

FRANKEL, C., Bibliography on international education, *Exchange* 1 (4), 58, Winter, 1966, US Advisory Commission on International Educational and Cultural Affairs.

FULBRIGHT, J. W., New channels of communication and Communist exchange programs in the mid 1960's, *Exchange* 1 (1), 32–43, Summer, 1965.

GARDNER, J., Testimony on international education, *Exchange* 1 (3), 42, Spring, 1966.

GREENBAUM, M., Some experiments in a new approach to the teaching of World History, *Indiana Social Studies Quarterly* 16 (2), Autumn, 1966.

HOWLAND, H., East–West Center, *Exchange* **1** (2), 33–43, Autumn, 1965. US Advisory Commission on International Educational and Cultural Affairs.

INTERNATIONAL BACCALAUREATE OFFICE, *1967 Progress Report*, Cologny.

INTERNATIONAL SCHOOLS ASSOCIATION, *Newsletters*, Nos. 1–45 inclusive, (1958–67).

INTERNATIONAL SCHOOLS ASSOCIATION, MS., Minutes of Official Business Meetings (1951–67).

INTERNATIONAL SCHOOLS ASSOCIATION, *Report on Conference on Primary Curricula in International Schools*, Geneva, 1966.

INTERNATIONAL SCHOOLS EXAMINATION SYNDICATE, *International Baccalaureate*, Cologny, 1967.

INTERNATIONAL SCHOOLS EXAMINATION SYNDICATE, *International Baccalaureate Conference: Papers for Commissions A and B*, Geneva, 1967.

INTERNATIONAL SCHOOLS EXAMINATION SYNDICATE, MS., Minutes of various organs and commissions (1963–7).

INTERNATIONAL SCHOOLS SERVICES, *List of ISS Schools*, 1965.

INTERNATIONAL SCHOOLS SERVICES, Council of overseas schools representatives meeting in New York, *Newslinks for Overseas Schools*, September 1966.

JAFFE, A., Intellectual life in Roumania, *Exchange* **1** (3), 1–7, Spring, 1964. US Advisory Commission on International Educational and Cultural Affairs.

KEPPEL, F., Facts and figures on educational exchange, *Exchange* **1** (4), 64, Winter, 1966.

KNIGHT, M. and LEACH, R., International Secondary Schools, *Yearbook of Education, 1964*, London, Evans Brothers.

LEWIS, S., *Towards International Co-operation*, Oxford, Pergamon Press, 1966.

MAUNG, H., MS., letter to Russell Cook, UN, 3 October 1962, Baghdad to Geneva.

MOWAT, J., Vers un Baccalauréat International, *Tribune de Genève*, 19 January 1967.

PETERSON, A. D. C., Un Examen International, *Tribune de Genève*, 21 February 1967.

PETERSON, A. D. C., International Exam, *Times Educational Supplement*, 3 March 1967.

POSTLETHWAITE, N., "International project for the evaluation of educational achievement", *International Review of Education*, **12** (3), (1966).

PURKISS, R., MS., Thesis on International Schools.

RONSHEIM, S., MS., Thesis on International School of Geneva.

UNESCO, *World Survey of Education*, Vols. 1–4, Paris, 1958–66.

US ADVISORY COMMISSION ON INTERNATIONAL EDUCATIONAL AND CULTURAL AFFAIRS, Aspau in French-speaking Africa, *Exchange* **1** (2), Autumn, 1965, p. 58.

V. R., L'École Internationale envisage de créer un baccalauréat reconnu dans le monde entier, *Tribune de Genève*, 15 October 1964.

VALENZUELA, R., Ms., Why UNESCO?, 1967.

VINING, E. G., International Christian University, *Friends Journal*, **12**, 16 August 1966, Philadelphia, Pa.

WINKS, R., Century of misunderstanding—Canadian–American cultural relations, *Exchange 1* (2), 6–18, Autumn, 1965.

WORKING COMMITTEE, *Proposal to Establish an International School in Washington*, 1965.

ZWEIG, M., *Idea of a World University*, Carbondale, Southern Illinois University Press, 1967.

INDEX